The End of Hardware

augmented reality and beyond

The End of Hardware

3rd edition:

Augmented Reality and Beyond

ISBN: 1-4392-3602-X

ISBN13: 978-1-4392-3602-4

Printed by BookSurge Publishing
To order additional copies
visit www.booksurge.com

Contains bibliographical references and index

BISAC: COM057000 - COMPUTERS/Virtual Reality
Keywords: Augmented Reality; Virtual Reality; 3D;
Mobile Computing; Media Technology; Holography

1st edition: March, 2006
2nd edition: October, 2006
3rd edition: May, 2009

to Sigrid

THE END OF HARDWARE

Foreword

I was captivated by the last edition of „The End of Hardware" on a round-trip flight to Los Angeles. This book is not only an in-depth introduction to the concept of head-attached displays for augmented reality (AR), but also a great source of inspiration for many professionals - at least it is for me.

The augmented reality community has carried out extensive research and development for many years to make the vision of AR come true. So far, head-attached displays have not found their way to the mass-market. One reason for this might be, the technological foundation still has too many limitations to become an efficient and widely applied user interface.

In „The End of Hardware", Rolf R. Hainich puts together concepts and ideas that he has collected for years from a large variety of fields to sketch out his vision of eye-worn displays. He explains, how advanced optics and electronics as well as electromechanics can be used to build personal displays that have the potential to overcome the limitations of today's devices.

Being a technical guy, I particularly enjoyed reading his technical design chapter which, in this new edition of the book, has been greatly extended with many details on holography, light fields and MEMS. Despite a technological focus, the book is written in a popular-scientific style - and therefore allows easy access to the material - even for non-experts.

If I were to characterize this book in a single word, that word would be „inspiring". I can only hope that one day, someone will pick up and realize these ideas. For although, this might not be the „End of Hardware" - it could well be the beginning of many new and exciting interfaces to the digital world in which we all live in.

Weimar, 23rd of March 2009
Oliver Bimber

The End of Hardware

Content

part 2: Fiction - Adventures of a Four-Eyed *99*

part 3: Technical Design *153*

Publications integrated since the last edition

This edition integrates the following new papers published by the author in university lectures, conference contributions and on the book's web site http://www.theendofhardware.com. A few are didactic or prose, most have been first publications.

Eye operated cell phones (Apr.2, 07), 207
Auto holographic displays (May 27, 07) (only mentioned here) 334
'Bionic' camcorders - drop the bricks (July 15, 07), 345
More on mask displays (Aug.20, 07), 259
Light field displays (Oct.12, 07), 243
Coaxial scanners (Nov.5, 07), 200
Light field encoding (Feb.24, 08), 349
Visual flow eye tracking (Mar.25, 08), 181
A new class: Ghost objects and devices (June 3, 08), 73
Holographic optical elements (Aug.1, 08), 232,387
Piezo electric micro motors (Sep.16, 08), 211
Monocular depth pointing (Sep.16, 08), 393
Contact lens displays (Oct.3, 08), 250
The 1ˢᵗ Implant (Oct.19, 08), 291
The world in a nutshell (Nov.9, 08), 142
Retina trackers (Jan.12, 09). 187

Please note that this book contains many more new materials and updated parts, exceeding this list. The fiction part in particular, has been greatly expanded.

3rd Edition

When the first edition of this book appeared, in April 2006, a certain revival of Augmented Reality (AR) could already be noticed, yet almost entirely limited to research projects in software and to industrial applications. The idea of AR for private use had always been widely ignored except for a few pioneers, manly exploring it as an ingredient to wearable computing. In Wikipedia for example, simply none of the myriads of possible everyday AR applications had ever appeared before.

The book I therefore originally wrote with two main objectives in mind: bringing consumer AR back into common discussion, and promoting the development of dedicated hardware. The hardware issues are however exceeding the capability of almost any academic research facility, and without resolving them, most people have difficulties figuring out all the many possibilities with this technology. The typical AR research paper deals with rendering issues - hence software - and off-the-shelf hardware. Sometimes, quite similar issues are being taken up just with new hardware every some years.

The optics necessary, as it turned out at a closer look, can be approached in a way understandable by anybody with just a basic school education, even including often mystified topics like holography. So indeed anybody from other research disciplines will surely be able to evaluate the possibilities, and this is necessary to move anything here.

Lots of things happened since the first edition appeared.

Besides several university lectures, in the meantime I've been invited for a keynote at the ISMAR 2008 conference in Cambridge [123], where I took the opportunity to present the new metaphor of focus steered ('ghost') objects to a greater audience, along with many other materials that I had published in lectures and at the book's website since the last book edition. You will now find all of them in this 3rd edition as well.

Said conference also contained the first full fledged optical analysis of single mirror near eye display optics [103], and there it was proven that it would work, even without any electronic geometry or focus correction already. Another especially remarkable contribution was a paper about gaze steering [104].

Someone approached me about 'contact lens displays'. Pretty far fetched, but researching it a bit I discovered that some misunderstandings in the news media required the real possibilities to be addressed. So I added a few pages about it.

In the last edition of this book, I identified the eye operated cell phone as the likely killer application for general use AR and in May 2007, I proposed a version with double use optics at the book's website. Shortly after, a renown manufacturer of laser scanners [15] displayed an imagination of a spectacle phone on their website, seeking cooperations with cell phone manufacturers. Instead, micro projectors are now the next gadget being developed for mobiles. Projected screens however cannot replace near-eye displays, and the very same company also acquired a major public grant for the development of laser based display glasses. Another remarkable project is ISTAR [118]. So the topic is taking up momentum, and hope may be justified that these developments will be resulting in real products not too far away.

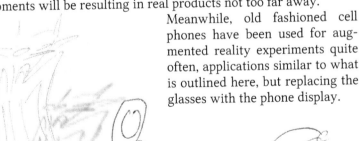

Meanwhile, old fashioned cell phones have been used for augmented reality experiments quite often, applications similar to what is outlined here, but replacing the glasses with the phone display.

This is not the real thing of course, people walking around pointing their phones like crazed vampire hunters.

Several interesting hardware developments have occurred that I wanted to include in the book. One is advances in piezo-electric micro motors, a promising solution for the dynamic adaptation we will most probably need for any kind of AR display, adapting it to the never ending dynamic movements of our eyes and allowing for focus adjustment and other goodies to come.

Not only hardware news are fueling this edition. I introduce the new 'ghost' objects already mentioned above, consisting of many layers that can be activated one at a time, according to the willfully changed distance accommodation of the beholder's eyes.

In the book's first edition, I proposed holographic encoding instead of the object oriented MPEG extensions usually tried for representing three-dimensional images. Just shortly after, it turned out that others were also following this idea [83], including practical experiments and conversions between holographic and light field representations. In this edition, I included new ideas for a light field display as well as multi camera acquisition and encoding, refurbished the holography section, and added a thorough introduction to holographic optical elements.

Many more new or extended ideas and insights, about virtual worlds for example, improved and new explanations, made this book many pages stronger than the last edition (see p. 11 for an overview). The fiction part received many and new items as well. I think it's space well spent.

Rolf R. Hainich

The End of Hardware
augmented reality and beyond

Preface

Mobile phones will soon have hundreds of gigabytes of storage and replace a camcorder, a PC, anything. But how to use all this? Traveling with 2 pieces of luggage, looking for my connecting flight, I just imagine fumbling around with this thing, trying to see any informations on its dwarfish display. Taking a pen, trying to stab little blots on the display, doesn't help either.

This technology, getting as near to the *personal communicator* as anything so far, will surely hit the wall in the near future, simply because there is no acceptable display, and rollout displays or projectors won't do.

Long ago I realized this problem, and now technology is ready to solve it. We need to eliminate the screen in favor of a near-eye projector, glasses with a tiny add-on that could finally weigh less than 20g.

Forget those ancient virtual reality goggles. Forget anything hampering direct sight. It can be done way better.

Virtual objects, virtual devices will surround us, everywhere. They will soon replace most of today's user interface hardware, screens, keypads, entire installations, and they will do a lot more. Nevertheless, these virtual things won't clutter up our view at all, because other than with some classical approaches to augmented reality, here they will be seamlessly integrated and fixed to the real environment, rather than sticking in front of our eyes.

We will have to envision entirely new applications and usage habits. It's a new world to explore.

No more desktops mapped to a computer screen, but operating systems mapped to the real world. Available anywhere. Boosting productivity beyond any expectations.

When I started my activities back in 1993, generating steady, high quality images merged into natural sight was already resolved, and the only major obstacles were computing power and small high resolution displays.

Ten years later, these obstacles were gone, but very little had happened in all the other fields. Somewhere, programs and joint projects were launched whose aims looked ten years old. Basic parts of augmented reality technology still deliver themes for theses all over the world (fortunately at least this happens), but it's usually a matter of chance if somebody, maybe from institutions not generically involved in the thematic at all, picks up this or that problem because of necessity. Very few researchers around the world are dedicatedly concerned with the thematic, and a few small or medium enterprises are developing in this field. The funding of this research is still microscopic compared to that of large screen display technology, for just one example.

In the beginning, only Japanese companies built camcorders, i.e. had the full spectrum of technologies at hand for tiny display glasses. Meanwhile, mobile phone technology delivers the best starting point and it is available in many countries. This is just good luck, not the farsightedness of managements.

Only a very small number of books cover augmented reality, and even fewer really deliver a strategic view. Some of the most important issues, visual orientation and mask displays for example, are hardly treated or not even at all. So I literally had no choice but to write this book. It has two main objectives:

- showing as many applications as possible, because this already induces a lot of thought and inspirations about realization;
- demonstrating the feasibility, i.e. naming the technological approaches as well as calculating the results achievable. Delivering the recipes. Otherwise, the usual skeptics could just too easily do anything away as mere speculations.

It should be readable to the (interested) public, but it can't be entirely popular science, as it has to treat several issues in a way that professionals can profit. Yet this isn't such a contradiction, as professionals from different disciplines also usually don't know a lot of each other's field.

Many augmented reality projects now deal with screens all over the place, projected items, lots of additional installations. In the context considered here, this would be sort of installing phone booths everywhere, rather than using a mobile phone. It may be the right thing for certain applications, but generally shouldn't we try to reduce hardware and costs, not to multiply them? Recent studies say copper will get rare even in spite of recycling. So will other resources. It will therefore be wise anyway to push forward technologies that reduce large appliances, office space, wiring.

We will see that the actual IT hardware of the ultimate perceptional interface could fit in a sugar cube and take less than 10 milliwatts of power. Micro and nano technologies will be very important here. Some tasks will turn out easier than anticipated. We don't need tactile feedback all the time: nobody wants gloves. We don't need gestures: too complicated. Pressing virtual keys is so simple to implement, you wouldn't believe it, but even this won't be the end. We'll finally operate anything by just looking at it. It will be like magic.

Current near eye displays won't do. We need something that dynamically adapts to eye motion, incorrectly sitting glasses, focus and aperture effects, geometry changes. Also of course something that does not impair direct sight at all, has very high resolution, a very large field of view, and a *mask display* to make virtual objects non transparent.

It can be built, and for the basic functions somebody will already have to reinvent the wheel, as many of the problems have long been solved in some military projects. Yet the entire technology still doesn't have a really supporting structure, no powerful industrial basis. In the academic field, mainly the ISMAR conference developed into an important platform during the last years. Yet it is not done with research papers covering this or that mathematical or programming problem on still inadequate interface hardware. It is not done with fancy demonstrations or utterly expensive industrial installations on the same basis. The central topic of this book - in spite of its title - will have to be hardware, the new, better one, that is, and these issues still are missing most of the time.

What is necessary in this field is an entire, ambitious, multi threaded development program that involves, or better, is initiated by major industrial companies, has adequate funding and a sufficient time scale, and aims for nothing less than perfection.

The device that we are aiming at will require:

- *Eye tracker*
- *Mask displays*
- *Position cameras*
- *Dynamic image generator*
- *Dynamic fit and focus adaptation*

⇨ **No straps, no screws, no belts, no clamps**

In current products, hardly anything of this is realized at all. It's not only technology that we have to deal with. First of all, applications have to be envisioned, fantasy has to be stimulated, the entire way of thinking has to be fully comprehended.

I remember when I had my first programming course back in the 70's. Nobody could afford a private computer back then, but I had heard a lot about it. I knew digital circuits, but I wondered about all those silly articles describing 'thinking' machines.

This couldn't work, so what? After writing my first lines of code, I knew. This thing wasn't meant to think. Within minutes I figured out how to build one. It was all simple and clear.

The important issue was not how to do it, but first to know what it should do. Just as with all innovations:

The most difficult and important step is not to find the answers, but to ask the right questions. So it is here. We know there is something that could do amazing tings. We have to do a lot of thinking about what it could realistically do and what not. Once the goals are defined, we will be able to build it. Hence, this book is meant to ponder the technology as well as its applications. The entire scope.

I went as far as to write many pages of fiction, in order to make this more colorful. Only by exercising our fantasy and delving into the scenario will we be able to find new applications, and there are many.

Utterly important here it is to sort out the impossible and the unacceptable, or this would really be nothing but fiction.

Just „can't be done" is not an option. I've seen quite some examples where would-be experts said something wouldn't work, and a short time later it had been accomplished.

Applications dictate the construction. I try to define the necessities and the technologies that could do it. You'll see that it will finally be working. We will be able to build those ultra light plastic glasses that don't even look as if they got any super technology in them. We will have to face all those problems arising from the everyday use of virtual objects. And a lot more.

Displays and especially optics have been widely neglected. Maybe nobody realized the potential of a really good solution? So I'll address this extensively, including new ideas like holographic optics and image generators that may change things entirely.

The main chapters in this book I started to write in 2004 and 2005 (even 1993 in some detail, as nearly everything in the earlier papers is still current and true).

First is an introduction, outlining the technological and economical basics and a lot of applications. Then a piece of fiction, that in my opinion will say more than any of these brittle tech ideas and that is, as said, crucial for the comprehension of the entire thematic.

The applications list is also continued in part 4, with emphasis on virtual media. There I'll also address themes like 3D and surround cinema and holographic and light field encoding.

Part 3 goes into technical detail, exploring possible solutions.

Even this is meant to be understandable to the general public as well as to experts from a wide variety of fields. This 3rd edition contains a lot more optics basics that I collected in an appendix to get a more readable main part.
This may also help anyone interested in actual construction work in figuring out what to do and how. Sensitize technologists and managers to new possibilities. Motivate people to become involved in this new development, or at least to keep it in mind with their everyday decisions.

This book is not primarily an overview of current research nor a summary. It is an investigation of technology and its possibilities, and in the course of it we will develop many entirely new ideas as well.
The objective is to fill all the gaps, at least in theory, that are parting us from the ultimate vision, in order to prove that it can be done, and to show how it will probably be accomplished

As soon as a first - even a simple - implementation succeeds, drawing competition and accelerating the development, it will start an avalanche. An eye operated mobile phone integrated into a pair of glasses, for example. A killer application.

John Doenuts just discovered these surgical telescope magnifiers to be an ideal mobile phone accessory

The End of Hardware

part 1: Introduction

Virtual devices

Quite some time ago, new technologies in image processing and presentation were promising the next step in the evolution of user interfaces. Virtual reality (VR) went beyond commonly used graphics by linking computer generated images to real world parameters such as point and angle of view, location and movement in space, and to physical interaction. In [1] and especially in [2], I had suggested several improvements in this field already, introducing virtual devices and other things now called Augmented Reality (AR). The first chapter of this book is partly based on these original papers, of course updated and vastly expanded with new ideas, many pictures and examples.

In the beginning, in times of Virtual Reality, the user was totally shielded from his surroundings and interacted in a totally virtual environment. Bulky, low resolution displays caused more headache than fun. Even nowadays the available devices are calling for tons of improvements. A first step towards Augmented Reality employs a near-eye display, inserting a virtual computer screen into a user's natural view, but fixed to one position inside the user's field of view [3]. This type recently became very current in military applications.

A real merging of reality and virtuality definitely demands for virtual objects merged into the natural scene, at positions defined by this scene. The first technology meeting this definition were military flight simulators, combining a real cockpit with a virtual outside view (example: CAE FOHMD, see p.38).

Another current type of object insertion simulates the projection of maintenance manuals and drawings into real machines. Such applications have long been in use in aircraft and even sometimes in automobile maintenance, but almost always it has not been more than just a flat projection of blueprints *onto* the machine.

For practically all interface solutions trying to bring virtual objects into the real world, Augmented Reality has meanwhile become the common term.

Under this label however a wide range of different approaches are summoned, some that create virtual objects by projectors and screens, some that refer to the 'augmented' experience from ubiquitous computing, chips and devices strayed all over the place, some that draw augmentation from the experience with 'intelligent', computer equipped clothing. In my view however, the most interesting aspect of AR technology is the *minimization* of hardware, not its maximization.

Moreover, all known applications so far have accomplished but a small part of the imaginable. They do not efficiently utilize our capabilities. Human beings can handle large numbers of different things simultaneously, by arranging them in space. We all have a very strong dedicated processing unit to do this (our brain), and we make extensive use of it in any natural environment.

A user interface of an information system should exploit these capabilities. Hence, an operating system should show data and applications in 3D (3-dimensional) spaces, and even much better, in the real 3D space around us. All of which quite obviously can't efficiently be done on a 2D computer screen, but could be done with a stereo vision simulator, with transparent display glasses.

What is essential, that we do not restrict ourselves to passive display objects, but design these objects to become interactive, behave like real machines. This will appear very similar to a windowed operating system, and not by accident, because the metaphor that made these OS successful was the imitation of devices and operation modes that we were used to. The next logical step now will be, to pull these devices and objects from the computer screen back into the real world and to use our entire environment as a giant 3D 'screen'.

In and out of the screen
The evolution and re-volution of paradigms

A simple look onto a present computer screen reveals interesting insights, if we just lean back and reflect what we are actually seeing there.

There are those windows of course, representing documents. There may be a TV window. There may be a folder window. And there is a wallpaper. Any of this could be in a room. What we don't see is a desk, but it's not accidental that we call this screen surface itself a „desktop".

With basic document windows, it is just this - a desk-top. But it can be more. These documents already are more than paper, they have controls and maybe they can even calculate. They are more like devices rather than passive objects.

The TV is even more like an apparatus, and a flight simulator for example brings an entire airplane into our screen, and the world around it as well.

This is a space more than just a desktop, a complete environment, obviously, if we for instance start a contemporary game application. The 'wallpaper' can as well be a landscape.

All this is not by chance, the Windows approach has been developed to be just this, a reflection of the real world, in order to make computers more intuitive.

This ingenious paradigm of interaction had first been developed at Xerox a long time ago. It was then called the „Star" system, and even the mouse was part of this development. Then it became popular with Apple's Lisa and Mac computers, and the ultimate mass market success took place in connection with the PC.

This paradigm of man-machine interaction did hardly change, during several decades meanwhile. An astonishing success story indeed.

But now time has come, for another revolution. Imagine we could take these windows right from the screen, drag them into the room and position them somewhere to stay on their own. Each window in another position, another direction, like a separate screen. The area available for these objects would be as large as our entire field of view, and - if these windows would stay just where we leave them - as big as the entire world.

Remember, these objects are virtual *devices*, and a TV or other appliance could be among them as well.

And this is not all: those monsters from the computer game could be populating the room like a holodeck, and the room could turn into the cockpit of an airplane or into a surround cinema theatre.

The screen area of such an environment would equal hundreds of conventional PC screens, offering us almost unlimited capabilities. But how may we accomplish ?

Simply, as we have learned already, by display glasses that are projecting images of virtual devices right into our eyes. With a sophisticated 3D rendering software, intelligent position sensors and eye trackers caring for motion, and all this contained in a device just as convenient as a pair of modern light weight glasses, of course, as we want a technology that everyone can use anywhere, and also wants to use anywhere.

What has gone into the screen will come out of it again. 'Back to the real world', as a first tiny survey of the first emerging, vague and still very incomplete augmented reality ideas had once been titled.

And there is more to it. Not only the infinite operating surface, but also new methods of interaction. Finger pointing may be familiar from touch screens, but we will also and predominantly use eye pointing, and like the old screen our new 'world' screen will be loaded with special areas, links and icons, allowing us to navigate through any kind of information on the real and virtual objects we see, or about anything else there may be.

„Hyperlinking the real world" a journalist interviewing me titled his article, exactly hitting the point: this will be the seamless integration of the real with the virtual, the ultimate information machine.

Surfing the world this way is more powerful ad also more serious than just web surfing. 'Popups' for example, in this context would not just be nagging, they could become a hazard. Nevertheless, this enhanced power of information handling will be mastered and made useful to an unimaginable extent.

This has actually been the vision from the beginning on, but in the course of development, augmented reality as it was christened somewhere along the way, became more and more a specialty for design, laboratory and 'professional' niche market applications.

Bringing this into everyday life first proved to be too difficult with the technology available, then literally became forgotten and even vanished from imagination, in some peculiar way.

Concurrently, efforts to make these display glasses convenient got widely neglected at last, necessary technology for it received hardly any attention at all, and even projects that were started in the course of what could be a revival of the original idea at the beginning of the 21st century, approached and still are approaching the subject from a viewpoint of special applications only, despite of the fact that technology meanwhile could readily deliver the solutions for a really advanced device, seamlessly integrating into any aspect of everyday life.

What I intend here, is to thoroughly explore the newest possibilities, in the course of it also reviving some almost forgotten ideas and integrating them into the full picture of an upcoming, revolutionary technology that will radically change our lives, as radically as the automobile changed the live of our ancestors almost exactly one century before.

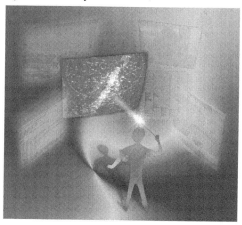

Future vision: windows unleashed. Just a tiny fraction of all the possibilities with AR, of course.

Early ideas about AR

Ideas about merging the virtual with the real are really dating back as far as 1968, when Ivan Sutherland at Sun Microsystems constructed goggles with tube displays.

By restrictions of the time's computing technology, just simple line graphics could be displayed of course, but if we remember the fascination that even the first simple cartoon-like pictures of the first 'flight simulator' on an AppleII made at its time, it was surely impressive back then.

In the early 1990's already, nearly perfect simulation was possible (FOHMD, more at p.38), but it took entire halls full of the times' finest computers, way beyond reach for anyone with a normal budget, least to talk about *portability*.

One of the earliest serious industrial applications was the support of wire tree assembly (Boeing HUDset, 1992). Most remarkably, when augmented reality was sort of 'rediscovered' a few years ago, some of the first new industrial projects emerging didn't look much more advanced than this, at a first glance.

Virtual hardware
The Virtualware* concept

In a perfectly simulated 3D space, we could replace real hardware with virtual objects - that is, software - saving lots of material and energy, and the equipment doing this would, for the first time, fulfil the paradigm of the really universal communicator. Indeed any software application is just very similar to a hardware device, except for the fact that it is not cast in hardware and has no real buttons to operate but virtual keys etc. instead.

A motorcycle or a chainsaw of course, are not ideally suited for a virtual implementation. We have to concentrate our effort on

---

* This term was introduced for the concept of virtual hardware in conference papers from 1993 on [1], [2]. Some people meanwhile also used it as a name for some entirely different things in software technology, that should not be mixed up with our theme.

information machines, like PCs, screens, cell phones, notepads, and - generally - any keypad or panel of any machine there is.

Now this represents a huge advancement already: with some sophisticated display glasses (I call this a vision simulator* until somebody comes up with a catchier name), we could replace all these machines or partial machines with just one piece of hardware and - obviously - an appropriate piece of software. What needs to be developed are display glasses that are able to produce a perfect, high resolution image under all circumstances, that are not dependent on a special fixture to the head, that can totally compensate for any kind of head movements and perspectives and thereby generate the illusion of really *immobile* objects.

Another necessity are ways of seamless interaction with it by hand or finger pointing, eye pointing, speech, etc..

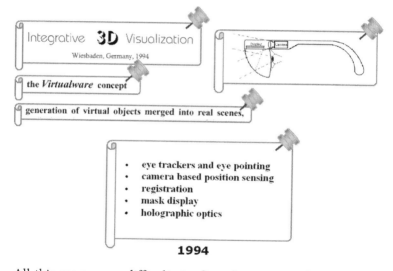

All this seems very difficult at a first glance, as we have to guarantee that a device essentially not bigger than ordinary plastic glasses, should incorporate perfect position sensing, eye tracking, its own cameras, and so on. Not to mention high resolution displays, optics, and of course some audio components.

---

* Introduced in 1994 [2].

The augmented reality concept presented here is open, communicative, and inherently mobile, as virtual objects are not bound to any specific installation but to real locations and objects that could be anywhere. Different people may work with the same virtual objects, and objects may be made available to anyone anywhere, by wirelessly distributing their appearance or contents. Beneath virtual objects, an advanced vision simulator would also offer novel and yet unmatched capabilities to provide the perfect 3D movie display, something not practically possible with holography or conventional stereoscopy.

With conventional high definition TV, even the novel flat panel displays are quite bulky and expensive things that could advantageously be replaced by vision simulators, even much for the better, because even a cinema sized screen could be simulated in economy sized rooms, or the screen paradigm could just be abandoned at all. The vision simulator is the equivalent of many large screens at once, as it can simulate them all concurrently, in different directions.

Within this first chapter, we will now systematically develop the paradigm of virtual devices and objects, review the necessary technologies, outline many possible applications and finally try to address the effects on economy, environment and society.

A classification of virtual objects

Virtual objects and devices come in several varieties that we will now systematize, also in comparison with traditional screen objects as in window based operating systems.

Virtual objects : Images *

Devices

Images: 2D - Image,
        - Cross-Section

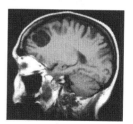

3D - Volume
    - Surface
    - Solid

---

* New Bight international airport, Cat Island, Bahamas

Devices = images with controls

2D - Typical Windows screen objects
- Virtual 2D display devices
- Virtual paper

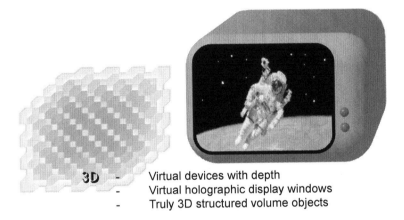

3D - Virtual devices with depth
- Virtual holographic display windows
- Truly 3D structured volume objects

We see that most applications for virtual devices will only require 2D or 2½D presentation in the real 3D space.

Some new types of devices will also be designed, making full use of 3D representation. Many of these will be unlike any real predecessor, and will enable entirely new experiences, as being able to grab into 'solid' or transparent 3D structures ('ghost objects') or dissecting or manipulating them just by eye pointing.

What will also be very different from a screen based system, that we may arrange such objects and controls in the real environment where we have many more degrees of freedom, and more ergonomic ways to operate them.

A virtual workspace

This is an illustration how virtual devices would replace current computer screens, and more:

The only real items in this picture are the desk and the keyboard. There is no computer monitor, not even a simulated one. Instead, several program windows are freely positioned in 3D space. They are operated with fingers or by just looking at their controls or fields. The usual window controls and the surfaces are activated as virtual buttons. Instead of a mouse, a mouse pen is used for more difficult inputs.

Everything virtual you see is just simulated in the display glasses. We have a spreadsheet up front, a text processor (tilt backwards) to the left, a virtual stereo in the right corner of the desk, and another window (calculator or notepad) on the desk itself.

Program windows alone however, are a bit boring. So I also inserted a real 3D object (could be a globe). It could also be operated (turned etc.) by hand. 3D models from computer aided design or art applications are other good candidates for these kinds of objects.

In addition to the office stuff, a virtual TV decorates the facing wall. Last but not least, the window: here we see the original (maybe a bit ugly) view replaced with a better one.

We could even consider to simulate the 'light' falling in from the 'window', by overlaying processed images from cameras mounted on the vision simulator to the real and virtual scene (we will see that we need these cameras anyway, as position sensors).

What is also visualized is the 'shadow' around virtual objects, that results from the inevitable fuzziness of the mask display (we will turn to this later).

We see that a single vision simulator can replace an entire host of monitors. It can lead to a much better utilization of computing power, a more natural and powerful way of interaction, and a better oversight.

As we use the same display to show all these monitors in all directions, we get a virtual resolution for our virtual workspace being many times larger than that of our actual hardware. We would need several giant screens with ultra high resolution to achieve this the conventional way.

This is but a tiny first glimpse on the new possibilities, still very close to the old 'windows' paradigm of known operating systems.

A lot of imagination will be needed to unleash the full power of such a system. A whole new class of operating systems will have to be written to implement all the new features. New classes of object will arise, with properties never known before.

Let's now have a look at the one device that will make it happen. There are many shapes it could take or technologies it could use, including fancy things like holographic displays and mirrors. I will also address this extensively later on in the design chapter.

The vision simulator

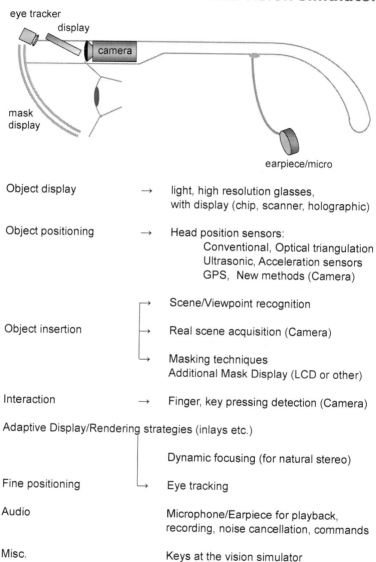

Object display	→	light, high resolution glasses, with display (chip, scanner, holographic)
Object positioning	→	Head position sensors: Conventional, Optical triangulation Ultrasonic, Acceleration sensors GPS, New methods (Camera)

Object insertion
- → Scene/Viewpoint recognition
- → Real scene acquisition (Camera)
- ↳ Masking techniques Additional Mask Display (LCD or other)

Interaction	→	Finger, key pressing detection (Camera)

Adaptive Display/Rendering strategies (inlays etc.)

Dynamic focusing (for natural stereo)

Fine positioning ↳ Eye tracking

Audio — Microphone/Earpiece for playback, recording, noise cancellation, commands

Misc. — Keys at the vision simulator
Headlamps (e.g. infrared for night vision)

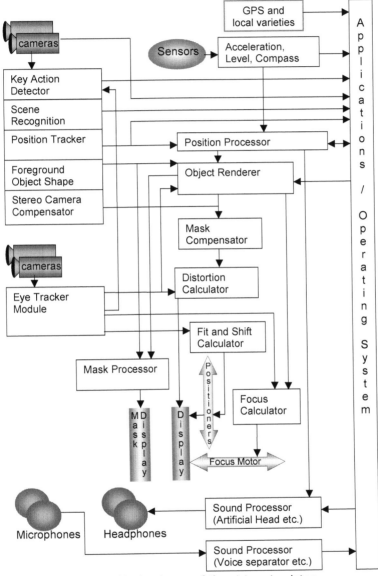

Principal block scheme of the vision simulator
and computing device (hard-and software)

Displays

The largest difficulty on the way to an acceptable virtual reality device lies in available display technology and optical designs.

With displays, making them small, light and crisp enough is quite difficult. One problem are the small pixel sizes, difficult to achieve with technologies usually developed for large screens.
The maximum currently is at 1280x1024 pixels in applications. and first 1920x1200 display chips are announced. If we want to simulate a computer screen of just this resolution, as is common today, we would like to have about 2 times as much, as we need not only to show this item itself, but some surroundings as well.

This implies that with display chips, some more development is still necessary, even though a lot has happened during the last years. Several technology and design problems with micro displays have been resolved or will hopefully soon be resolved by pioneering enterprises ([33], [51]). The issue has been neglected by most of the major manufacturers, because hardly anybody seems to have envisioned a market large enough.
Useful display technologies for example are LCD, LED, OLED and DMD displays*. Another solution is the laser scanner, writing an image directly into the eye. Holographic display chips, currently in prototype versions, may also become an interesting option in the future.
What has not yet been realized anywhere (other than practically unusable research installations) is a mask display that can cut out parts of the real sight in order to achieve non transparent virtual objects. Except for LCD, far from being optimal, there is nothing in sight so far to solve this. Nevertheless this is utterly important and I'm sure there will be a solution.
In the applications area, there were and are many exciting military and scientific projects, like flight simulators or helmet displays for pilots, but these are scarcely published.

---

* We will further discuss display technology in the design chapter.

Scientific and commercial implementations are also heavily used in some fields, but they are also not very convenient and pretty expensive.

As stated already, display glasses should be as transparent and lightweight as possible, serving the only purpose to project pictures into the user's otherwise totally unobscured viewing area.

To illustrate this, let's have a look at one of the first projects that already implemented many of our desired features, in a display helmet for a flight simulator. The FOHMD (Fiber Optic Helmet Mounted Display) development was started as early as 1981 (first prototype 1984), and other than most military applications that are simple data displays even today, it was the first really earnest approach to virtual environments.

Head Mounted Display System (FOHMD) for out-of-cockpit view of the Tornado Low Level Flight Simulator (photo courtesy of CAE)*

This project is especially important for our thematic, because it already involved advanced eye and motion tracking technologies to produce a stable virtual display, something not to be found in almost any other display or application even today.

---

* From 'Proceedings of the Workshop on integrative 3D visualization' [44]

Acceleration sensors and motion prediction stabilizing the images against head movements and compensating for trivialities as the one frame delay of any video system, are working perfectly here. I say this because these issues are still reappearing as problems in scientific papers. Apparently with all new technologies, many things tend to be reinvented several times.

The FOHMD has a very high resolution display with external projectors from where the pictures are transported to the helmet by (expensive and fragile) glass fiber bundles. A high resolution, eye tracker operated picture inlay boosts the resolution at the center of view to an equivalent of about 3000x3000 pixels. The field of view is 67^0 vertical, 127^0 horizontal (both eyes). This is far more than anything one could buy in a shop today.

The computer installation supporting it filled rooms of course, at that time. For our objective, we will need something many times lighter and less expensive.

Even now, more than two decades later, there remains a lot more to develop until we will have a mass market product. While computers in general have taken giant leaps, several other technologies necessary in vision simulator glasses, including optics, are way behind.

Several end user products with more or less limited capabilities have been built meanwhile. The resolution available in this price class is normally 600x800. A few professional or semi professional see-through glasses go up to 1280x1024, (Saab, NVIS, Cybermind) but are still a bit heavy, between 700 and 1300g. Some interesting developments have been announced by Microvision [15].

An overview of current products you'll find at page 163, and in [29] or [50]. For military technology, an interesting source is [37]. As stated, we would need about 1600x1200 pixels at least (better twice as much) and the device should weigh less than 100g.

I'm confident that even less than 20g could finally be achieved after about one more decade of development. There can be little doubt that Display devices for vision simulation glasses will be an important key technology with a huge market, especially as they will replace many traditional screen displays.

Optics

The human eye is quite good at seeing, isn't it? Optically, it's a mess. All the rest is done in the brain. I think this is a very smart concept after all. If nature had tried to give the eye a 'perfect' optical design, our ancestors would probably have long been eaten, as it is impossible to achieve even only a fraction of our eye's capabilities with a conventional camera design.

We should learn from this. The major problem with today's display goggles is that they are attempts to perfect optical design. This can't work well. It gets heavy, the field of view is small and the optics have literally to be screwed to the head.

As we can only see sharp in a little area around the center of view, a display with dynamic focusing and eye trackers does not require an optical design delivering an image that is crisp everywhere. It could be dynamically focused to the area being looked at. Optical distortion should as well be compensated electronically, resulting in simpler, lighter, and cheaper optics.

The system also has to compensate for image size changes due to dynamic focusing and for image position changes due to eye movements and position changes of the glasses towards the head. No fixtures should be necessary anymore.

Dynamic focusing is indispensable anyway. Most 3D systems cause headache because the apparent stereoscopic distance seen, does not match the required eye focus adaptation. A dynamic focusing system should solve this problem by changing focus according to the distances of objects seen in a virtual scene.

With laser scanners, focus is said to be always crisp. Which is true for low resolution displays only, by the way. It could be an advantage or a disadvantage, as it may also be irritating.

Finally, display glasses should not disturb normal sight at all, yet offer the capability to project virtual images over the entire field of view. This sounds ambitious but has already almost been achieved with quite conventional optics, by placing the displays to the side or over the eyebrows, out of view, and mirroring the picture before the eyes. What's obvious, that a large viewing area definitely needs a curved mirror, unlike most current products.

Eye tracking

An accurate and artifact free positioning of virtual objects will be essential for the acceptance of the technology.

Parallactical errors, e.g. angle differences that result from looking through the display more straight or more sideways, should also be eliminated.

As the display screens of our glasses are positioned near the eye, just simply looking about will move the pupilla relative to the display center and (depending on the optical design) may shift the entire image relative to the user's virtual position. This would not be desirable, as would destroy the virtual steadiness of the picture and could be one possible cause of vertigo (dizziness).

Varying positions of the device towards the eye are to be expected as well, at least if we do not want to use those special fixations that are part of almost any current 'VR goggles' and are making these devices so unbearable.

So we will definitely need an eye tracking system, that determines the position of the pupil relative to the display. Such systems in principle are state of the art. They simply use a camera and some image processing software to track the user's pupil.

They are still expensive in the professional area, but cheap versions have already been built even into cameras and camcorders, guiding the autofocus (Canon EOS5, 1992, and Movieboy E1, 1994). What we need for our purpose, would be much faster and more accurate, but this is simply a matter of chip complexity.

Some applications of an eye-tracking system would be:

- Dynamic focusing in order to keep the eye adaptation aligned with the virtual distance of virtual objects or details of 3D scenes displayed.

- Creating picture inlays of higher resolution in the center of vision, as with the FOHMD flight simulator display.

- Exploiting eye-pointing in an advanced user interface.

- Automatic adaptation of the display system for best sight in any constellation.

Position sensors

In the field of relative position sensing, there are many companies with excellent products. The most common solutions use electromagnetic fields (e.g. Polhemus sensor) or camera recognition of light spots connected to the target object.

An intelligent visual orientation system however, based on image processing, would promise a much better solution and could induce a radical change in the ergonomic constraints of virtual reality.

It will be absolutely important that virtual objects can be defined to appear at a certain place in real space, to stay there and only there, which implies they have to disappear when the place or room is left, but also have to reappear when the same place is entered again. This requires the recognition of environments, which can also be achieved by cameras attached to the Display, in conjunction with appropriate image processing.

Such a system would indeed also be useful as a very precise and direct position sensor, simply by exploiting the geometrical object data gained from the recognition process. While this is inherently a bit slow, things are greatly improved by adding some cheap and accurate acceleration sensors to keep track of fast movements, a method already used in aircraft simulators in order to improve the efficiency of triangulation and eye tracking systems.

Another supporting technology is optical flow detection, well known already from the optical computer mouse.

It is important to note that visual orientation would not actually have to separate seen objects, or to identify their nature. The entire difficulty is reduced to the acquisition of 3-dimensional basic structures and their comparison and alignment with stored references. What we need is a system that can swiftly compare stored 3D structures, regardless of perspective.

Basic orientation can be simplified if we include a GPS system. Since the first introduction of the proposed ideas in 1993, GPS[*] receivers have become unexpectedly small and cheap.

---

[*] Global Positioning System. What your car navigator uses. Exploits timing differences of signals from a number of earth satellites.

With a differential GPS transmitter nearby, an accuracy of about 1m can be achieved. Yet we have to keep in mind that GPS reception cannot be expected everywhere, especially not indoors.

We could also envision systems that work like GPS but are confined to local environments, like buildings.

Illumination

If we want to generate natural looking objects, we must show them in the same brightness and light color as the surrounding scene. We must also try to simulate directional lighting, according to light sources the vision simulator cameras and software are able to identify. In order to do this, image analysis has to find the light sources either from directly seeing them, or, more difficult, from shadows cast by real objects.

Then we have to decide whether virtual objects should cast shadows. This is not really simple, because we could only do this appropriately with the mask display, hence not sharp (more next). It may also be wise not to try this much realism, as it would always be safer if we could identify virtual objects as such.

Object merging – the mask display

Image presentation would be significantly improved, if we could cover up light from real world objects at those directions where virtual objects are located. This would simply keep the virtual objects from appearing translucent.

With constructions intercepting direct sight with optics, or even replacing it entirely with camera pictures [25],[77], it would be easy, but these approaches aren't acceptable for everyday use.

Another method would be 'subtracting' the brightness/color values of the real scene from the corresponding pixels of the virtual objects, an approach that works well to a certain extent and has yet been thoroughly investigated with projectors [19]. In our context, there would however be a frequent problem to cover exceedingly bright lights or objects in the background.

Real masking is, in principle, not so difficult to achieve. A cheap black-and-white transparent LCD display panel could dim direct sight at locations of virtual objects. This would however incur some light attenuation due to the polarizer filters necessary with current LCD technology, not optimal for night applications.

There are some other display technologies perhaps better suited for this, especially considered that a curved device would be nice to have. We'll discuss this later on, in the design chapter.

The fact that the mask display is always out of focus, e.g. appears with blurred edges, is not so much of a problem, as you'll see in some sample pictures below. I already proposed this in [2] but it's still a principle widely unknown.

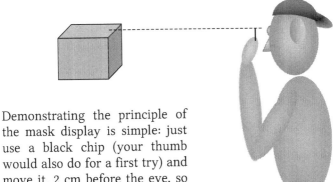

Demonstrating the principle of the mask display is simple: just use a black chip (your thumb would also do for a first try) and move it, 2 cm before the eye, so that it just covers up exactly the edge of some distant object.

It may be surprising that this results in a pretty sharp edge of total obstruction, even though an area of half transparent shadow remains beneath it. Use some thin masking object to verify that even tiny distant objects could be cut out quite selectively. The proper size of the mask also depends on your pupil diameter. A real mask display would have to be corrected for this, and also for edge diffraction effects. The reason why this simple masking works so well we'll explore in the design chapter.

Generating the correct masking shapes of course also requires an entire knowledge of the real scenery, hence cameras, taking pictures from approximately the locations of the user's eyes.

Simulated insertion of virtual images into a real scene

Original view of a perfectly white wall with a rectangular section cut out (covered by mask display with typical unsharp borders). This is from an original digital photo taken with a camera with an opening similar to the diameter of a human eye's lens (2.5 mm). The distance to the mask was like in a real display assembly (2.5cm).

A Virtual image has been inserted into the cutout section. This simulation was done with an image processing software, taking the image as 100% transparent. The image is slightly larger than the 100% black area, therefore a little of the background light shines through at the edges. Of course, if one chose a naturally darker background, this effect would be smaller and the image insertion would be less obvious.

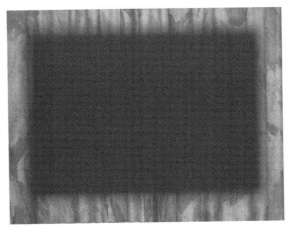

In this example, the masking is applied on a more natural background

Obviously in this case, the masking process is hardly visible anymore.

If the background texture is known (by the position cameras for example) we could also modify the edges of the displayed image, in order to compensate for the blur of the mask.

Foreground object overlay

Another issue we must address for a really hassle free augmented reality representation, is the appearance of real objects in front of a virtual object. Otherwise, the resulting scenery could be very irritating. For example, a virtual keyboard should not hide the user's hands, or it would be unusable.

This was recognized a dozen years ago (e.g.[2]), but is still subject to basic research (e.g.[62]) as many of the themes we're discussing here, because augmented reality has been neglected so much during all this time.

For the virtual object to behave correctly, we have 2 possibilities:

1) to cut out the shape of the real object from the virtual object and the mask display, in order to uncover it, or

2) to overlay a picture of the real object, as taken from the position sensor cameras, over the picture of the virtual object.

The method of choice would usually be 1), at least as long as the image resolution and processing capabilities of the VR display are limited. We could use the position cameras to recognize objects and cut out an appropriate shape from any virtual image supposed to stay in the background.

This is not really so difficult. No object would have to be really 'recognized', it would be entirely sufficient to spot structures that are positioned before the virtual object, starting from a cross correlation of two stereoscopic camera pictures.

In case of general orientation, there are some situations that may not so easily be dealt with. For example, we may consider an entirely monochrome, featureless surface: correlation would be useless here, the distance could at best be constructed from the borders, and some heuristic approaches would also be necessary for reasonable results.

With the foreground overlay of a hand for example, we wouldn't have this kind of problems. There we always have enough features to exploit for a reliable object recognition.

Not always will foreground objects have to be non transparent and solid. The handling of overlays with these 'ghost objects' we will look at a little later.

Virtual keys and Icons

There will be many kinds of interaction possible with virtual objects. One essential difference to most of the current approaches, is that we don't rely on gestures, nor on tactile feedback. Gestures are hard to detect. tactile feedback needs gloves (who wants that).

A frequent type of interaction, in my opinion, will be touching part of an object with a finger. This may be a handle or a virtual key. Feedback will not be tactile but visual and/or with sound.

Eye pointing is even more elegant. It works hands free, which makes it perfectly fit for all mobile applications at least, and it allows for unambiguous pointing even at distant objects.

'Staring' at an object could be a quite distinct action, safe enough for practical use. It could be accompanied by blinking or eye widening for example, allowing to implement very ambitious operation modes with sort of 'click' or 'double click' actions or drag and drop operations, entirely without using the hands.

Not before 2008 had first experiments been carried out about interactions using dwell time and blinking. The result was that dwell time alone was a bit unsafe. A Method called half blink was introduced, already improving things a lot [104].

Essentially, I think that eye operated modes together with speech, and mouse pen or finger inputs for text, will lead to a very convenient and efficient user interface.

Virtual start menus and task bars

Displaying any items fixed to the user's view should normally be avoided. Exceptions could be virtual start menus, task bars or the like, that will probably remain a method for primary access to applications. Virtual bars and menus would usually carry one or more virtual keys. They would, contrary to 'normal' virtual objects, often be transparent, and would appear in areas not primarily inflicting with visual orientation. Above the center of view, for example. Virtual taskbars could be activated in various ways, e.g. by touching a real key sitting right on the vision simulator, on the handles or at the edges of the glasses.

Hardware add-ons

Earpieces (headphones) and microphones are very important add-ons to any vision simulator. The device could then be used as a versatile 'personal communicator', replacing handheld phones, notepads, music players, and, with the anyway included cameras, a camcorder. It would probably be a good idea to integrate microphones into the earpieces, which would also result in an 'artificial head' microphone assembly (something already available under the name 'Soundman', actually working with the real head of the user instead of a dummy), yielding a perfect directional reproduction when listened to with headphones later on, and the possibility to derive normal surround sound channels with the help of some advanced audio processing.

The two cameras of the vision simulator would naturally provide for 3D pictures, something not yet very easy to use for video production, but maybe it could become of interest with future developments in image processing and display technology. The vision simulator technology will promote 3D video anyway.

Really useful would be the already mentioned buttons right at the vision simulator, that could be used to trigger some actions: just touch your glasses and the options menu for the home appliances appears in front of you, for example. Or, even better, use your eyes to point at something and start an action on it by pressing one of the buttons.

It's trivial that we will need some sophisticated radio, cell phone and network connections. The vision simulator has to talk to its computing unit, to local networks and to other vision simulators.

With RFID and active tag technologies, a dedicated radio transmission unit for these could also be helpful. Very simple RFID chips of course require far too much RF power to react at all. With smarter units, solar powered active price tags in supermarkets for example, that could carry their own transmitters and receivers, or just show visual codes pointing to the frequency of a central site network, establishing a communication would be no problem. It would depend on the provider of these units, who could communicate with them and to what extent.

Realization

As we have seen, a display for the virtual devices concept will be a fairly complex system, involving up to four microcameras with image processing (two scene cameras and two eye trackers) and up to four displays (two high resolution color screens and two mask displays), not to mention acceleration sensors, possible acoustical interfaces, communication links etc. The miniaturization necessary won't be a problem, since there already are hosts of affordable microcameras and other very small devices available. The processing power necessary will still be high however, and will most likely have to be provided outside the interface itself.

An intermediate step, prior to the full implementation of all features, could be a system for stationary professional use like in medicine, where the display might still be acceptable at weights up to 300 grams, while the computing equipment could be placed in an extra unit. Yet with chips already used in mobile phones, one could probably build a battery operated wireless glasses assembly real soon now, weighing less than 100g.

Necessary Software for Vision Simulators

Object Presentation	Rendering
	Correction of display optics
	Adaptive resolution
	Adaptive dynamic focusing
Insertion	Image adaptation
	Masking
Positioning	Image/scene recognition
	Fast structural matching/search algorithm
	Acceleration or other sensor interface
	Anticipative positioning
Interaction	Finger or Hand recognition
	Eye tracking
	Voice
	Others
Operating System	Standardized software interface for object presentation and interaction (3D-Windows)

Applications

As stated, the technology outlined could replace many of the information technology devices currently available, the PC screen being but the most obvious.

TVs are another very obvious candidate, of course, then all kinds of control panels, and many more.

In the following I will illustrate several types of example applications. Some more will follow in the media chapter.

The most vivid overview may be the fiction part that follows this chapter. There are many remarks and sidekicks in it, scratching themes that might inspire your fantasy. It's a collection of various pieces of prose that would need a real novelist to make it a thriller, but I hope you like it nevertheless.

The "laptop back" (humpbackus aeroterminalus), a civilisatory disease

Goggle phones

Let's start with an application implementing only part of the functionality, as this is easier for a first product and can be a technology test bed that is sophisticated but still manageable. Just have a look at these very small cell phones that are now equipped with cameras and a lot more things. Their hardware would already be light enough to fit into some (not yet perfect) glasses, it's only built the wrong way.

During his sabbatical, John successfully demonstrated the feasibility of light weight display glasses

No joke at all: it is absolutely possible with available technology right now, to integrate a complete mobile phone into a pair of glasses at fairly convenient size and weight ($\approx$50 grams). A one-eyed, fixed vector display would be sufficient. Considering the increasing habit of wearing micro headsets, it's quite conceivable that such a device would encounter a great demand. Iris or retina recognition could replace passwords, eye pointing could be used for menus and dialing, and the virtual screen size possible would enable full featured web surfing, where users could click on links by just looking at them, just to mention a few of the possibilities.

Such an application obviously lacks about all of the environmental integration that we are talking about here, yet it allows to develop, test and improve a lot of the underlying technologies in the context of a real product, that would already pave the way and create the demand for more sophisticated ones.

Virtual control panels

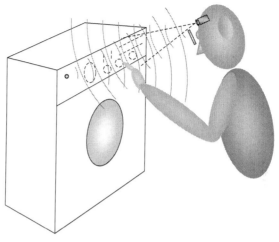

This is one example of the hardware savings potential of vision simulators. The washing machine has no classical control panel. Instead it has an empty surface, possibly with some markers or codes to help the position sensor cameras. An infrared or radio emitter and receiver element are the only real features required.

The machine sends an image of its virtual control panel to the vision simulator, which then makes it visible, in the correct perspective and position.

An important advantage of virtual control panels: they can be customized.

Some day, users will be able to download various skins for any appliance there is. Users will also be able to re-use the same skins for almost any brand of microwaves, or of washing machines or whatsoever, so they don't have to get used to different designs all the time. A device could also be enabled to identify different users by their look or by transmitted codes for example, giving them a customized user interface any time they appear.

Skins can also be much larger than the actual hardware, simplifying access to small devices. Using a virtual control panel follows straightforward the already mentioned virtual key paradigm.

Here, the real (empty) panel provides for tactile feedback, so it is feeling real some way.

Key pressing or other actions will be reported to the washing machine by transmitting infrared or other wireless signals. So this is indeed a two-way communication.

Another advantage: virtual control panels do not have to stay in place. Once activated, we could take them off and operate them from a more convenient position. Radio operated panels could be made to appear wherever desired, so we could operate any equipment in the house without ever leaving the chair.

Remote remotes

TVs today don't hardly have control buttons anymore. Everything went into the remote, and there are reasons. Obviously, nobody likes to jump on his feet and run towards the TV any time the commercials are starting. Remotes also allow saving money on control panel hardware.

Now would we equip a virtual TV with a remote control ? - I guess not really, because these remotes tend to clutter up tables. The better way would be virtual controls beneath the display window, like with an ancient TV set, but operated by eye pointing. Eye pointing would indeed be perfect for this. Eye trackers can detect the user's viewing direction at high accuracy.

Our vision simulator could serve as a universal remote control for all kinds of classical devices as well. A lot better than any we have now. This may even be one of the first most frequent applications for AR glasses.

They could even identify devices by their look and download the right panel look and infrared codes from the web.

All these virtual control functions could already be implemented with the simple 'goggle phones' mentioned above, by replacing the eye operated virtual control panel of the phone with that of another device and adding an infrared or radio transmitter for the remote codes.

Mixed 'virtuality'

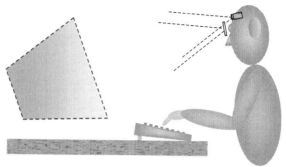

Combining a virtual monitor with a real keyboard

Virtual devices are not a dogma. It would often be smart to combine real parts with virtual ones. A keyboard, for example, can be clumsy to operate if only virtual. With a foldable keyboard, we would still have a very portable solution.

Pens or mice operated on a real surface are other examples for this approach. Game applications need some real joysticks, grips for virtual swords, bats, golf clubs. Certainly, the gadget industry won't die out.

No Force

Some people think that omnipresent tactile feedback would be indispensable for augmented reality. Here I strongly disagree. Not only don't we need this for the vast majority of applications, it would also require the use of gloves, something absolutely unacceptable for everyday use. There are several professional applications that use force feedback and sometimes also hand movement recognition built into special gloves, but these are mostly virtual – not augmented – reality, and there is enough literature about them already. The really revolutionary feature of augmented reality will be eye pointing, hands-free.

Virtual writing

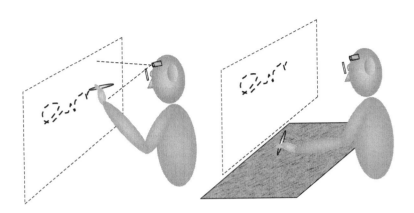

One of the most obvious applications:

A special pen (with acceleration sensors and perhaps a modulated LED light or other markers) could be used to ensure easy detection of the user's hand movements to the position sensor cameras. Virtual lines are drawn when the pen is moved inside the virtual paper plane.
This writing plane would normally better be chosen to fit to a real desktop's surface, or at least to a drawing board, to provide a tactile surface.
Another possibility is to write on a desk with a mouse like pen or a mouse, but to view the results in the virtual window. This would work exactly like a normal mouse with a PC. It would be intuitive, hardly need any processing power and be very reliable. The mouse or pen could also be switched between multiple virtual PC application windows, by eye pointing for example.

We could also think about mixed mode operation, moving the cursor with the eyes, yet clicking and writing with the pen.

Under way

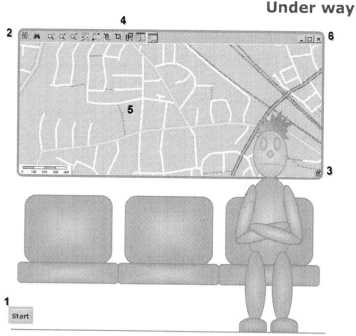

Here is nice example, illustrating the use of simple eye operated applications: suppose you're riding the subway. Wondering where to go next, a city map would come in handy. So you shortly peer at that start icon at the edge of the glasses' display range (1), select the map from the transparent menu popping up (not shown here), place the program window by shortly peering at its desired corners (2,3), and the program starts. The guy facing you is still in front as the window has been 'looked' onto the wall. Now you may select functions from the icon menu (4) or drag and zoom the map (5). Eye lock can be engaged or quit by blinking. Having looked up your target, you close the application by peering at the exit icon (6), or you just leave the train and let others wipe up after you (a joke, that's the *virtue* of *virtu*al devices, they don't litter). You think the guy there may wonder about your strange looking about? Don't worry, the mask displayed for the program window will shield your eyes from him.

A medical application

A quite complete implementation of the technology, yet with lower requirements at least for image resolution and orientation, can be accomplished with medical applications. Displaying images from online diagnostics at their very location of origin results in substantial ergonomic advantages with surgery under NMR (magnetic resonance), CT (computer tomography) and ultrasound imaging.

- Open NMR, Ultrasound and fast CT typically deliver black-and-white images of 128x128...512x512 pixels. So relatively low resolution, even black and white displays can be sufficient.

- The objects are flat (simply cross sections). So we need but simple algorithms for rendering. Showing multiple cross sections would be easy as well.

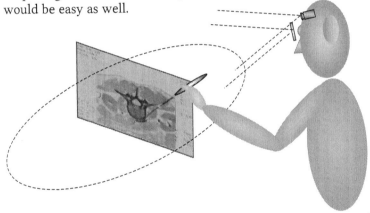

The picture shows a cross section of the human torso, taken with an NMR, that has been set to a perspective similar to a virtual look 'inside' a real patient lying in front of the surgeon. The bone structure of the vertebrae appears in black. The NMR image is from a real minimally invasive operation, where the tiny instrument used is also visible (slanted black line to the right).

The operation shown was carried out under continuous NMR control. A virtual display as visualized here, would have largely facilitated the operation, as it would have eliminated the necessity to repeatedly look up to the monitor and back to the instrument.

Several more or less similar appearing applications have meanwhile been implemented. Nevertheless, dynamic head position and eye tracking have been thoroughly addressed but very recently in [4] (an application with offline data but nevertheless very close to our general concept of virtual devices).

In such an application with a single surgeon carrying out minimally invasive therapy, a simple 2D or 3D flatscreen floating just above the operation field could also be used, as in this case no cameras need to take up the operation field or the surgeon's hands and there may not be much to see that this screen could cover up. As a simple solution, this would at least deliver a convenient viewing position for the surgeon, but in case we want a realistic perspective, we would still have to measure the surgeon's head position and calculate the image accordingly.

Another option would be to show several adjacent layers simultaneously in a transparent way, giving the surgeon real 3D information with very little computing effort. This only works with a display like ours, that allows for dynamic looking around by head movements.

It is a very important fact indeed that dynamic image presentation can be used to exploit the vast 3D processing abilities of our brains. For example, if we would use a normal ultra sound device and project its echo image just into the body at originating location and in real time, the beam 'flowing' around inner structures would just appear to depict them three dimensional, if it can be moved rapidly enough to let these images appear timely related in our visual system. It is also possible to use raw data from tomographic scans, have them perspectively displayed in a transparent way, and have this entire 'pixel cloud' either move itself or being viewed like a virtual object that the viewer can look at from different angles. Without rendering any surfaces at all, a perfect 3D impression will emerge (Dornier medical once experimented with this). More about this at p.73 (ghost objects).

Cooperative telemanipulation
(remote surgery)

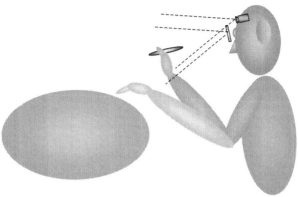

This is a quite complicated application, in that both participants here see their own hands as well as the other's. The operating surgeon sees the patient (a dinosaur egg) directly, and he can also see the hands of the consulting surgeon.

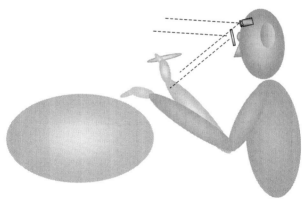

The consulting surgeon sees exactly what the operator sees, and he cannot only give acoustic advice, but also point directly to parts of the operating area. His hands are filmed by his head position cameras and the picture is transmitted to the operator.
So this is truly a 2-way communication, with speech and images.

Integrating external infrared or radar pictures
(virtual headup display)

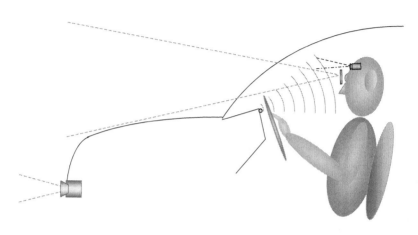

An example how to save expensive hardware by using a vision simulator. A radar sensor mounted to the car's front, or a far infrared camera, are delivering images for better sight at night driving or in fog.

The vision simulator here replaces an expensive headup display. The picture is transmitted by an IR or radio device in the dashboard.

Perspective correction information for the virtual overhead display is provided by the position sensor cameras of the vision simulator itself.

The car's instrument panel could also largely be replaced by a virtual version of course, like with the washing machine example.

A routing guide could also be transmitted to the vision simulator and seamlessly be integrated into the field of view, probably much better than with an LCD device mounted somewhere on the panel, and also better than with a classical headup display, because any information could seamlessly be integrated into the real landscape.

Intelligent sunglasses

As to their high intrinsic absorption, currently available solutions for the mask display will not be suited for night driving.

Nevertheless, if we find a better technology, the mask display could also serve as an anti blinding mechanism, selectively dimming the headlights of approaching cars.
The position sensor cameras would provide information about extraordinarily bright lights, which we would then use to darken appropriate areas in the mask displays.
Correcting for the slightly different perspectives of the cameras and the user is very easy, as we only need distance information that comes from correlating the camera images.

This way, blinding lights could be dimmed without affecting the entire field of view. With such an equipment, one could perhaps even directly view into the sun (nevertheless, don't try this !).
Especially when driving, anybody would probably highly appreciate such a feature.
For day driving, it would of course work with a simple LCD mask display already.

Avionics applications

Avionics exhibit some similarities to the automotive application presented, yet here the vision simulator could also replace the headset, even with advanced features like noise cancellation.
Nowadays, advanced color screen displays are replacing classical instruments even in general aviation. These units are a major advancement, but they are pretty expensive.
As headup displays are already appearing in cars however, these will also be seen even in low budget general aviation airplanes.

If everybody would use a vision simulator as discussed here, displaying would almost entirely be done with it. The only hardware add-on for an airplane to keep up to date with the most modern features, would then be a data link that transmits all information from the 'classical' instruments, and also receives some input from the vision simulator.

The vision simulator could generate a very versatile display, head-up style for example, and a lot more.
It still needs software to process instrument data and operator inputs, to generate an ergonomic display (instruments, maps etc.). Some orientation features, like virtual maps, GPS, etc. would just be part of the vision simulator anyway, but a necessary addition would be electronic air maps, approach charts, ATIS and other avionics information, and all software for processing and display.

Radio hardware should of course remain part of the airplane, it requires a lot of RF power and special hardware features that won't make sense in a vision simulator. The same applies to most of the 'classical' instrumentation. We would not even have to drop any of these to make room for new displays. So the entire concept would be one of great redundancy. Which doesn't mean that it would come for free. Instruments and sensors need data links to be integrated into an advanced system.

What's most important: the virtual display would not only save the costs for the extra screens, it would greatly surpass them.
Blocking direct sight, like huge conventional instrument boards tend to do, would be a thing of the past. We could use images from cameras outside the airplane and generate a virtual view through the walls, introducing an entirely new level of visual overview and situation awareness.

Maps, trajectories, also a predicted flight path of our own airplane and of others, could just be projected into the landscape and the skies, and be visible through walls and wings.
First steps in this direction have been tried, in [38] for example, but anything like this will need a good affordable vision simulator to get into common use.

Virtual Radar

Every airplane has a device called transponder, a radio transmitter that continuously transmits the aircraft's altitude and ID code. This usually helps radar to classify echoes and to generate an informative display for traffic control.
There are plans to have transponders transmit GPS data as well, because then it would be simple to get a traffic overview without a radar, so a relatively simple device could provide any pilot with a virtual radar image of any traffic within radio range.

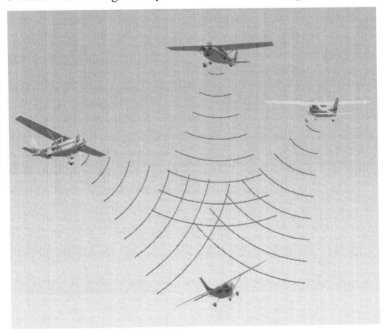

A vision simulator could make this up as a really 3-dimensional picture, letting the pilot see other aircraft right through the cabin wall or the wings, removing any of the usual dead angles.
The aircraft itself would not even need to have a built-in GPS, as the vision simulator would already have one, yet it would be better for safety (redundancy) of course.

Speaking of redundancy: Multi function color screens always come in pairs, to have a backup if one of them fails. With Vision simulators generally available and probably cheap enough (this would not be specialized GA stuff but consumer electronics), having some spare ones wouldn't be a problem at all. It would therefore come out a lot cheaper than today's high end instrumentation, without any loss of safety.

Virtual conferencing

Vision simulators could easily be used as a videophone. If the user places himself in front of a mirror, the environment cameras could pick up his image and transmit it. In turn, his own simulator could display the image of the communication counterpart(s).

The impression however would not be ideal. In order to display the communication partner(s), a central part of the mask display would have to be darkened, otherwise the user would see himself and his partner as a mixed image. This would cause his vision simulator to look like dark sunglasses.

A simple solution would be using the eye tracker picture. We would need a very good eye tracker for a good vision simulator anyway, one that should cover the entire eye. So this picture could easily be inserted into a face picture, resulting in a true and real reconstruction of what is actually there.

The only problem here could be that we probably use infrared lighting for the eye tracker, and other light sources could be dark. Hence, color wouldn't necessarily be accurate. We may have to reconstruct color. Not a big problem, if we only once before provide the system with a true color picture of the user's eyes.

In a room with several cameras installed, an entire array perhaps, more options would be available. Virtual perspectives could be generated and merged into one virtual room. Still then, eye contact has to be established. With many participants involved, this can be tricky, maybe an eye simulation is necessary to adapt the different perspectives. Simple one-to-one videophone talks by the way never needed such sophisticated approaches, here it is simply possible to use a 3D picture taken by a stereo camera and turn it into a virtual 2D camera view from inside the screen, just form the place where the conversation partner's eyes appear to be.

Simple speech connections will undoubtfully remain a frequent application as well, especially when walking, driving etc.

Videophone technology has been overestimated all the time, anyway. When it was expensive, nobody bought it and since it is a cheap function in any computer or mobile, hardly anybody uses it. In most cases it only makes sense if you haven't seen your conversation partner before or if you also want to show him something. And it doesn't work when on the walk.

Our new hardware will improve this application a lot. It also enables new ways of dialing, hands-free.

Meet my avatar

Another method of virtual meeting would work with avatars. The device could be taught to 'know' how its bearer would look. It could also pick up eye movements just by the eye trackers. If we would add some micro cameras to record the face (just near field down from the lower end of the glasses maybe) and to eliminate the dead angle in gesture recognition, a sufficiently intelligent software could generate a quite vivid and exact simulation of the user's actual look, even without the obstruction by the simulator.

It would even be possible to synthesize position and environment. The user could, for example, lie on his back at a beach, while the software would depict him sitting at a desk in an appropriate business outfit. It could even compensate physiognomy changes that result from non vertical positions. It could also shave its user, and so on...

Quite a peculiar concept, but anyway, physiognomy, look and gesture could become entirely realistic, so the main objective of video conferencing would be achieved. Needless to say that such a concept could be expanded to several partners simultaneously, that they could be arranged in a virtual conference room independent of their actual being sitting, standing, of their outfit or environment. We could even generate perfect eye contact between all participants, something extremely difficult with any conventional teleconferencing system.

I have very little doubt that this can be achieved perfectly enough to be totally acceptable as a professional tool. There already are some experimental tele-conferencing systems using image processing and perspective correction to restore eye contact [10], so the solution discussed is not so surprising at all.

The downside: one could also abuse such a system, not only to look better, but to deceive people in many ways. Anyway, this is not too bad if people know about these possibilities and are prepared to be suspicious about what they see. A manufactured communication avatar is not too different from a faked document, is it? Another nice side effect of avatar imaging: Bandwidth requirements are extremely low. Indeed, the capacity of a simple classical telephone line may suffice to transport both good sound and a crisp and vivid image. With today's rapid increase of available bandwidth in most of the communication channels available, this may not seem so important. Nevertheless, bandwidth will always remain a cost factor, and the difference between a really good TV transmission and what has just been proposed here, is tremendous. So in case of wireless communications, or a satellite link, this advantage may still count a lot.

... or me, in person

When bespectacled people meet face to face, an automatic *data* communication link between their vision simulators will prove most useful. The important thing to solve is identification. Just wireless data transmission alone cannot tell the devices that they are really talking to each other. The transmission source has to be identified. This can simply be done by transmitting the own visual appearance. Facial appearance of the bearer, or a picture of the sim device itself or a visual code on it will serve the purpose. Another possibility would be a transmission of time coded optical signals, an infrared emitter for example, or an entire display picture, maybe even a modulation of the mask display and/or an intentional defection of light from the own sim display. All of this could be recognized by the other sim's cameras and brought into correlation with radio signals received.

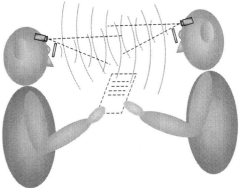

Once the proper radio source is identified, a secure channel can be established and visual concepts and documents can be made visible and accessible to all partners communicating.

Virtual Worlds

While *second life* for instance meant a whole lot of new experiences to many people, to an IT specialist it's core technology is essentially a no brainer. What you need is a graphics and physics simulation engine as in any game from flight simulator to Quake. Linking such games for multi user experiences in a network is something that has been done for decades. Usually, any participant in such gang games had his own copy running on his own machine, but all of them with the same pre-defined scenery set, and anything special was the other participants appearing in the scene when appropriate. With web hosted games and 2nd life type applications, the blueprint usually goes like this: all of the virtual world is hosted and run in a remote server park. Individual users send their intended position and motion and get the model based description of their view back in turn. That's nearly all about it.

Of course the user has to define his avatar appearance before-hand, and there also are physical feedbacks from the model about his motion parameters, he can also express wishes or just buy changes in the virtual model (adding an estate, getting virtual goods etc.), but it's still simply a distributed game application in the end. What makes it different, is the more complex social scenario and the fact that the world itself is variable, can be 'developed'. Therefore it is also better if the world scenario is hosted in the servers, as it can be changed by anybody anytime. The experience is technically limited as long as only simple PC screens are used, but it may be intensified by imagination, just like the simple text based adventure games in the early days of computing. An invented world is already a good place for experiments and imagination, of course. With the *real* world rebuilt, this is possible as well. There are a few models of real cities under construction already, but roaming in them just by the screen interface makes hardly more sense than with an invented world, so the question remains, why should we bother with realism in such an application. For orientation and exploration it will surely make sense however, as an extended Google Earth for instance, but there the social factor is not as important.

Virtual travel

Assembling a complete model of the real world will be utterly simplified as soon as the better part of the world's population will be wearing vision glasses. Assuming the presence of numerous webcams, and even more so personal goggle cams anywhere, anytime, we may assume that there will be no place on earth not being recorded at least once a month, or more likely even once a minute or second, and in many different views as well. This will enable the calculation of a more or less current 3D model of any place there is, just by merging the many available views, of course requiring some pretty complex algorithms for matching all these pictures. Such a merging of simple pictures to 3D worlds has already been demonstrated [100]. Adjustments for lighting, shadows, weather, distortions, etc. will be necessary, and temporary changes caused by moving objects, cars or pedestrians, will have to be eliminated. Form a 3D model once established this way, almost perfect real time views from any position can be synthesized if even only one current view from an occasional goggle or web cam can be obtained for some hints about current light, weather, and so on. The entire scene pre-rendering and real time adaptation should occur in a server that would only have to be given the desired viewpoints and trajectories and that could then return the perfected scenic impression in a compressed format, possibly containing vector and texture representations as in game engine based applications, or MPEG-like motion based compression for a more photo realistic rendering.

The ongoing digitization of the earth would for instance allow us to choose any really existing in- or outdoor location for virtual events. Having a meeting in some nice place on the other side of the globe would be no problem, even special places could be provided for the purpose. People could even meet in plain air, floating amidst the falls of Iguaçu, for example, or sitting there at a flying table talking to each other (or down in the jumble, in between the howler monkeys, more adequate in some cases).

The scenery could easily be a real-time 3D rendering from a few simple high definition webcams. It could even be calculated locally, at each client's computer in this case. With only a rudimentary real counterpart at each participant's real location, a chair and a table supporting tactile impressions, this would feel quite real. Actual paper documents could be used and handed over, being turned into virtual thereby. Which would only work with single pages of course, or if the system already knows the contents. Otherwise, images of already virtual documents would be better. Just using this for stupid video talks would however be ignorant. Virtual travel would be a much better idea, being able to explore any place anytime, and for free of course (providers could place ads into the virtual presentation, seamlessly on house walls and real signposts). Social simulations could take place in the virtual twin of the real world, many parallel worlds could be created, and so on. More of this in the fiction chapter (p.142).

Eye Steering

The real potential of eye steering has hardly been recognized so far. A simple but impressive example may illustrate this: quite recently I had the opportunity to test a research setup of a simple computer game that could be operated by mouse as well as eye pointing. Nine little 'holes' were depicted on a screen, and inside them a gnome randomly appeared. The task was to point at him by the mouse pointer or by the eye, so it would disappear.

Although I'm pretty quick with the mouse, my eyes performed twice as fast. No wonder in a way, as focusing to sudden events as quickly as possible, must always have been very important to man throughout his entire evolution. So eye steering, properly implemented, is much quicker than manual steering, and if you fear this would tire the eyes, just try to watch how many movements your eyes are performing unconsciously, all the time. They are never at rest. Even when staring at one point, they are performing little movements, 'saccades', even necessary as without them, things at rest would disappear from our view within seconds, and we would only be able to see things that are moving, like a crocodile.

Hence, „*the eyes have it*":

- eyes look where the action is, intuitively
- and almost without wear
- are faster than our hands
- and more accurate
- and can work at a distance.

Gaze switching

Objects meant to be eye-operated will usually be virtual, and located at distances different from that of others in the same direction. This means, display glasses with stereo eye trackers will surely know when you look at any of an object's controls rather than anywhere else, and it can simply discriminate the intent to switch something if you are keeping your eye on the control for more than a third of a second.

Meanwhile, first research has been done on this approach, delivering valuable insights into the dynamics of eye switching [104].

Squint-and-touch

Eye pointing can seamlessly be integrated with finger pointing, yielding an utterly powerful interface:
- We usually look where we want to hit
- The software only has to watch the area before the key, for things looking like a finger appearing in the camera picture.
- Hence, the entire complexity of this approach is far lower than with the usual hand recognition schemes.
- Not only this: We could grab right into a complex 3D structure and pick out an element.

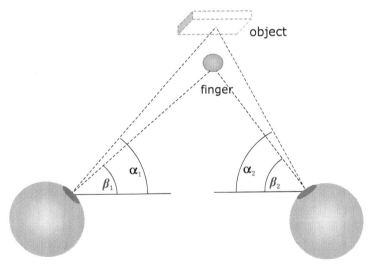

The complex and powerful options this delivers are hardly recognized so far. It leads way beyond the conventional ideas about virtual worlds. So let us explore this a little further.

Ghost objects and devices *(Vaporware?)*

This is introducing an entirely new concept, expanding the possibilities of virtual objects far beyond those known or imagined from real ones.

Some time ago I took a new look on some old ideas, considering what would happen if we could actively use our eye accommodation to pick out spots in three dimensional point clouds.

Raw tomography data for example is fairly huge by the number of pixels and therefore hard to rotate in real time. Calculating features and surfaces for a solid modeling is even more difficult.

Our brain however, if we are looking at nothing but rotating transparent raw data pixel clouds, gives us a perfect 3D impression even on a 2D screen. Alas with this simple approach, many features are just occluded by others, even so if we render for optimum transparency and actively look at features from all sides.

Just confining the rendering process to the center of view, steered by eye tracking, has long been tried and may reduce calculations.

But what if we also use depth accommodation, focus and eye parallax that is, to render just one depth area, that we are accommodating to, denser and crisper than others?

It would save a lot of computing power as well, as we only have to render each pixel for a small area of main interest, 1/1000 of the volume for example, and anything else at far lower resolution.

Literature, reveals a few hints on confining rendering efforts actively to area and depth, but only for solid modeling. Only one paper deals with manipulations of pixel cloud rendering by eye steering, in this case by certain *eye gestures* using a single eye tracker [95].

This medical application is however just one out of many possible others that could profit from active depth steering.

In virtual and augmented reality, entirely new things could be created by exploiting active accommodation.

This new approach would use the eye parallax or accommodation, giving the actual distance of the point of interest, to render crisp only things in this distance, and others before and after it progressively unsharp. Concurrently, we could make the foreground components more transparent.

All these are features not known in reality. *Real* objects can also be transparent, but even despite of parallax and focus effects, we will always have difficulties seeing details within them.
With virtual objects reacting to eye directions and parallax, uncovering the detail being looked at, this will be totally different.

We could build virtual devices that are transparent, have features distributed in 3D space rather than on surfaces, and can be accessed throughout all their physical volume. An entirely new world of designs to explore.
So a genuinely three dimensional device could have controls over all of its volume, in many different layers. Like with 2D and 2½D devices (any real machine is 2½D, as its interface consists just of its surface), the combination of eye peering with finger pointing delivers an entirely unambiguous signal of intent.

There are many more possibilities: imagine virtual objects being like faint vapor when not in use, staying in place while just hinting their existence, but becoming solid all of a sudden when you accommodate to their proper distance.
Or several layers of windows on your computer screen (to mention the most old fashioned stuff), not simply being transparent but changing transparency and crispness according to depth accommodation, of course requiring different eye parallax and focus to look at them.
Then it would not only be possible to see a window quite well through another, transparent one, we could even operate controls on the background window, by eye as well as by finger pointing, without mistaking the action as being meant for the foreground window. This means *real* operation in 3D, something not even possible with physical 3D objects.

Other than the transparency of current window managers, hardly being useful at all, this could really be working, but of course here we are at the limits of conventional displays again, as it would really be hard to accommodate by parallax on a screen that cannot deliver the appropriate focus as well.

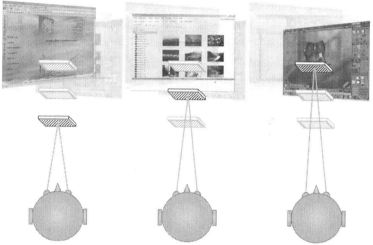

Nevertheless, 3D eye pointing can also be used with conventional 3D screens to a certain extent, if both eyes can be accurately tracked from a distance. Accurate distant eye tracking has been demonstrated with many different applications already.

With display glasses, things are all different and of course a lot better. Virtual windows could not only be arranged all around us but also in several layers, enabling not only dozens but many hundreds of them for concurrent use.

Moreover, we could not only enable virtual looking through walls, but fully automate it, making the wall disappear as soon as we look towards infinity, changing its humble appearance for a view from outside cameras, or for a giant screen cinema event.

Several layers of virtual bookshelves stacked in front of a wall, all kinds of gadgets, devices and utilities shown as vapor or faint outlines when not in use (Vaporware, anyone?), but getting into life if you eye-point at them in three dimensions. A virtual globe for example, in the middle of your living room, five ft. tall but not activated by an icon, instead by looking at its own faint preview.

These virtual objects should of course disappear as soon as you are approaching real ones covered by them, just for safety.

This is an unknown realm leaving a lot to be explored, as it is not obvious how the interaction with such objects would feel.

Would a 3D solid dissected this way, giving the impression of a super microscopic or ultra narrow depth-of field view, interact with our visual system in a convenient way?

Would the reactions of the object make our accommodation go astray? Could we easily learn to willfully accommodate towards 'nothing', beyond or before things that we really see, to activate the others still hidden?

These are very complex questions that no one can currently answer. A properly designed system might work well, while a poorly designed one might cause headache and eye strain.

Nevertheless the enrichment of the virtual experience by these things would be overwhelming, and any research in this field will be very rewarding, given alone the numerous fancy applications we could imagine. In 2D, we are actually seeing but a tiny speck of an image crisp at a time. Our eyes move around, picking up part by part and giving us an impression of the entire scene.

So we could suspect this to work for the depth dimension as well. Then we could assemble within our mind a total, three dimensional imagination of an object, without big effort. With our brain, being genuinely a 3D machine, it should be possible to accomplish. This visualization method could be of advantage not only for virtual objects. It would greatly enhance and facilitate tasks like virtual looks inside engines in maintenance jobs, virtual looks into patients in surgery, simulated see-through for guidance and orientation of any kind.

There can be many varieties of this approach. Instead of dual eye trackers measuring parallax (squint), we could e.g. use a refractometer assembly measuring eye focus though the lens.

The little extra effort of an accommodation sensor (see p.392 and on), can create a monocular goggle phone almost as powerful as a full fledged virtual vision system, even without motion tracking and object registering. Transparent vapor icons and buttons could be used, and activating them by eye pointing would become very secure, as it would only work when accommodation would fit as well. Eye-pointing onto a link inside a virtual, transparent web page would also be depending on proper accommodation, so if we look at something further away, the link wouldn't react.

The page could of course become fully transparent at far accommodation and reappear at near accommodation, half transparent then for example. Hence, using complex virtual interfaces in the real world would become a lot easier even if the device would not support any real world placement or registering of these objects. In the end, 3D eye pointing will be utterly convenient. Many other applications will be possible that we can't even imagine right now.

A short summary of possible applications:

- gaze selecting among transparent 3D layered windows or objects
- simulated transparent views into real objects (engine service)
- 'seeing' through walls
- dissecting three dimensional structures
- moving virtual objects around, by eye-pointing
- really three-dimensional objects (3D chess game)
- dynamically looking through walls (3D+ Quake)

Overlay handling with ghost objects

There is a profound difference - not in appearance but in ways of rendering - of making transparent a real or a virtual object.

With the virtual object, it is utterly simple, we just have to let the background shine through.

A real object we can only make transparent if we have a picture of what's behind it. Outside camera pictures for example if we intend looking through a wall. Pictures from several cameras would have to be rendered to the one right perspective for the viewer, of course.

Corrective glasses

Quite obviously a vision simulator could in some cases replace corrective glasses, by overlaying sharp pictures from the position cameras onto the real scene. The different perspective could be mended by image processing, and an advanced vision simulator should be able to position the overlay precisely.

How this would look and feel isn't yet foreseeable. It may be a lot better than varifocals, but with short sightedness we would require those overlays all the time. The better way in this case may be individual corrective lenses added to the display glasses for far adaptation, reserving the overlay feature for the close-up range.

Surgical methods for eye correction are another option. Correcting just short sightedness by laser ablation has literally become a fashion. Yet this doesn't help with the reading problems due to lack of near adaptation, experienced by most people over the age of 50. It appears that replacing the entire lens with a soft synthetically one might entirely restore adaptation. There aren't enough long term experiences with this so far, but maybe in the not-too distant future it will be possible to correct any sight problem the surgical way. Glasses could then become a thing of the past maybe. So you may ask, why introduce them again by wearing a vision simulator? Anyway, there's no other way so far to make a minimized man machine interface; and after all, why are so many people walking around with sunglasses even at night ?? There are even at least two products integrating an MP3 player with sunglasses right now. All a matter of fashion.

Seeing with the ears

One class of partial implementations that we shouldn't forget concerns sound: generating spatial sound impressions complying with the pictures of virtual objects is something that's necessary for a vivid impression with both virtual devices and media, and definitely needs to be a component of the vision simulator's software. This leads to another thought: we could also generate sounds just from the images, letting things start to hum, whistle or crackle.

Entirely weird? Not at all. There are people who can't see but have learned to orientate themselves just by making noises and listen to the echoes. It can work extremely well. Even a special generator for these echo blimps is already available.

Yet couldn't it yield an even better sound image if we use the camera images and generate spatial sound as if the objects were actively emitting it? Spatial discrimination improves a lot if we can turn our head and listen for the changing sounds (which the device could simulate). Many things already have a very characteristic sound image (knock at them and you know). We could also encode object color, size and speed with different sounds. So vision simulator technology could even provide for a very efficient and affordable implementation of solutions for visually impaired people. Imagine the cameras recognizing signs and inscriptions from ordinary objects and make them sound different. Eye or finger pointing could then tell the device to read the text. The cameras could recognize persons from a distance, recognize many other things and just tell about them, and so on.

This is all not as far fetched as it may first appear, and indeed there is already at least one project with similar objectives [59].

Let's consider this further with the vision simulator in mind: many visually impaired people are still able to use eye pointing to a certain degree of accuracy. Imagine different applications windows arranged in 3D space clearly separated, sounding according to status or content, also clearly separable, and reacting to pointing by reading their contents or accepting entries, perhaps with a mouse pen. Imagine a person wearing the specialized vision simulator device taking a book, opening it, and the position cameras would right away start 'reading' it loud to the earphones. With eye pointing, the device would also know when to start reading and if at the left or the right page. In addition, finger pointing could be used to select certain paragraphs or sentences. All absolutely intuitive, ergonomic and natural.

Using the position cameras for general orientation needs some additional thoughts. Simply recognizing locations, what we typically require of a vision simulator, does not require to identify objects in a way that would determine their nature or meaning. It does not even require separating different natural objects from each other. Meaningless scene details are entirely enough.

Image recognition in the classical sense, as we would require for an intelligent orientation support system, is different. We would need a lot more sophisticated software and probably some support in case of ambiguities in the image interpretation (a glass door, for example is a difficulty), or in case of insufficient light. In these situations, an additional depth sensor - maybe a simple ultrasound device - would help quite a lot. Many things to develop, yet certainly way easier than creating the complete perfect vision simulator, especially because we won't need those high end displays here.

There is also an amazing project with an entirely different approach, as it translates pixel patterns directly into spectral patterns, sort of a sweep signal [58]. Surprisingly, people can learn to interpret these patterns very well, and actually 'see' the image that a camera delivers. It's astonishing that this works at all, and once more it reveals how flexible a human brain can adapt to the environment, although the learning curve seems to be pretty steep.

Currently this works with a single camera and is about to be extended to stereo view and more. The most fascinating development is a version that works on a camera mobile phone and is nothing but a free software for the phone. Minimum cost and maximum effect.

This may as well be a basis to add some of the features discussed above, like automatic object recognition or classification, automatic reading, spatial sound impressions and so on. Just imagine what could be achieved if mobile phones were already built like vision simulators. This could lead to fascinating products very fast, even in numbers allowing for a commercial amortization. Being based on a widely used, common vision simulator technology, these would be very affordable as well.

Sharing a virtual object

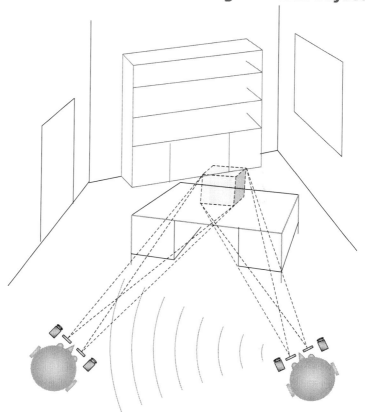

We've already touched upon the handover of virtual objects. It's a special variety of object sharing:

The right user has defined himself an object (maybe a virtual monitor) sitting on top of a real desktop in an office. This object is real to him, stays fixed to the real environment and is obviously no more accessible if he leaves the room (like any real object also wouldn't). He can make this object visible and accessible to others by selecting this feature (how that is done, is defined by the 3D operating system he uses), then his vision device transmits the object's data by infrared, radio or similar, so others can receive it. The receiver's vision simulator then produces a picture of the virtual device in the perspective correct for him. Depending on the sharing allowances given, the other user may also operate or even move the device. In game applications, he could even steal it.

Virtual holography ('holodeck')

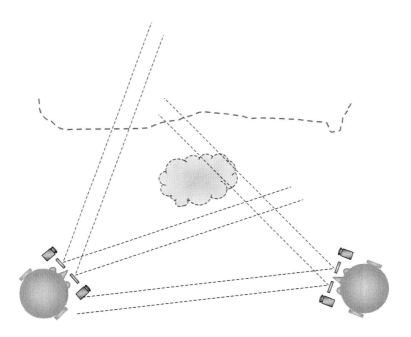

It is self evident that a vision simulator with appropriate software could generate the illusion of totally immersed 'real' objects, as with a 'holodeck' that everybody knows from the Star Trek series. (of course, without tactile feedback or the danger of getting hurt; the simulation of real intelligent beings from fairy tales will also take some more time to develop).

Virtual showcase,
Virtual exhibition, public objects

In a radio networked environment, anybody could set up a node that transmits object descriptions and possibly communicates with vision simulators passing by.

Imagine virtual window dressings, or an entirely virtual art exhibition, especially useful for sculptures.

Nodes delivering object descriptions also have to transmit some data for their location and orientation, descriptions of real objects in the same environment for example, references to their own appearance, pictures or block codes, and virtual object position relative to them. They could even serve differential GPS data to further facilitate the task (information about the actual deviation of GPS at location).

Objects Types

Objects may be static, moving, interactive, restricted to certain users, for free, or payware. They may be shared by groups of users or just be generated for one.

Detailed type descriptions should allow to determine if a certain object should be accessed automatically, by user command or not at all.

Object allowances

Sometimes it needs to be secured that public objects do not cause hazards. Street traffic for example has to be protected from such interference.

Objects should also not be allowed to molest anybody.

Therefore it will be necessary to establish rules and licensing structures that inhibit the abuse of public objects.

We will return to this in the Design chapter.

More applications

- Virtual advertising towers, placards, posts etc.

- Virtual attendants, guides, policemen, road runners... (should only be possible if authorized).

- Location dependent information: signs, road signs, labels and popup windows of all kinds.

- Virtual environments, guidance etc. in shops.

- Virtual road and town guides.

- Virtual Internet everywhere, with all services imaginable.

- Virtual media: this is a wide area also comprising novel recording technologies. It will enable truly holographic films and many other things. See media chapter.

- Virtual cinemas (would it really make sense? sound, effects and snacks could still be real; the virtual display makes perfect 3D and surround possible; more on this in the media chapter).

- Virtual training and job guidance, showing how to do things, hands-on, with explanations, virtual hands and tools showing techniques, even intelligent observation and commenting of user actions.

- Virtual training on 'unreal' things, like 4-dimensional or quantum worlds...

- And still many more

Additional applications will appear in the fiction and the design chapter of this book.

Some others - that don't need the fully implemented vision simulator - are outlined in [3].

Markets

For highly complex products, there are typically three major market segments that can provide for a stepwise amortization of development costs for new technology: Military (partly), Office and Home.

Other professional applications (medical, industrial, architectural etc.) will only create niche markets in comparison.

In military applications, costs are typically not most relevant. With defense budgets sometimes under pressure, it is also important to know that simple pilot applications could easily be implemented in medical environments. This could well be helpful to lay the foundations for a new technology trend.

Not only a trend though. Expect a revolution.

Yet core technology developments for such markets only are generally not recommendable. Although medical applications are an ideal area of experimentation, also with lower technical requirements, and even though there are some military products that have to be rugged but can be kept relatively simple, the billions to be invested into the new technology may only be amortized with millions of pieces sold. Being 100 or 1000 times smaller than the office or home markets, specialized segments might well accept higher product costs, but scarcely 100 or 1000 times as high.

I won't try to guess any numbers here, but from the applications it is obvious that the market impact of this technology will be extreme.

Many major manufacturers will have to rethink about their abstinence from certain consumer or business relevant markets, especially the camcorder or the mobile phone market, where a lot of manufacturing and component technologies for future vision simulators are located. The same applies to the ignorance about certain components, e.g. high resolution micro displays.

Ecological and economical implications

The ecological and economical advantages of virtual objects technology will be immense.

Today, fast changing technology obsoletes equipment every 2-5 years. This will not be different with VR equipment, but with our virtual devices concept, only very small amounts of physical equipment will be discarded, while virtual devices are simply reprogrammed. With such an interface, virtual paper would finally have the potential to really replace its physical counterpart, because ergonomic constraints are far better met than with any present concepts.

Power consumption is another paramount advantage. Displaying a picture directly into one's eyes may take up to a million times less energy than providing the same image brightness on a large screen. Button head phones typically are 10.000 times more efficient than speakers. The power drain of computer and signal processing chips will also drop dramatically in the near future, so the entire personal information systems will need milliwatts where today's devices are drawing watts (hundreds of them).

In conjunction with a communication network supporting virtual offices and work at home, not only office buildings will become obsolete in great parts, but working environments will be reduced to a minimum as well. Virtual devices will replace traditional hardware and filing concepts, and working conditions will become independent of location.

Given these effects, and the even broader impact on everyday applications, this technology will be for the 21st century what the car was for the 20th.

Anything we're considering here, is a logical part of the advent of information technology, or the 2nd industrial revolution. It's already a fact that even though we should have learned something, some mistakes of the first industrial revolution are obviously being repeated.

As any new technology, this one may require major conversions. Well, it's trivial that people do invent technology to save work or resources. It should increase wealth. Everybody's, hopefully (cars don't buy cars).

The economy is not to blame if changes don't unfold in a smooth way. Businesses are to earn money, nothing else. Even if they know better, their lobbies are only there to multiply individualist interests which, if turned into politics, could as well turn out damaging or suicidal to their very originators. Preventing new technologies or seeking cheaper labor instead of investing may be short term strategies for one company, but turn out bad for all in the long run.

What is due in many more aspects as well, is to adjust the legal system to entirely new facts and circumstances.

The diligence to create appropriate structures is due politics. Alas quite obviously, people in charge often don't meet the challenge so well, in a society where many important players are still carrying a mindset from the 17th century (or even the Roman Empire, as they would probably even proudly concede), without having or even wanting a clue about production technology, economics of scale, nor the very essentials of system dynamics or evolutionary processes, too lazy to calculate, simulate or really question anything there is, just talking all the time, still thinking in their stomach that the most effective way of production would be slave work, and that creativity as well as technology are sort of an obscure substance that can be traded like lean hogs. In fact, not so many people seem to have a real clue about what's going on in these days at all.

Politicians have got the mandate, the power and (in most cases, we're hoping) also the will to act adequately, but are too often lost in the labyrinth of opinions and propositions flooding on them. Lobbying runs wild nowadays, more than ever.

What we are talking about here is an utterly important matter. Information may become more valuable than hardware, and the plains are open and the wagons run. Some people already are trying very hard to get an unfair share, you'd guess.

Bottom line: it's every single citizen's own responsibility to take care about this. Not just deciders, but anybody has to *really learn* about technology. Voters at least have to ask for whom 'their' candidates are really acting, or who pays their campaign for example (takes just a few mouse clicks!).

Big Brother

With everybody wearing a vision simulator, having orientation cameras recording anything being seen, connected to wireless networks, it may well be possible that crooked governments want to have access to all this data.

The better part of the possibilities may be that pictures of terrorists could be distributed and an 'intelligent' software in the vision simulators could ring alarm if it sees them. In the worst case however, everybody could be tracked by secret services just anywhere, anytime.

With enough storage capacity, the vision simulator could also do less controversial things, like finding the lost keys, because it recorded where they have been seen last time.

It could amplify memory by photographing texts and numbers we see. With some intelligent algorithms, the device could also select those informations that are relevant and dismiss others.

Otherwise, if somebody succeeded to pirate a vision simulator, he could spy out the user's secret numbers and passwords. Just as with any computer. Yet with the new technology, even murder could be committed, by sending someone faked road scenes when driving, for example.

This however would require a severe hacking of the vision simulator's software, which is only a real danger if all safety measures are neglected.

It's not an impossible scenario, anyway, if operating systems are further delivered in a default state that is just utterly unsafe; and despite of all the warnings, this is still the rule.

'Secure computing', understood well, could inhibit unauthorized changes to operating software, if not greedy copyright advocates would steadily be pushing laws and technologies that deprive the user of his capabilities, force unwanted communications and information transfers, and inevitably open barn doors for possible attackers.

The really important copyright to address, is not the copyright to any pseudo cultural kindergarten stuff, but anybody's copyright to his own thoughts.

Privacy will really be a paramount issue. Computers, even today, have practically become extensions of our mind. Information stored must be protected from governmental and other intrusion, or we will more and more get an equivalent to thought control, not to mention the security threat to businesses, institutions, the entire society from criminal or terrorist attackers.

With a device that is used by anyone, anywhere and all the time, this applies even more. As vision simulators are just the last step before implanting chips, all the issues that would then finally arise have to be addressed in the course of this evolution. What's evident already: computer privacy is a human right [68], [69].

One step further out

A propos implanting chips. This is something that would not end with just interfacing.

Simple memory chips may soon be implanted, as an 'external' secure storage for vision glasses for example, not critical in terms of privacy as long as no RFID is involved (see p. 291).

But just for fun, let's speculate a bit further: It is easily foreseeable that information processing structures will one day surpass the density of comparable brain structures. They will also be able to reproduce typical brain structures [12]. Logical elements like gates will almost get to the size of single atoms.

As early as 1965, Gordon E. Moore stated that the number of transistors on a single chip doubled every 2 years. This has been proven true ever since. Today we have chips running at 3 GHz (billion cycles/second), having 1 billion transistors with 45 nm structures, consuming up to 100 watts.

It would take 30 years until the absolute limit of structure size (atoms are approx. 0.3 nm) is reached, or only 15 years for a structure that could still work like current chips (2nm). This would yet be chips 1000 times as complex. As smaller components also get faster, we could see a 30 fold increase in clock rate or alternatively a 30 fold decrease in power consumption after the same time. A chip of 1cm^2 could have more than 1000 billion transistors and either a clock speed of 100 GHz (even many times that, with some new semiconductor materials) or a power consumption of only 3W (at 3GHz or a lot more). In less than 20 years, a tiny very low power chip as capable as a today's PC could be an integral part of super light vision glasses or, if the connection problem is solved, even be implanted for permanent personal use. In maybe 40 years, a single layer 'brain chip' of 100 cm^2 could have 1000 transistors for each of our 100 billion brain cells, take about 1 watt and *run a million times faster* than any biological structure.

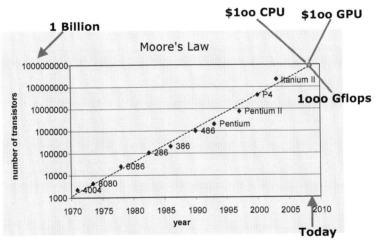

Evolution of processor complexity on the example of Intel processors (dashed line: doubling every 2 years). 2008, we still are perfectly on track!

Such tiny structures are subject to data error by simple electrical noise, or hits by gamma rays that are usually transgressing us all the time, but error correction schemes dealing with this are already available. Quantum processing may also be an option, not only resembling many of the pattern processing capabilities of the brain but most probably surpassing them. The problem with current quantum approaches however is their need for temperatures near absolute zero. So this may take some time.

A problem one could bring up is wiring. Yet a single glass fiber can theoretically carry about 10^{15} bits/second (read out an entire super brain chip in *less than one second*). A formidable tool for interconnecting even in an ultra large and complex structure.

The myriads if single nerves transgressing our brains could hardly be replicated by an electric chip wiring, but on a smaller scale, a matrix of wires with switchable connection and disconnection elements, could in theory enable even the most complex interconnection schemes, and with entire flexibility.

Brain chips could also consist of numerous flexible computing units (like programmable gate arrays) interconnected by a packet switching super high speed web. Hence, a single brain could in some way resemble the Internet. But probably our biological brains are already using similar principles of parallel operating, networked units in this or the other way.

Even though the complexity of the human brain is fascinating, the potential of computer chips to improve human intelligence* is many orders of magnitude greater than anything hypothetically achievable by genetic engineering, mainly due to the extreme speed advantages both in signaling and switching speed of electronic or photonic components. The biological brain, although performing the most formidable parallel processing we could imagine, does not offer many options to enlarge it without sacrificing a lot of speed.

---

* You may object that there is no conceivable method of interfacing. Yet consider that our two brain halves are interconnected just by a relatively narrow trunk of 'only' about 200 million nerves, the corpus callosum. In the past, surgeons have experimented to cut this apart for the treatment of very severe epilepsy. From the results, one can conclude that people survive this but that many cognition processes must normally be communicated through this connection. If we imagine a chip reconnecting the brain halves and thereby tapping the wires, so to say, we could conceive that a 'third brain half' could be implanted between the two natural ones. Where it could get its energy from would of course be another problem. This is all extremely spun and quite irritating, but it shows that speculations about such technology are not entirely clueless. Simple neural adapters like cochlea (inner ear) implants have long been in use now. For some current research on neural interfaces, see [66] and [67].

One could of course speculate about inventing entirely new genetic codes, creating nerve cells being fast a CMOS gates, and nerves as fast as wires or optical fiber. Hard to say if something like this may really be possible.

Probably even more useful and easier to accomplish as well, would be a genetically engineered interface enabling communications with external structures like brain chips, possibly also providing a comprehensive 'mind backup' feature. With this, biologically grown and technically produced brain structures could literally meet half way, combining the most efficient parts of both worlds.

Mere speed and density, of course won't turn any artificial structure into something with superb 'thinking' abilities. This could only work if we know how to replicate the brain's structure at least, or even better if we would actually find out how it works (even if this may not be absolutely necessary for the purpose). The actual time scale for these developments may therefore depend on the progress in neuroscience rather than in chip technology, at least if Moore's law really persists for a few more decades. Decoding the brain within said 40 years seems not really that likely, indeed.

Nevertheless, in conclusion it will some day be possible not only to implant chips, but also to use them to think, provided that a suitable interface technology can be developed. It may be that our natural brain will then play a role just as it is currently taken by the cerebellum. Due to its higher computing power, practically all of the personality may finally reside in the chip.

One might argue that intelligent machines could also emerge, that some day would compete with us for predominance. Well, I don't buy this. Computers are depressive. Making them independent beings (such with a real will and ego) would require to implement unrestricted self preservation (the instinct that makes us tick), and any sane human beings would violently prohibit any appearance of it. Terminator won't happen.

The dangers of 'artificial' intelligence* may also be vanishing compared to the dangers of genetic engineering, at least as long as there is not enough intelligence and computing power available for actually engineering DNA in a reasonable way, thoroughly simulating any implications, instead of just creating hulks and 'Smarty Smurfs', following the intentions of moronic parents or the fantasy of horror movie directors.

All these sorcerer's apprentices will have to understand that the power of evolution lies in diversity. For example, if we were all the same, a single virus could kill us all, 100%, within days. Fortunately, our bio-diversity lets even the most terrible virus kill just a fraction of the people infected. Evolution scientists have known this for long, that there is no and has never been the really 'fittest' for all beings, whatsoever.

What is realistically conceivable in my opinion, is a continuous mind migration from brain to 'chip', first expanding and then accommodating an existing human being's mind. There might come a time when bearers of such chips would refer to those still using vision simulators as the 'four-eyed' (now you know why the fiction part of this book is called „Adventures of a Four-Eyed").

As it is quite likely that a 'brain chip' - contrary to the biological original - will have a backup feature, it may become possible to copy an entire personality. Then we'd get some copyright problems, you bet. There would also be profound dangers of privacy breach and slavery, to say the least.

The advantage of all the hassle could be some sort of immortality. Therefore if such a technology would work, it would certainly be developed. Especially as it would not only mean to snitch aging, it would also mean sort of security against accidents (how long would be the average lifespan of people if it was limited only by accidents? - still not too long, really). This simple truth, by the way, doesn't only concern beings, it concerns all kinds of information.

---

* replicating individual brain structures into chips doesn't even create artificial, but natural intelligence.

Rotting paper and gnawing greed

Librarians for example, are bemoaning the limited lifetime of digital media. Absolutely pointless. Digital media are a lot more secure than even paper, as any number of copies can and should be made, over and over, for being stored in different places. Paper has never been nearly this safe.

When copies were difficult to make, burning down a single library (Alexandria) could extinguish a great part of all human knowledge. Water, bugs or fire consumed most paper documents during the ages, so even if some lone Papyri still survived thousands of years, it is by no means correct to say that this was their average life expectancy. Only after the invention of book printing, things became safer as many libraries were now holding copies, at least of the more disseminated works.

Any real danger for cultural or scientific knowledge nowadays does not lie in the life time limitations of media, but in copy protection of any kind. Copy protection is - by general principle - doomed to fail its intended purpose anyway. The only thing it will always achieve and this for sure, is to imperil the safety of the information it is being used on.

Given these facts and their implications, it may be considered necessary to prohibit most types of copy protection or activation schemes, sooner or later.

This even more so as there is the alternative of watermarking [107]. Since the last edition, several major vendors even started to sell music without any of this (some have watermarks, but those are naming the vendor only).

The *real* matrix

The intelligence achievable with synthetic brains, as said, will be overwhelming. Such a being could simultaneously 'talk' to a billion people, if sufficient communication channels were established. The world would become a village.

It's also obvious that the information constituting a mind could be transferred, could live in any kind of 'body' or virtually in a computer network (similarities to the Matrix obvious here). Sending all information of a human brain over a glass fiber or a laser beam takes less than a second, if we use all the bandwith of this communication channel. 'Beaming' a person in this manner will be possible.

People could chose a body upon arrival, as we nowadays do with rental cars. It could be synthetic, natural, mechanical, of alien biochemistry. It could be of an shape useful, or it could essentially be a machine like a boat or an airplane. Certainly we can nowadays hardly assume the emotions of such future beings.

Not too unfamiliar, these ideas, SciFi writers have written comparable things decades ago, but usually they assumed a conscience to be transferred entirely immaterial, by sort of soul travel. Most of them thought that thinking wouldn't occur in the brain but in some occult, mysterious way inaccessible to physics. Apparently, many scientists haven't overcome such ideas even yet, or the peculiar discussions about our brains forming decisions before we consciously 'know' wouldn't occur at all.

From a sober, scientific point of view, all of the artificial brain speculations mentioned are based on facts and only need scientific knowledge be turned into technology. Warp drives in contrary are not, as there isn't the faintest reasonable idea so far how to overcome the speed of light. Only that most SciFi writers won't realize it. Some others even still believe in the - actually very limited - prospects of gene manipulation.

Not even Augmented Reality is really present in SciFi. The best AR movies so far, this is where many researchers agree, are Harry Potter, even if the effects there weren't meant to be provided by technology (but many of them could, indeed).

So as none of the story telling gifted took up the topic, I had to write some prose of my own, not as thrilling but scientifically sound and in this aspect a lot more imaginative, I hope.

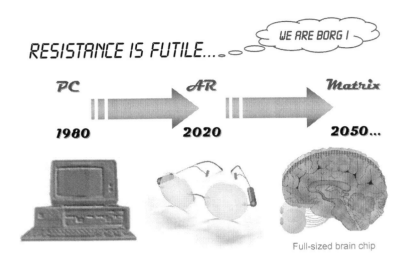

RESISTANCE IS FUTILE.... WE ARE BORG !

PC → AR → Matrix

1980   2020   2050...

Full-sized brain chip

With the Matrix in mind, it may be worth thinking about the meaning of 'real' and 'virtual' once more. There is no absolute border between them, obviously. Man is information.

Anything happening in virtual environments has relations to the physical world. For example, a guy has already been murdered for having 'stolen' a virtual sword in a computer game. Virtual representations, called simulations, are influencing real decisions all the time. Have always been, most trivially, indeed: 'it's all in your mind'. And to an advantage, because this way, 'real' damages and failures can be prevented.

Evolution is being moved into virtual worlds, while in the real one, the cruel 'survival of the fittest' is replaced by a more gentle 'creation of the fittest' (necessary footnote: evolution theory was never based on these simplistic selection schemes spread in popular literature, but on much more elaborate and efficient ones).
It's a bit as with quantum computers, if we think of the virtual world resembling the complex possibility relations within the machine, that would finally condense into irreversible reality once a 'measurement' is performed. (Of course, all of physics is

working like that quantum computer, where of all the vast numbers of possibility states we will always only see the real events arising from them).

As man is information, any suitable information processing structure could be a viable habitat, be it a thinking device in a global computer network also providing a virtual world, or any biological or artificial body desired, in the real world. Frequently changing between these could become usual, and travel would just consist in mind transfer, into a new body at destination, if so desired.

The time frame for the described radical change of our physical existence to emerge, will be much less than a thousand years. In cosmological terms, the current stage of human development would then literally only last for a second.

Hence if we are looking for extraterrestrial intelligence, we should keep in mind that we may be looking for super intelligence in (quite exactly) 99.9999% of all cases.
These would probably not be interested in talking to us at all. Real aliens wouldn't talk to stupids who would most certainly develop racism against them, as they would mistake them for 'machines'. If they use quantum computing for thinking, they may also feel most comfortable near to absolute zero temperature. Yet anyway, as a science fiction writer once put it, we might currently just be an ant hill beneath the highway.

Fortunately, we won't need super intelligence to develop a perfect vision simulator.

Conclusion

The evolution of information technology tends to minimize hardware and connect the user interface as closely to the human senses as possible.

Replacing Hardware by virtual devices and reducing the remaining parts to the absolute minimum, would be a logical step in this development.

This Technology will save material and costs while offering an overwhelming area of new possibilities. Its openness to the environment versus the seclusiveness of classical virtual reality, along with its communicative capabilities, will lead to new applications not yet even thought of.

As many traditional products will become obsolete this way, it will be crucial for any information technology business to be present in the new markets evolving from the developments considered.

Virtual devices could definitely save a lot of natural resources and generate additional wealth.

Dumping a 20g vision simulator is not as bad as dumping a 20 kg monitor, for just one example. Saving material may even become an inevitable economic necessity, as recent studies predict that many rare elements (like Tantalum, Gallium, Indium etc.), necessary for high tech electronics and displays, may be 'used up' within a few decades [122].

So even as there are many connected issued to be solved, this development should in the end be to everybody's advantage.

The materials presented here have originally been found in the ruins of one of those ancient office buildings that became obsolete during the 21st century. It may be quite amusing to see the difficulty of life before brain chips.

part 2: Fiction- Adventures of a Four-Eyed

Home office

This place here is not very inspiring. I guess I should change the wallpaper. No problem, although the edges of the furniture look a bit soft with all the pieces of virtual wallpaper inserted between them.

Maybe I should just tare down these walls, replace them with some panoramic view. There are these super webcams, 360 by 360 degrees high definition. These guys are making a living by selling the ultimate view. Considered that people are paying millions extra for an apartment, just for the view, it's no wonder how good these webcams are selling now.

Swiftly I find one on a Caribbean island, on a hill, overlooking a gorgeous bay. It's night, like here. Now the walls and ceiling are gone, it feels as if I was really there. Well, let's dim the light, it creeps in at the edges of my glasses. Spot on the desk, it's the only real thing remaining, and the working windows are of course still there.

Hey, a little too real. No, not simulated mosquitoes. But that disco across the bay is really too loud, and then there are those little frogs chirping in the tree beneath me, those super loud little ear killers. This really hurts.

That the neon light of the disco are displaying some ads is OK (this is a free webcam), but what have these polar lights to do in the Caribbean, also forming ad texts all the time? This is annoying. Fortunately, here's a better webcam. The only thing still missing is some breeze. I tell my computer to start the ceiling fan, blowing upwards, so it makes some whirl. Quite OK now.

With daytime scenes, it's a bit harder. I can simulate sunlight by adding some light on the real objects simply with the goggle display. Sun heats. I might install an infrared beamer at the ceiling. This would complete the illusion (and make me sweat).

What I really did next day, was to create a room with cathedral ceilings, carried by marble columns giving way to a free view over the ocean. For this ocean view I chose one of these notorious sunset webcams. And a glass floor I added, of course, letting my room float over the emerald waters of the lagoon...

The link

Then that 'wall breakthrough'. We have a branch office in Springfield, and sometimes my wife or I are looking for our business there. So we had the idea to connect the houses.

First we thought about display wallpaper. It comes in nice rolls of 20" by 80" that are glued on like ordinary wallpaper, edge to edge, and then connected by some clamps screwed to the wall.

We would still have to set some cameras right into the wall, and even though these tiny devices would come with optics only 1mm wide, any of them would require a hole in the wall as well as in the display, and they would have to be wired.

One company offers an integrated system with this, but then these very tiny cams have low resolution or suffer from snow. The perspective also isn't always right with such a simple screen. It can calculate it for one person, but if there are two, each has to wear glasses to allow for time multiplexed mode, and this even applies if only one person wants stereo view already.

The next choice was a 12-projector multi perspective cell system with a holographic mirror wall. It concentrates light from the different projectors to different areas of the room, dynamically generates perspectives if someone is there, does not stray ambient light and is transparent in directions not programmed to reflect. So the cameras can also sit behind it and need no holes. A very nice system but most varieties do not allow for different pictures for each eye (no real stereo) and even then they're too expensive.

As if this wasn't yet expensive enough however, they also showed me an 'auto holographic' system, generating dynamic projections to each eye of any viewer in front of a large screen, using holographic techniques [88]. Quite nice, but it needs expensive displays, it is not flat, and draws lots of power for computing.

So as we wear our little vision simulator glasses almost all the time, why bother and spend a fortune? Just cameras and mikes we'd need. Well, I found a vendor who proposed a grid like assembly, vertical tubes with several cams and mikes each, that are connected by horizontal tubes at the floor and at the ceiling. Looks like behind bars, I told him, and he was not so amused.

Yet another conventional system then proved convincing enough: an adaptive light field display, consisting of several vertical segments of 6 ft. high and 2 ft. wide, with interleaving dent lines at the sides providing for a secure plugging together. It contains an array of many pixel sized cameras that are also used in light field mode. Software derives any perspective from the numerous low resolution partial images, fitting all these together is accomplished first by a calibration run together with the light field display calibration, and when in use, an adaptive mode keeps up with distortions of the not too rigid display pane. Even an array of tiny microphones and of piezo speaker is included. They provide an almost holographic sound field. The salesman in that Floppy Hints shop didn't promise too much, indeed.

This system works amazingly well indeed. I often think she's really here. Three times I ran right into the display, which fortunately is all plastic and well backed against the wall. Now I know why they gave it such a soft surface, as in a padded cell.

Excuse me, I think my door bell is ringing. A tunnel to the front door opens. It's Rudi, our dog. I point to the control field of the virtual tunnel view and the direct camera picture appears in front of me, together with the door controls. It also establishes the speech connec-  tion. I say „come in" and open the door. OK, let's continue with...

 just a minute, there's a virtual owl bringing an e-mail. It's pecking at the window, wanting me to really open it, instead of flying right through!! At least this obstinate bird can't bite. The envelope opens and releases a giant dragon's head, giving me a fireblasting „you forgot to charge the car!". OK, I plead guilty. I guess she had to hook up to one of these 'in-drive charging' services that load your fuel cells while driving on the highway. They're also called 'high-chargers' (for obvious reasons). At least the extra expense saves you the wait at the gas station.

A final remark about this 'wall breakthrough': you may wonder if the broadband connection (it's high definition of course) wouldn't suck up my wallet (the large screen display is luxury enough).

This turned out quite cheap however. The networking people told me that one single optical fiber, with multi spectral modulation, could carry 10 millions of those connections at a time. Amazing. I guess they're even still too expensive.

After this installation, my wife noticed that the real look of our rooms also needed a facelift. No doubt. It Actually looks a bit like a bunker, with careless installations all over. Especially in the morning, before taking the goggles, it's really enough to look into the mirror, the house around it should at least look a little better.

Only the virtual room dressings, ambience lights and so on are making it livable. No good. I should do something about it, but currently I'm just out of time.

Our daughter is just going out in a new designer T-shirt. I can't resist to tease a bit: „How much are they paying you for showing around their brand logo?".

Workspace

After all the virtual 'home improvements', I really have to get back to some work. Finishing this book went almost out of control. I had so many documents and notes, and in order to forget nothing of it and to check the entire material for consistency, I had to keep many files open at the same time. If I had nothing but one of these medieval display screens, it would have been a nuisance, cluttered windows all stacked upon each other, not really good to use.

Maybe electronic folders are way easier to use than real ones, but if you work with many files at once, there is no match to the method of pinning everything to the wall. In a software project we once had all the walls of a big room covered with listings. It really helped. Except that we had to jump around all the time, just as the CPU would jump from subroutine to subroutine.

This here is even better. All the docs are arranged around me in all directions, like controls in a spaceship. I guess these are a hundred or so and still all visible and in reach.

My wife just comes in to ask something. Could have used the link. Anyway, the windows in her direction are automatically dimmed as the position cameras register relevant motion.

She needs a document I have. It's just one of the windows in front of me. I grab it and throw it to her. A paper pigeon flies off. She sees a display appearing, asking if she is willing to accept. She looks at 'yes' and the sheet appears in front of her.

This feature is called SEEHIS or See-How („see it how I see it") in contrary to SEEWIS or See-Where („see it where I see it"). With the first method, an object is placed to someone else in the same relative perspective. This is good for copying documents. The other method is for cooperative work. It does not copy but shows all participants the same object in the same place and allows any to manipulate it. Public objects also use this method but cannot always be manipulated by others.

Ok that's managed, let's go on with the work. To activate a window I point at its controls with my eyes. I even move the cursor this way. For writing and other inputs when working with documents, I like to use a mouse pen.

I could write directly into the air with the pen, but that's far too jittery and tiring. I remember when those parcel guys always presented me with an electronic notepad to sign as a recipient. I wonder if anyone has ever tried to verify who did those chicken scratch figures the device had stored. Writing without a support is something for a professional painter. I prefer to write on a desk. This pen that I always carry with me works like a PC mouse, on any surface. I do not need a keyboard because all applications now are able to recognize handwriting.

Now the work is getting schematic. Proofreading, and I'm sure I won't get all errors even after a dozen passes. Could also use some stimulation while doing the boring stuff.

As these windows clutter up the virtual wall TV that I normally use, I open another little TV window that I can sort into the crowd. If there weren't as many of them it wouldn't matter, as my giant screen usually covers the entire wall including the book racks, sparing only the sideboard and the armchairs, so it's the entire wall used for the (even three dimensional) display and a few items in front don't matter, the real ones even help to avoid running into the wall.

This little window by the way looks pretty conservative compared to some fun skins they once made for such applications, but this is not unnormal, designs always revert to the simple if that proves to be the best.

The satellite viewer application however sticks out, it comes as a virtual 3D globe that can be flipped around by just touching and turning. It only transforms into a flatter shape when closing in on some place.

TV's and icons

I really guess I need a break. The TV application follows me step by step as I walk around in the house. Any of those 20-something different virtual TVs that I've set up in the home just show me the program I was tuned to. Normally this is what's intended, but now it sucks. I touch the switch on one of those, and all turn off at once. Actually they are reduced to little icons that I can point at to reactivate. I could have used the option to revert them into virtual paintings, but the little artifacts of the mask displays stop me from defining these virtual room decorations all too often. It only works well if the TV was defined onto an already black part of wall. The icons use no mask, it is not bad if they are transparent and the advantage is that there can't be any artifacts.

Reactivating them if they are not in reach, is no problem. I have configured most of them to 'staring' mode, i.e. just looking at them for more than a second will do it. If I rise my eyebrows it even works instantly. My daughter just twitches her nose for the same purpose. Her sim has an ingenious electrical field sensor to record physiognomy. Mine still relies on a 'flies eye' stripe of optical sensors along the lower rims of the glasses.

I'm just figuring out what it would have cost to buy this many TVs, not to mention the space and the energy they would take and the wiring as well. Meanwhile these TV apps for the vision simulator cost nothing, they are always included or can be loaded as freeware. Given the fact hat I could even set up a giant movie theatre wall anywhere I want, or even a full fledged surround theatre, that it can even display fully holographic images, there is just no comparison to ancient screen technology.

Just in the sleeping room I have another large display (a laser projector pointed to the ceiling, controlled by infrared distance eye trackers) and speakers, as it is not always convenient to carry even these very light glasses that I have now.

The downside of the cheap supply is that eventually all rooms get cluttered up with virtual items like chess boards, pets, stickers, controls and icons of all kinds, maybe even a leftover monster from a video game. Fortunately I can hide or dump them without needing a real trash container.

Outdoors

A bicycle ride through the woods will be perfect right now. Let's do that. The dictating function of my sim is really useful here. Being able to activate it just by eye pointing and just to talk into the machine what comes to me, is way better than with any ancient recording device. Works hands free, allows to assign files to where they belong from the very beginning, stores everything with timestamp and dynamically backs up anything over the radio network. I like this especially as many of my best inspirational ideas come to me outdoors. This way I don't forget anything. It's also pretty useful in a car or any other busy situation of course. Orientation is another advantage. Not the usual stuff. Bicycling in the wild, I really appreciate the satellite pictures that show me what the environment actually looks like.

A very versatile way of seeing them is the 'transparent landscape' mode, that lets me see behind way bends, buildings, hills and woods. It lets me see certain things even miles away. Simply merging the satellite picture into my field of view would obscure it and be dangerous. The subtle methods of blending in the see-through information you can get now are much better. Getting astray is not an option anymore.

A friend of mine uses the view-ahead feature even for car rallies and racing. Seeing bends ahead with this virtual tripmaster allows him to speed like mad, and seeing obstacles like stranded cars improves safety. This also applies to normal street traffic, of course.

I remember when in the old days I once traveled on a highway, the traffic radio warned of a horse running around on one highway nearby, an armchair sitting on the left lane of another, and a car going the wrong way on a third one. Fortunately not on my route. Stranded cars are easily announced by their emergency transmitter, but for things as those mentioned above they've fortunately invented the voluntary 'anticipation network', that either delivers pictures directly from sim to sim, or over the street safety network. So you can literally see through the eyes of the guy ahead, intelligently filtered for importance and timely and spatial fidelity, of course.

But that's not the only way to profit from a sim in outdoor activities. The night vision capability of the sim cameras proves perfectly useful all so often. Even the strongest flashlight won't be very helpful in the open, but a combined thermal camera and light amplifier - this is something different. Pretty new technology that's already getting affordable and that I couldn't resist to buy. It's even fast enough to use with driving or bicycling, especially as with the perspective correction of the sim, it blows away anything formerly used even in high grade military equipment.

Cooking for beginners

Bicycling makes me hungry. There's a recipe service that promises to guide you while cooking. I once logged in and it worked quite well, picking up my kitchen inventory through my sim's cameras, telling me what I could make from it, then guiding me through any steps necessary, timing the cooking, and so on.

The downside was that afterwards my cupboard and kitchen walls carried some lists of things missing, but also several ads with 'one-look order' functionality, and my stove received a sticker „look here to buy a new one" and another for a service contract. It took me an hour to get rid of all this. So much for free recipes.

Intruders on the loose

But that's not the worst. Trojans are now spreading that are causing your sim to record your eye movements and even your sim camera pictures, to find out what you are looking at. They cannot whistleblow everything of course, due to bandwidth limitations, but they're usually getting active in front of shopping windows, when you're watching TV ads, shopping web malls. All in the name of targeted marketing.

Not enough, adware can now turn your entire world into a campaigning theater. Refurbishing any normal advertising surface with its own materials. And this goes almost unnoticed, as only if you take off your sim you'll notice that some things have changed their appearance. For the side effects it may have, covering necessary street signs an the like, these sneaky ad bugs are meanwhile prohibited, but that doesn't keep people off trying.

An even worse offense can be avatar trojans. Once I noticed people staring at me al the time, until I asked somebody and he told me that I had literally turned into a signpost, the avatar function of my sim transmitting an appearance that I was entirely unaware of. These dirty little apps can do a lot more havoc and are a popular trick among school kids, you'd guess.

Even burglary can now be committed, virtually. It started with online games already, and in virtual worlds. But nobody ever expected that anyone could steal a locally installed application right from his computer screen. This simply wasn't possible. So it shouldn't be possible to steal a virtual TV from my living room, or should it? Well, there is a certain difference. Sims are more open than classical computers. Definitions of virtual goods are allowing for a handover to other persons. It's inevitably necessary for virtual documents, paper and such. But this function can also be abused, of course. Usually the problem isn't so severe, as documents for example are being copied, not 'moved' when being transferred. But there are other cases. Objects could be copyrighted, prohibiting them from simple multiplication. Hence, sort of 'stealing' them as with physical objects is indeed possible, with some manipulation.

To me this happened only once so far, as I'm pretty cautious. I simply didn't take care enough of the permission settings of a virtual book I'd bought, so I left it on a table in public place and before I noticed, it was gone.

Virtual money would have been worse to lose, fortunately this is better protected. What bugs me most is 'stealing' of information. Usually this is just copying, but it happens all so often, as people don't care about proper encryption, for example. But that's an ancient issue, people and also most companies have been utterly careless with this all the time.

The bagman

A common nuisance nowadays are popups. Not the harmless little windows we formerly knew from web browsing on old fashioned screens. Nowadays, they come as a full fledged simulations of gadgets or persons, whatsoever. Last Saturday, a virtual sales agent suddenly appeared in my living room, while I tried nothing but to look up some information about vacuums. Instantly he began spilling dust and dirt all over the carpet from a bag, grabbed a vacuum that he'd brought with him and started to suck up the dirt, relentlessly babbling at me all the time, explaining the unsurpassable virtues of this ingenious marvel of a machine. This wasn't just a simple 3D movie however, as this obtrusive guy actually responded to my objections and my requests to stop this silly demonstration, trying to convince me that it would be a terrible mistake missing even a single second of his performance. A lot of artificial intelligence technology spent on rubbish, and even quite risky as these push sales agencies are always across with the law. But spam still seems to pay.

Concerto

Doing sports myself is much better than watching, but nevertheless I appreciate nature films or live events that use the full surround technology.

The triathlon last week was one of those in several ways. Most fun was the helicopter ride above the swimmers, bringing this immersive experience to the max.

The athletes were also using vision simulators, not all in the water (although the cameras can provide crisp underwater view with laser based units), but certainly afterwards when bicycling, because it allows for total orientation and control and, of course, they are perfect sunglasses.

Some people also like the virtual sitting in the football stadium, but that's not for me.

I better appreciate nature films, that really get exciting this way, as many visitors of surround movies had experienced even in the olden days. Back then, one had to go to a special theater. Now I can have this at home all day.

This evening they transmitted one of these holodeck like events: A violin quartet with artists, recorded by a complete surround camera array, that could be displayed right in the middle of my living room.

Not that I always prefer this kind of music. Yet being able to go around the orchestra and hear any instrument clearly separated, with this perfect spatial simulation, is something really attractive.

Having the news speaker sitting almost bodily in front of you is just nothing compared with this one.

I could even choose to have the walls and ceilings of the real concert room displayed, but that's dangerous if you walk around, as you will definitely run into your own furniture, or the safety function will rip the image. It's just an option for sitting in one place.

Needless to say that the full spatial sound requires to use the headphones, because speakers would just involve the acoustics of your own room. I only use them to enhance the bass, as those headphones could never make your stomach feel it.

Fairy tales

Recently the fairy tale channel featured the 'history of media', a 3D movie with total surround, virtual characters running through the room, and so on. Yet do they really think even a child would now buy it that 'once upon a time', they tried to prohibit recordings of TV transmissions? In this story it must even have been illegal to play old vinyl disks with a digital amplifier (as this could mean digitizing) or in presence of friends. As this was no interactive game movie, I could not test these suspicions myself.

It went on with storage crystals getting so powerful that the entire 'cultural' heritage of mankind could easily fit onto something the size of a sugar cube*.

Inevitably, just this kind of gadgets emerged. Those 'Final Chips' were heavily prohibited, but it couldn't be stopped because nothing that people want can be stopped and they had been so totally deprived of all their consumer rights that almost nobody had any sense for legality with these things anymore.

It also proved what experienced technologists had known all the time, that it's an illusion to stop such things by technical means, or the damage gets way bigger than the benefits. During this time - they called it the 'media prohibition'- crime was booming again, as for outlaws it became another license for money printing.

Some guys with trick or treat hats then asked to install surveillance cameras in any home to see if anyone played illegal stuff. As this wouldn't work with vision simulators, they finally asked that any private computer should be entirely accessible to them at any time. It became finally evident that ill designed laws had led to a point where there could either be no copyright or no privacy anymore. The backdoors to computers and 'magic mirrors', opened by some copy protection schemes, had then already contributed to billions in damages by attacks of villains and evildoers that eventually even paralyzed the entire kingdom and destroyed colossal amounts of data.

---

*A simple, ½"wide plastic surface with apparently random nano engravings, can secretly store over 10000 movies or 100mio. books or pictures. Replicating it by injection molding (like DVDs) is dirt cheap and done in no time.

A more harmless occurrence was a TV virus that caused certain politicians always to appear with puppet strings attached and their suits stuffed with dollar bills all over. Well deserved.

Scientists presented studies that the costs for implementing and maintaining this 'technology' and for the collateral damages it caused amounted far higher than its benefits. As if it hadn't been enough already, huge problems that cybersquatting[1], patent sniping[2] and patent landmining[3], accompanied by clueless law-making apparently had accumulated over a long time, added to all the disaster. Rightout bizarre, bits and bytes had been assigned more rights than humans, and digital slavery[4] was spreading.

The 'intellectual' property mania turned against the entire economy. Any engagement with hardware or programming became as heavily restricted as money printing, small IT businesses couldn't emerge nor grow anymore because they could neither afford enough patents nor meet the security requirements for dealing with classified chips and algorithms. Education in IT and electronics became confined to a small caste of shamans, and progress had been frozen forever.

Everywhere, signs like this were harassing harmless pedestrians:

> This text is copyplighted. Reading it and storing it in your brain is a violation of the devious malicious copyplight act of 3001 and constitutes a filial crime.
> Please move to the next frolice station immediately and report your crime. Do not surf over GO and do not look away $200.

---

[1] Hijacking rights on data paths, information resources, web addresses, trade marks on common words, names, colors, genes, natural substances etc

[2] Hoarding rights on trivial ideas, common knowledge etc.

[3] Landmining by issuing numerous trivial patents.

[4] Depriving persons of their informational rights and possessions.

At this point, just before the guys in the white jackets came, everybody realized that this couldn't lead anywhere, and politicians - who had taken two generations of evolution to acquire some knowledge about information technology - established new rules, a legislation granting both fairness and freedom (hey, don't they always claim doing just that ? and what's the result ?).

The wide acceptance of the new regulations made copy protection almost unnecessary after all.

They also declared it unlawful to track anyone's physical movements, personal business, private life or communications without a court decision. So the intrusion by tireless data collectors also finally came to an end.

Most important, a law was passed, that granted the privacy of personal computers ('mind extensions'). This was even turned into an amendment to the Constitution.

Nevertheless, could anybody even in a fairy tale[1] be naive enough not to recognize that no property is safe without freedom, as only freedom can grant justice and only justice can protect property? Privacy in turn is essential to protect freedom, isn't it. So protecting property by taking away privacy is a contradiction in itself and anybody trying this will shoot himself in the foot.

In this story, Orwell's prophecies [11] had almost all come true. The reversal came shortly after some lobbying groups like 'Take Them to the Cleaners' or 'Privacy is Crime' had in a last effort, tried a little too hard to oppress their opinions onto the world's legal structure in a fictitious '2nd Cyberwar'[2].

Sometimes, things are turning for the better and all live happily ever after.

---

[1] Probably it hasn't escaped your attention that in reality, even more bizarre and sinister developments had been pushed ahead once upon a time.

[2] It had long been recognized that all knowledge and legal structures also belonged to what had initially been called 'cyberspace'. So this 'war' didn't take place in the web, and no viruses were used to fight it. The main weapon in this 'war' instead were law proposals tirelessly written by hosts of lobbyists.

This was made for kids, of course. Issues like 'private' banking and the virtual goods black market weren't mentioned, these in reality induced even more tendencies to install Big Brother in any computer, because it impaired tax revenues. Unsurprisingly, in these cases no business lobbies were ever asking for more control. Some official's greed for information got so bizarre, that they entirely forgot that privacy is a human right [68], [69] (yet did any of these law poets ever care about constitutions and such?).

I'd really like to know what your Senator would say if just after the postman, a snoop would regularly appear at his mailbox, open all his letters and read them thoroughly. Of course the guy would put everything back in afterwards, nice, ain't it. As secret communications generally can't be stopped, not even proven (if data are hidden in sound or picture files by steganography), it finally turned out that total control will ever remain an illusion and one had to turn back to more conventional methods of investigation.

Since the laptop days it had also dawned to just anybody, that the possibility of the perfect digital copy never made any difference at all. Most people aren't even able to tell the quality difference and if so, they usually don't care anyway.

Inhibiting all varieties of copying requires to place a policeman in every living room. 1:1 hardware copies cannot be inhibited unless the technology is entirely sealed and locked, and playing them cannot be blocked unless there are only playback devices that only work when online connected to a dedicated 'rights server'.

It turned out that such stupid makeshift stuff would never work in any acceptable manner at all, unless an entire host of also makeshift and likely unconstitutional laws would be pushed forward, trying to enforce the functionality of an inherently flawed technology. As digital goods are totally different from hardware in that they can be reproduced and distributed at very little cost, implementing the equivalent of a daily house search for everybody just for their control is meanwhile considered brainless anyway, and just a fundamental failure to adapt to the market. Nowadays, the fight of the plastic carvers against the web is often mentioned alongside with the fight of the gas companies against electricity. So it finally became common consent, that the primitive crowbar technology once named 'Digital rights management' (DRM) was clueless and even counterproductive, as nobody was actually willing to buy anything without getting to own it, even less so from the very same people who would just use the money to promote even more 'legal' atrocities against them [75].

The 'six postulates' became standard in any engineering textbook

I.   It's impossible to prevent any physically identical copying unless the entire information technology gets classified and restricted.

II. It's impossible to prevent any content copying unless the entire information technology as well as analog technology is classified and restricted.

III. It's impossible to manage any detailed digital rights without an entirely classified and restricted digital technology and enforced communications to and surveillance by centralized servers.

IV. It's absolutely dangerous to bind any information content to any specific hardware, as such content would be destroyed if this hardware becomes unavailable.

V.   It's absolutely dangerous to bind the usability of any information content to any remote servers, as such content would be destroyed if these servers become unavailable.

VI. 'Digital rights management' can only work in a perfect police state. The only thing that digital technology contributes here, is that the perfect police state can be implemented much easier.

Fortunately, the archaic habits of distributing media on round pieces of plastic are now long forgotten. So an entirely different system came into being. If I download something really valuable now, it might contain my name and the originator's signature[1] in an asymmetric watermark[2], but then I can do with it what I like.

---

[1] A hash (sort of checksum) calculated for a data set, using a secret key. Anyone can check for integrity of the entire set using a related public key.

[2] Making at a large number of subtle (invisible/inaudible) pseudo random changes in a file, determined by a secret key. A related public key allows to derive enough of the changes for a very safe validation of the watermark (even from only a partial or format converted file) [111].

Remark: Since the last edition of this book, insight has grown that customers aren't the enemy. Several of the most important online distributors recently started to sell music free of DRM *and* personalized watermarks.

Only a few special releases or expensive software are now sold personalized anyway. Nevertheless I'm entitled by law to sell them second hand, perhaps involving a bit of bookkeeping.

Most kinds of copy protection and software activation techniques have even been outlawed in the mean time, so this is nothing new (see p.94). There has never been anything wrong with pursuing people for causing damages to, or making money from the work of others, assuming the use of methods that comply with human and constitutional rights. Nonetheless it would be *nuts* to even think of making '1984' a reality just for the sake of greed.

Well, we have had this already. Tom Britsome, commonly named „Unohu", had recently taken over the well oiled machinery of one of the world's most ancient and unsuspecting democracies that, for some time prior to this, had been sliding silently but inexorably into a police state. Trying to distract from the economic chaos brought about by his ruling the country into the stone age, Unohu had outlawed the common use of information technology, and even resorted to starting a war on the most feeble of pretences. Fortunately, this only resulted in his comprehensive defeat within a few days, due mainly to his army's technical and logistical inferiority brought about by his stifling regime.

The entire story had originally started with jailing people who simply refused to reveal the passwords to their computers. Some years after came the installation of so called 'black boxes' recording any e-mail and any website visit nationwide, and it didn't even end with the installation of real time tracking of all citizens. The perfect Orwellian dream machine it was, ready to be abused by any tyrant haphazardly stumbling into the scene.

Only after the dark age of Unohu's tyranny had ended, after people had learned it the really hard way, privacy got subsequently restored as one of the most important fundamental rights.

By the way, even the antediluvian, 17th century patent system has now been reformed and replaced by general copyright. You can post your ideas to a government wiki site and if anyone uses them for profit, you get compensated the same way as if you had written a song and someone used it for his own interpretation.

Flight scenes

Yesterday I went to Tampa, via New York JFK airport. Needless to say that I had booked my ticket online and the certificate was loaded into my pocket computer, so I had nothing to do at check in but to take the glasses off shortly for a face control (their system wasn't really up to date). Booking was all done wireless. I only had to OK that transaction once for the sake of safety. Again I was happy that I didn't have to use a mobile phone or other ancient stuff that would occupy my hands and make me run against lanterns while trying to read the display.

As usual, the onboard movie was as bad as the music from the armrest. I also wonder why they still have these screens built into the back of the seats. They already have transmitters as well, sending a vision simulator the movies, the music, and having it display and operate the virtual controls for it.

The only time I enjoyed an onboard movie was long ago, when they played Apollo13, when it was all new. Good that I have my own harddisk in that pocket thingy, that can simulate a giant movie theater with the high resolution glasses and carries my entire movie collection. Yet once you have it, it starts to bore.

At least they don't tie these nickelodeons to the hardware any-more, as some did once upon a time. I've never had a computer that actually *itself* liked watching movies or listening to music.

Just being able to download personalized files without insane restrictions is much less inconvenient. Some retail stores may even still burn disks for you, if you live in the digital outback. So my shelves are no longer filled with plastic garbage that's only been invented to make the stuff look more 'valuable'.

I decided to ignore that inevitable psychotic B-movie. Tuned to the outside cams of the plane instead. Hey, that's the best thing ever invented. Especially as I didn't manage to get a window seat. I gave it a try and let the entire plane interior vanish in favor of the outside picture. These cams merge together quite seamlessly, so the impression is absolutely perfect. It felt like flying without any plane at all, just alone in mid air. Quite disturbing the first time.

Then I tried to have the seat blended in, so that it wasn't looking as if I was sitting on plain air (as a default, these goggles never hide your own body, so you won't get disoriented), but then it looked even weirder. I wondered if they shouldn't replace those seats with broomsticks, that would be looking quite cool. The first class could offer dragon's necks instead.

The flight attendant suddenly brought me back to the inside. The motion detector had decided that she needed attention and blended her into the picture, the same time blending in the plane interior by 50%. This surely destroyed the illusion.

After she had handed me the drink, I stayed with the outside view most of the time, except for some phone calls and a little web search. The clouds were spectacular this day.

I have been told that in the past, some airlines prohibited the use of camcorders and even cassette players in their aircraft, because they feared interference with onboard electronics or radio communications. Really mad. I understand that they didn't like the use of mobile phones, but didn't they have any engineers to tell them that all these other devices emit a thousand times less power?

Actually, I think that just some yellow press campaigns had impressed people more than facts. Maybe I should wrap this book in yellow ?

General aviation

I remember renting a general aviation aircraft last year, doing one of those useless dinner trips just for the fun of it.

You guess that even the remote rustic restaurant we headed for had these virtual menus that let all dishes appear right before you on the table as soon as you're seated.

A little chef was growing from the middle of the table like a mushroom, starting a quite dramatic presentation of today's cuisine's highlights. Looking quite funny to me. Obviously, each of our company saw his own little chef, and the performances started at different times, so this character was generated separately for each guest, obviously. As he was even talking French for no reason, I couldn't resist saying „I'd have some hamburger with French fries". The little guy gave me a look as if I had stabbed him, „mais monsieur, c'est impossible...". „OK" I said, „never mind, I take the red snapper, all right? - and a glass of Merlot". Again he faltered, made a begging gesture „mais Monsieur, du vin rouge avec le poisson...". „OK, Chablis" (from the supermarket I was tempted to say, but this time I pitied him). Who in all world got the idea to install this freakin' blabla-machine in a rustic seashore restaurant?

The bill became enormous, of course. Since the oceans had been skimmed of anything edible and jellyfish took over, fish had become extremely rare, and even freshwater fish had risen in price beyond belief.

The airplane we used also had virtual gadgets, but more reasonable ones. I could see all the other aircraft around, virtually, right through the cockpit walls. It also had a really good set of external cameras, so I could see anything out there as well as in the big airliner. Quite nice, really. I never did such a soft landing before in a rented plane: I could actually see the landing gear and the runway right through the bottom. There were even some thermal cameras that would go through fog and would make night flying a cinch. Fighter planes have been operating these for a long time of course, and the ability to aim and shoot those disk rockets to all directions at any time made dog fights a little obsolete.

The real-world mapped navigation system is really so much better than just a conventional GPS. You'll know when you have learned how difficult it sometimes is to find small airports from the air, in all that haze, even if you know that they must be right ahead of you. I have seen many experienced pilots having the same difficulties. The reason is simple: you only see things if you know what to look for. From the air, landscape changes a lot with weather, time and season. I remember once canoeing with a fiend and just for fun I didn't change directions when we were right approaching an alligator. He didn't see it before it just ditched into the water only 10 ft. away. I only saw it because I knew what to look for. So in unknown environments, a direct insertion of directions into the real scene is a huge advantage.

These virtual sight applications are quite common now. With my sailboat, the sonar provides 3D pictures of the ground, that can be seen through the bottom of the boat, and outside cameras let me look right through the sail. Also no toys, these ones, could really avoid collisions or falling dry.

Games and sims

I'm not a game fanatic. I just run some of them from time to time, to check out what's going on with technology, but generally the flight simulator is the only one I really keep (that's not actually a game though).

Escapism has been a problem with computer games from the beginning. People fled into virtual worlds, and some even got insane with it. High end vision simulators also offer much less dangerous and more useful things, like dressing the rooms for free or having that million dollar view just out of the backyard window. The borderline between the sane and the insane will always be hard to draw. With these shoot-and-run games it has become really dangerous. People have been reported running into cars or falling down stairs, just acting on virtual scenes. Many games were completely transported to the real world, and some-times you see someone running down the street shooting at imaginary opponents with a real looking gun. Of course, those guys are usually caught quickly, if they are lucky enough not to be fired at by a nervous policeman. It went even further, actually: some gamers really thought they were immortal and jumped from buildings, some started to fight with real swords. Now you need a sanity check to join certain online games.

My Flight simulator is much safer. I still use a yoke and some rudders (how would you simulate these), but the cockpit is a 100% reality like 3D reconstruction that can actually be operated by any switch and control that it shows, though without tactile feedback. The good thing with this application, that it allows for a fully realistic VFR (visual) flight. The only downside, that flight figures are almost as likely to cause vertigo as in a real plane. Only gravity effects are missing.

They built simulators like this decades ago. Back then I could try out one of these ultra expensive installations and wondered when it would be possible to get something this good at home. Took some time.

What I still can't do in my simulator, open the doors and trample at the left one or the right one to steer, as in the real Airplane.

From the past

Back to the JFK/Tampa journey. After landing, I really enjoyed those green arrows on the floor, directing me right to the connecting plane. Even that virtual officer approaching me „Sir, you may miss your connection if you take this way". These guys always know your schedule. I think you can also ask them for the next restroom or so.

I remember a flight along the same route long ago, when right before landing they began to announce all the connections possible and their gate numbers. I don't know why, but somehow I mixed up gate numbers. After running through the Airport half way towards what I thought was the right gate, I looked at some screen wall and saw that we were wrong.

I was with my wife and a friend of ours, but they also hadn't noticed the error. Having made it back to the right gate (that was just next to where we had arrived), the airline guys had already checked in some people from the waiting list (our flight had been late anyway), and only one seat was left.

Would a mobile phone or notepad with a guiding software have helped here? Certainly not: no hands free, no time, no way. Only a vision simulator could have done that.

They could offer us two more seats in a plane from La Guardia, going one hour later. We decided to give our friend that last seat and to head for La Guardia ourselves. Well, that was like an excursion into the NY underground: First a drafty roadside under a crossroads where we waited for the bus a long time, then a long and sometimes slow night ride through the wet and rainy industrial outskirts of town.

Finally arriving at La Guardia, we were so late that the front desk didn't even issue us new boarding passes but told us to hurry right through. Then a clerk at the baggage check didn't want to let us pass because our tickets didn't fit a flight from this airport. Remembering that our company would be waiting in Tampa probably with no idea where to go, I gathered the rest of my politeness remaining and shouted something like „Sir, I will definitely not miss this flight", together with a few other words unmistakably explaining what we had just been through. He must have felt that I was about to run right over him, so he gave way.

We got more to do that day. Not that I even remember meeting our companion and getting the car, but the hotel we headed for was a bit out of town and we had to find a tiny road going off the highway and then some more corners to take until we arrived about 2:30 AM.

I'm just telling you all this because I wish I had my vision simulator back then. There have been some approaches towards using mobile phones for similar services, but it's simply so that I need my hands when traveling, and the displays were tiny. A display that would insert a data screen at a fixed place in my field of view would also not be the real thing, feeling just like dirt on my glasses, and using a notebook even more so. There is no other good interface but the vision simulator.

A rental car

Entering that rental car, again I'm remembered at the past. They had stuffed more and more electronics into cars, making them more complicated and less reliable all the time. The only industry this was indeed that used information technology to make their products more expensive rather than less. A strategy only working for a while, as long as cars were an icon, but turning out suicidal in the long run.

A 'technology' magazine even once featured an article saying that soon some car company would probably have a CEO who was an IT specialist, because information technology would make up 90% of the value of a car. Rightout bizarre. When I was a student, I turned my car into sort of a gadget carrier, and I learned for sure what does *not* make sense. All my friends back then made the same experiences.

Fortunately, that's all over now. My own car is a car, has 4 wheels and is made for driving. All those electronic gadgets, those 26 stereo speakers, TVs in any seat, fax machine, even the radio, have been replaced with my pocket computer and vision glasses. The car provides the motor, some outside infrared and radar cameras, anti lock brakes, and so on, but most of the superfluous IT and media stuff went where it belongs: right to the user. I only added a subwoofer that gets its signal from my sim.

I really appreciate that they've made a law last year, requiring any car to have direct mechanical or hydraulic brakes and steering, with only a certain amount of simple, additional and independent servo support allowed.

None allowed that would depend on electrical or other power. It will save lives, I guess. That 'X-by-wire' stuff was a really bad idea, at least for the safety relevant features.

At the rental desk, the clerk had shown me several models by transmitting full fledged 3D pictures. I could go around each car, see it as real and in full size, open the doors and look inside, but I couldn't take seat of course (a guy at the next desk tried, you guess what happened). Fortunately, I had insisted on signed confirmation for my reservation price. With this particular rental company, I knew that they would always have 'forgotten' the reservation price and come up with a much higher one at the desk.

This time, before I showed my reservation ticket (a digitally signed virtual one of course), the clerk offered me an upgrade to a luxury car for $5 a day. After considering shortly I said yes, and then he came up with a rental contract almost twice as expensive as my reservation. I handed my confirmation to his sim, and now he surely was in a fix, because he had to give me that car for my confirmed price plus $5, which he had never intended at all.

Walking to the parking lots, I was wondering why nearly all staff at the airport looked completely identical. I had never heard about any cloning program going on.

We saw our car from 300 ft. away, through walls and floors, by a flashing light on top (virtual, of course), as if it hadn't been enough to see those guiding lights on the floor and walls all the time. The car unlocked when I looked at its door (the clerk had handed me the virtual keys just like real ones, only that it was a vision sim object), and when I got in, a short introduction to its controls, also the virtual ones, started to play, with illuminations and little hands pointing on anything being explained, switches virtually moving, and so on. I stopped it because I already knew this model. It had hardly any controls on its instrument board, that, except for the styling, was almost as Spartan as that of a 1957 Beetle. At least if looked at with the naked eye. The car could be conducted this way, but for convenience and safety, a vision simulator was recommended.

Well, a flashy firework of controls, goodies and gadgets appeared as soon as I started, and first I swapped the dashboard to show the radio controls (an unusual feature for a car today), so I didn't have to tune when driving. I could of course have used the radio of my vision simulator, but it couldn't really provide the bass this car could let loose (button headphones only provide good bass when they fit tight, and I hate that).

It was not so unusual for this rental car to have a stereo. Rental companies usually choose cars that can also be operated by technophobes, so this model did not only have the usual backup touch screen to access some functions in case one's vision simulator went defective, but it had some other 'real' gadgets as well.

On the other hand, it also had the now mandatory severe handicapped interface, allowing to steer it by eyes only, with help of a sim* of course, or to visualize outside sounds.

Sims are inevitable these days anyway. I can hardly remember how it was to drive without active sunglasses, the mask display of my sim I mean, that takes out blinding lights selectively. Be it headlamps of cars approaching, or the sun reflected in the mirror or rear window of a car ahead, those smart glasses will provide a tiny speck of dark before it and let you see at ease.

My glasses had automatically gone into 'car safety' mode. It's a largely hardware based (and therefore reliable) mechanism that prevents displaying any objects that are too large, too bright or entirely opaque, ensures that even dimmed down objects can still be seen, and forces any of my own software control windows to arrange with the control panels of the car.

My own radio controls, for example, would appear in the car's steering wheel, the secondary (virtual) switchboard over the front window, or the middle console, never on the road.

---

* Slang for 'vision simulator'

The middle console is entirely virtual of course, a big progress from these old fashioned cars with their overloaded consoles and tunnels that served nothing but to wedge the driver, as in a racing car. They should have delivered those ridiculous design monsters with sort of a shoe horn, to help people squeeze in.

As soon as I told the car where to go, those glittering guiding snakes readily appeared and lined out any single turn, even the right way out of the parking area. The headup display that the exterior infrared cameras sent to my sim, together with the anti blinding function, almost turned night into day.

I could see for miles now. The road ahead continued even beyond the visible horizon, and there, small and distant was my destination, although 35 miles away, together with the estimated arrival time. Even further at the horizon, some tinted clouds with little symbols on them predicted rain approaching from the west, but that didn't affect us.

The road ahead was now framed in green lines, not occluding anything ahead and unambiguously guiding the way. No guessing anymore what it meant when one of these ancient navigators told me „turn right in 200 yards" and there were three different exits in that range, leading right or half right (looking at the display in such a situation got me into difficulties many a time).

Even before we finally arrived, the guiding lines were already showing me where to turn in, even though the place was still hidden behind a long bend, and they were also showing the parking lot, not only behind the bend but also behind lots of bushes and several yards lower. Knowing the entire course ahead, no stupid illicit commands and nags dropping in, this really proved entirely helpful and no more distracting at all.

What I really liked with this particular car were its rear cameras. Not only for parking. I had forgotten to bring with me one of these convex rear mirrors that I'm used to, and the side mirrors also weren't my taste. Fortunately, I had a little software that could simulate me some rear mirrors from the outside pictures.

Most traffic signs were hybrid already, showing symbols as well as transmitting virtual appearances. These virtual enhancements can easily be changed and also be confined to be seen by drivers concerned only. Their use is limited however, for safety reasons. Suddenly, one of the conventional traffic signs flashed. The sim camera had seen it and thought I might be too fast, so it made a little overlay in the display. That sign however was meant for another road that ran beneath ours. One of the reasons why I prefer to steer myself instead of relying on machines.

There are still too many irritating traffic situations to leave it all to computers. After many years of trying, engineers had finally been able to sort out what works and what doesn't. Their machines, at least until now, never managed to match a driver who had 30 years without accidents, and there are many.

Maybe the 'superbrain' chips they make now could learn to act like a human? Rudi already has one and I fear he will be smarter than me some day. He is already good at rapping.

Yet these brain chips have to be trained. The problem is that too much general knowledge plays into some situations in real road traffic, and this can only be acquired by a complete human being. Hence, these chips indeed are just good as brain amplifiers, connected to real brains, rather than as autonomous units that would try to learn such a hard thing as safe driving, without a clue what's really going on at all.

Hardly on the highway, I soon got hungry. I increased the alien display allowance so I could see all these commercial road signs telling me where to find the next KrustyBurger's or such.

That's a real improvement: They could tare down many of those huge, ugly advertisement towers and replace them by transmitters. Only if I want to see what's offered I turn this function on and see all the ad posts littering the landscape.

Inevitably some people hacked the permits, just to show people signs they didn't want. Some also abused the capabilities of the feature: A business once displayed a very real looking, perfectly animated burning vehicle on the parking lane, with a flashing sign „we also roast beef". Bad taste, indeed (the sign, as to the beef I don't know).

Thinking of this, it suddenly came to me why all those guys at the airport had been looking alike. They must have been using avatar transmitters, and I hadn't set my sim to reject these things.

Merry Christmas

Some people have now started to use that road sign feature to dress up their home at Christmas. It's obviously cheaper and easier just to program virtual lights rather than climbing roofs and trees to install everything. The city supports it, because it saves lots of energy as well. You have to get a permit for your setup, only then everybody can see it, but apart from this it's really more easy than the traditional way. The permit avoids traffic jams and accidents caused by setups that are too distracting. The only ones suffering from it are the city officials, they have a hard time every year, drawing the border line between allowed and disallowed.

From the Attic

After Christmas, but not only then, people may be trying to get rid of things they don't need. The „track and recognize all" (TARA) feature of current sim cameras has led to the advent of *MonAttic*: a catalog of all 'junk' there is, in any backyard, in any attic or basement or garage, for anybody's access. Nothing in this world is wasted anymore, at least if people spend a really little effort listing their stuff. It's really all so simple: you go through your rooms, shelves and closets, the really intelligent software categorizes and estimates anything on-the-fly, and you only say yes or no to offering it and add a little extra facts in case. By the way: MonAttic now has strong security measures against searching for items from a certain person. Before this, it had earned the nickname *Burglar's Delight.*

In the mall

This evening I had to go to the supermarket, buying some necessities. A new gadget drew my attention when strolling along the shelves. They offered a virtual sewing machine. Quite peculiar. I peered at the price tag, and a short ad movie showed up.

Of course, should have known it, this was a toy, a simulation for kids. Guess I was a little flooded because I had programmed my sim to automatically extract and display the expiration date of any food products. It's a little freeware gadget from the consumer association, not really liked by the stores.

What they even like less is the second gadget I use, that looks at tags or reads out the info from these solar powered radio tags and automatically not only compares prices, but tells me if there are specials at another place in the store, also compares to other stores just by surfing the web in the background while I shop. Everything is of course displayed at the item addressed, never just stuck before my eyes.

Ten years ago, some guys even tried to lobby a law that would forbid using their active price tags as basis for a web search. Most peculiar for those times, they didn't succeed with it.

Some had even ceased to use radio tags because these allowed vision simulators or other special computers to sort out prices even more easily, for example comparing anything there is on that shelf within a second. Some encrypted RFID and barcodes, but that put off too many customers.

So now they try the old fashioned way, to name some products in a way just to aggravate comparison. As the only thing these price tags have is the printing, especially the bar code, that is read by the vision sims cameras, one anyway has to get the rest of the data from the store's computer.

I went right out with the shopping cart, and when passing the gate anything in it was accounted for, because it had already been registered by the cart through its RFID tags and also been assigned to me trough automatic interaction with my sim. Some items with classical barcodes had been registered through my sim's cameras and a certified piece of software. These carts could even register the weight of the entire load for a final check. When leaving the shopping area, the list of all items appeared directly on top of the cart, even with small pictures for each item, so I could control in real time that everything was accounted correctly. The bill was stored to my pocket computer and backed up via the next web hotspot. Everything under control.

I decided that I had a little time left, to walk about in the mall. This year they had replaced their Santa with a virtual one. Bad idea, really. How could that cyberfake lift the kids, like the real one? Couldn't even take a normal photo with Santa*. These virtual guys behave exactly like ghosts: cast no shadow and can't be seen in a mirror. How about wearing his head under his arm ? I guess they will realize, sooner or later.

These window dressings however galore. Some items look alive, I point at them and they speak (sort of „buy me", what else). Others start a little movie. And there are some that are entirely virtual. Some windows sometimes even display different goods for different people. Some are adults only, for example.

The fashion shop just installed a new system. Entering the store I'm being asked if it should do a microwave body scan to get my size. Well, that's not dangerous with data protection being quite rigorous now. So why not.

Now the mainly radio chip based inventory system highlights anything in the shelves and racks that would fit. I enter some styles and items I'd possibly be interested in, to reduce it a bit. Then just by looking at something, I'm trying on this and that. The system sends me a simulated projection of me with that garment, walking and turning in the aisle.

Quite silly, but much easier than trying anything on for real. I would do this as well if I'd really liked something, but compared to the tiresome shopping ventures I remember from the past, this is a lot less exhausting.

Some teens nearby also seem to use the system extensively, although they have to rely to the sleeve displays of their 'intelligent' designer sweaters (especially girls still don't like glasses and accept any hardship to avoid them).

At least they always have some equipment with them. Some people ('technophobes') still live without any computer, and just in case I have to show them a document or something, I took care that my new glasses have one of these pin head sized laser projectors. This unit is a bit power hungry however.

---

* My vision sim as well as some cameras can do it, by recording what I see.

Once the store has recorded my size, I can also visit their web shop to try anything on. So I may as well go home now.

Anyway, why buying garment if anybody wears a vision sim - could as well just simulate it.

Cyclops

The Cyclops online bookstore just sent me an e-mail advertising their new AR shop. Sounds interesting. I'm logging in, and their server asks me if it could have some information about my home's topology. This could be a security risk, but they run this in an encrypted session and our strict data privacy laws require them to handle this very carefully and to safely delete the information as soon as the session ends. So I give this a try.

Suddenly, all my tables and shelves are filled with their books, even my bed is covered with them. They seem to float above the real surface, probably to avoid that I tare things down grabbing a book.

In absence of tactile feedback (who likes gloves?) the books are handled a bit different from real ones. I can grab them by touching, and then they move into reading position. Changing pages runs by just moving my fingers over the volume. They implemented this quite well, intuitively and easy, and I can leaf through pages as easy as with a real book. Of course they don't let me read all of it. But this is not just a preview restricted to some random pages, this is like looking into a book in a bookstore, only (like there) the time I can do this is somewhat limited. Nevertheless, given the kind of survey provided together with the convenience of seeing all of a book before buying, and this as quick as in a real bookstore, I think this idea will indeed have a great future. Well, finally I did find something interesting, and I decided to order it in real paper. Until I have it, and even after, I can acess the virtual copy full time (of course, a feature existing with web bookstores since long).

This a really good idea I think, turning one's own rooms into a store, as it provides for an environment where to walk and roam in freely, being able to examine all merchandise in a very real experience. There have already been many stores letting you 'walk' their premises in a fully immersive, fully virtual way, but obviously you can only 'visit' such a shop like a ghost, using a joystick or something to fly around. Trying to actually walk here would let you run into walls and furniture of your real rooms of course. The Cyclops solution surely involves some additional complexity, as their software always has to design a new virtual shop inside the customer's home, but it is generating a really vivid experience and a convenient way to look at things.

Reading a book

Sometimes the old paper stuff is still useful. Before we had these ergonomically designed virtual interfaces, reading something on a computer was much less convenient than just having it in paper. Worst of all, the whole thing was confined to bulky machines (I also consider a notebook too bulky for the purpose).
There had been some attempts to build special e-book readers, some with LCD displays (not a good idea), some with those polymer e-paper displays (usually poor in contrast), and all with some major disadvantages, be it resolution, handling, and so on. Anyway, it doesn't pay to build a computer just for one purpose.
Now it's better, my vision sim can emulate a book where I can flip pages with my fingers and even make dents and other naughty things. I can even use it in bed, as easy as a real book or a dedicated e-book reader, but try that with a notebook.
What is not possible with all conventional solutions, just to lean back and read, the pages large and above in the air. I even like to write this way, for small corrections and such, even if I have to rely on virtual keyboards or eye-pointing and speech commands.
Nevertheless there are so many real books that I still use. I have set up an autostart to the scanner application that stores pages I have read, so I can access them anywhere later on. It does this simply through the position sensor cameras. It also 'binds' me a book of those pages and sorts them just by the page numbers it

recognizes. I guess a lot of people are using this feature. You never know. Companies have taken numerous measures to keep their employees from scanning every document they see, as well as from filming the entire site. But that's another story. Let me only say so much that it has been established as a personal right to record one's own life anywhere anytime, in picture and sound, except for using the data to trace others or to distribute things without allowance.

With implanted computers expected to become a mass product in a few years, this was mandatory. Scientists even expect that technology will soon allow anybody to acquire *biological* memory capabilities like certain 'savants'[1], without the disadvantages.

Here I perfectly agree. I remember when I was at highschool, I once tried to learn 20 pages from the history book for a critical test. After repeating the first half of it for many times, I suddenly noticed that I stored the remaining pages just while reading. I couldn't repeat this experience later on, maybe I was too lazy to try hard enough, but I'm absolutely convinced that everybody could achieve it. So in any case, forbidding anybody to record what he sees or hears is an attack on basic personality rights.

My sim now really ensures that I almost never forget anything anymore. At least if I can still figure out how to find it in those terabytes of data. If that app wouldn't also store an OCR version of texts, (that still cannot always replace the facsimile) and a signature of the pictures, I'd sometimes really be lost trying to find something again.

The most peculiar thing with vision sims and printed media are books and newspapers that have code stamps on their pages, or hidden[2] in the pictures, causing the reader's sim to display animated pictures (from the web) right in the pages, as in the ancient Harry Potter movies.

---

[1] Persons who remember anything unfiltered, for example thousands of books word by word. Usually also a disease as other capabilities are seriously affected, and as there often is no real control over the flood of data.

[2] Watermarks embedded in the pictures, too faint to be seen by the human eye but detectable by electronic cameras. Can contain quite a lot of encoded information (keyword: steganography).

The downside of it, before privacy laws were tightened, had been that you never knew if your reading habits weren't traced and by whom. Some books even charged you for reading.

Nowadays it's granted that you've already paid for the extra web content with the book. It's also a permanent value, as web add-ons of vintage books are routinely transferred to the world online library.

Some of my books don't even need this service, as they have built-in storage and radio chips and generators or solar cells, and can deliver their own enhanced media as soon as the book is opened.

Stolen

What I hadn't expected in this neighborhood: somebody managed to steal my glasses when I put them down for a moment to rub my eyes. No idea what he or she wanted to do with it. Those devices were so heavily coded that probably nobody could crack them. The only use would be as replacement parts, but who would care to steal a $5 laser unit (those items have become dirt cheap since they are built by the millions). The guy also couldn't hope to get into my computer with this device, as it would only work for someone with just exactly my iris pattern and anyway it would instantly lock up when the connection was ripped.

I had good web connection right before, so all data were backed up in a most current state. Only the last hours of the vision cams were lost, as I don't upload them to the public network in raw format. This kind of bandwidth is still not for free.

I just bought a new pair of glasses, the most difficult part of them being the corrective lenses for my eyes that I had to wait 2 days for, and reinstalled the last backup.

Fortunately, I had always refused to use any software with activation schemes or media with „Digital Rapacity Management". So I did not have to call a hundred companies for allowance to restore, and I also did not lose any of my media. Most people don't care for this and would get into real trouble when losing a sim.

Allergic

About two years later I noticed more and more incidents of occasional vertigo, and increasing attacks of headache. The vertigo seemed to come from uncontrolled eye movements that appeared out of nothing.

As it got worse from day to day, I consulted a doctor. He diagnosed vertigo (how do you know), did an X-ray, an ultrasound and an MRI of my head, then prescribed me some pills. Seemed quite weird to me, but he was the doctor, and his walls were covered with diploma (at least one of them was from an egg walk contest, but who cares), so I gave this a try. Shortly said, it didn't work. Everything got worse and worse. When I read into the info leaflet of these pills and found that they could dye your hair green,

I went back to the doctor and asked for better advice. As it is with these doctors when their knowledge fails them, he then stated my symptoms must be psychosomatic. He said he knew a psychiatrist (?!) who would treat me for the negligible contribution of $400 per hour. It appeared to me that when saying this, little $-signs were flashing up in his eyes (did he take commission from this guy?). Anyway, at this point I said no thanks and went home. On the street I saw all these people apparently having none of my problems. All of a sudden, I noticed something strange. Their sims all looked much lighter than mine, you could think they were simple sunglasses, but little attachments revealed they carried some technology. I realized that I hadn't paid much attention to new developments during the last couple of years. Here was the solution: I needed a new sim, a lighter and better one. My symptoms were easily explained as kind of an allergy against the imperfections of my sim, tiny movements and image distortions resulting from inaccuracies of eye tracking and motion compensation. The headache also resulted form the sheer weight of this model.

After the bills from that doctor, I wouldn't shop for the most expensive brands, an 'Eye-Phone' or such. I went to an optometrist to look for one with built-in corrective glasses at least. The models they had were all three times lighter than my old one, but also pretty expensive. Some had absolutely useless features, like gold coated glasses, where the salesman really tried to convince me that I would see better with them. 'High End' they use to label these rather esoteric tech gadgets.

So I turned to V-Flea (virtual flea market) and noticed that there were several shops offering sim frames for auction, with the strange note that once you had the frame, you could also order the rest of it, including optical glasses, for an astonishingly low price. Exploring this a little deeper I found out that these people were certified optometrists and offered the same equipment that I had seen in the real shop. Obviously their strange business model was designed to circumvent price fixing and other sales restrictions.

I gave it a try, and finally I had a brand new sim, a genuine „Unnoticed v.7" with all extras, for about one third of the price the cheapest regular chain had offered me (even though their TV ads always pretended that absolutely no one could undersell them).

I was still a bit suspicious for some time, about the quality I really got, but it all proved to be OK.

The 'allergy' was gone. This new gadget wasn't only lighter, it also had a larger display, higher resolution and a better motion compensation, resulting in a steadier image. Best of all, it had a new technology mask display with almost perfect transparency, and a perfect active edge compensation accomplished by the laser display .

Only one problem appeared, that despite of the much faster CPU, this device was a bit slower in handling than my old one, obviously because the new „Hasta" operating system that came with it.

So after a few tries I decided to do a clean installation of my old „X-Ray" and things went really slick from that moment on.

With the new gadget I will be able to avoid using an implanted computer for some more time. These devices still have difficulties and can cause complications (popular conspiracy theories even have it that the government can use them to control your thoughts, but that's just green ink of course).

6000 feet under

The last time my sim got lost, it caused me quite some discomfort, even though only a few of my most recent data were lost.

This time it could have even been worse, as it happened on a sailing trip, where a sudden wave happened to flush my sim into the sea.

Even though one could perhaps try to detect it by radio for some time, at this location the sea was simply too deep to retrieve it for a reasonable price.

Luckily, I had got a chip implant just a few weeks before. No, calm down, not a tag and not a brain implant: Just a simple storage chip, with huge capacity, yes, but with no other capability than to communicate with my sim from half an inch of distance.

This gadget is an ultra thin flexible silicon chip, embedded in tissue friendly plastic, and with a filigree structure that makes it slip under the skin without disrupting even the tiniest structures.

It communicates by a semi passive RF link in the Terahertz range, needs no power supply but the RF signal from the sim, stores almost a terabyte of data and communicates them with a speed of several hundred megabits per second while taking just microwatts of power.

Being an highly encrypted device, I used this chip as the main storage for my sim. The concept was so convincing - the sim just being the interface machine with the OS delivering the hardware adaptation and functions, the implanted chip being the 'harddisk' for all data and private applications - that I even skipped my general resentment against implants.

No one can now have access to all this data but myself, and if my sim gets defective I just get another one and enter a longish password (that is only remembered as long as my proper retina patterns are in sight).

That's about it. And for double safety, the sim may store all data in it's own memory as well, also heavily encrypted of course.

Now for this special event, having my sim swallowed by the waves, it was a matter of slipping on a spare one that I had acquired before as this went cheap enough, and all was mended.

New toys

Since two years before, a lot has changed in our home as well. The 'wall breakthrough' (some now call it V-gate) with this multi-user 3D Light field display has replaced the first setup that had nothing but a camera array and relied on our sims.

Not that we would really need this, but it is also convenient as a home theatre of the old kind when we are just tired, also of wearing glasses, and Rudi, our dog, can also see the picture...

My working room on the other hand, got a new stack of five *ghost* bookshelves at three of its walls.

It's actually a representation of the filing cabinet of my computer network, and for convenience these 'books' are lying flat, so I can read their back titles.

Having this many square meters of 'books', all easily distinguished by size and color, arranged from wall to wall and floor to ceiling, and now even in five and more focus selectable layers, proves quite ergonomical in a way, even though a bit old fashioned. At least some part of the full human range of motion and 3D interaction can be utilized this way. Yet it's only he topmost layer of the search tree.

By touching any of the book backs I activate whatsoever it holds for me, and this can for example be a text as well as a photo album unfolding into a three dimensional cascade of sheets or exposures, all individually accessible by gaze, touch and gesture interaction or by spoken commands if I want.

All the bookshelves and other cabinets and acess structures just vanish almost entirely, leaving nothing but thin fog, as long as I'm not intentionally focusing to them.

So does my globe, a simple app that I gave a nice skin from a web resource and that turns into a sectional enlargement or a map sheet when I zoom in.

With the virtual world function included, I can even dive into any location entirely, start a fully immersive virtual travel experience anywhere, including real time image enhancements from current webcam streams, and weather simulation of course.

Squint triggered outside view has revolutionized the feel of living in this house. Any time I want, I just look into the far, make the walls and ceilings disappear and see the perfectly realistic outside view assembled from a bunch of cameras. It's quite tempting to lie on the bed in plain daytime and watch the clouds passing by.

I couldn't even resist to install a starlight camera with a huge lens, that delivers an overwhelming impression of the nightly sky, even brighter than anything one could experience in the wild.

Key's gone

Usually I'm running the camcorder function of my position cameras all the time. They record anything I see. Sometimes this is really useful. Two days ago I lost my keys. Fortunately I have an advanced recognition software with a special object tracking feature. It saw and categorized the keys any time I used them, and allowed me to find the decisive second in my personal recordings in an instant. These cameras also catalog every item I store in the cupboards and allow a random search for it. The downside of the recording function is that you never know if the guy next to you hasn't rented his vision simulator cameras to the police or someone else, although this is heavily restricted now. When laws had been more negligent and total surveillance was quite common, even private sim cams were regularly tapped by the authorities.

Nevertheless it proved ever more so valuable to have continuous private records, as criminals developed a habit of collecting DNA traces of innocent citizens and depositing them at crime scenes.

Given the way police are thinking, it's no wonder that more than half of the population have meanwhile been accused of burglary or worse.

An unexpected bus ride

I never thought I would ever have to face this: my car in the garage for repair and my wife out with our second one. And then suddenly I need to go downtown for a meeting. I'll need a cab or a bus I guess. The weather is a bit gray but it doesn't rain and I'll use my mood lifter software to make the sky blue and add little patches of sunlight to the scenery.

I should get a hint about transport from the web. Well that's pretty amazing: the bus company has a new front-end that can lead me from my home just where I have to go, traces my location, displays guiding arrows and continuously informs me where any and each bus is that I could use, when I would arrive and what it costs. The app also lists alternate routes, by subway for example (it's obviously an application made by the city), or can even point me to a bicycle rental. Buses aren't always ideally scheduled or routed at all, but with this kind of guidance I guess they can be considered an option for occasional users the first time in history, even more so as they automatically schedule and call a cab for route parts they can't serve.

Nice, that one. When classical mobile phones came into fashion, people already thought about implementing something similar with them. But for no reason whatsoever, it literally took decades until a few working applications appeared.

Ignorance about ergonomical design may have been one problem: long ago, I once encountered a railway ticket machine that could quickly and easily display any line and schedule in the nation just by walking the menus with two big 'mouse wheels'.

I've never understood why nobody ever equipped mobile phones with mouse wheels. Plain stupid. Only after touch screens had made considerable progress, things were improving a bit at last.

The meeting of the ghosts

This afternoon we had a virtual conference with one of our overseas partners. They just upgraded their system. Now they also have one of these surround camera arrays, and their transmission quality allows for a perfect 3D reconstruction of each participant. No comparison to their old screen based system anymore.

Sometimes I have to pinch myself to realize that these guys are not really sitting here. This is so perfect that everyone can even walk around in the room, and around one another. This needs a host of cameras, and a lot of computing power and bandwidth (even though it always only transmits those details that any of the participants needs to see). But who cares, this saves a fortune in travel costs, and lots of nerves as well.

With the pseudo holographic acquisition hardware originally designed for media production, such setups can now be flexibly installed anywhere, and they have also become very affordable.

We have had this system for many years, in every office. Most of them being home offices of course.

The camera arrays allow to simulate virtual wall breakthroughs and doors in any direction, connecting these offices as if they were adjacent in the same building, or even in one big room. I can't just walk over to the next office of course, or I'd hit my - very real - wall (rubber walls are popular these days).

In this case I have to tell my vision simulator to virtually transport me there, so the rooms are merged. They also provide a silly 'beaming' effect if I want. After this, it just feels as if I was really there.

These camera arrays may be a larger installation, but they are definitely better than the cheap 'avatar' solution that tries to synthesize my own picture from just what my vision simulator can get.

The only real synthesizing effort with the camera array, except for perspective, is that eyes have to be simulated in a person's picture because one's vision sim's mask display will normally cover them in order to insert the picture of the opponent. The basis for the eye pictures is provided by the vision sim's eye trackers, so the merged picture is entirely real and accurate.

For just calling somebody, I usually just position myself in front of a mirror. This only works for face to face connections, but it's very simple and requires very little synthesizing.

But the video connection is mostly useless once you have it, at least for individual phone calls with people you know. Staring into each other's face makes little sense most of the time. A lot more useful is the 'see what I see' function. Showing things, or the TV program I'm watching, or the baby, these are the most popular uses of video telephony these days.

The world in a nutshell

Virtual tele-conferences were everyday business meanwhile. But once upon a time, we decided to have these meetings not in the office but abroad, at some nice places as can be found around the globe. The ever thickening grid of webcams and the billions of pictures and live transmissions from personal goggle cams adding to it, are making available visual data from almost any place at almost any time, often so even entirely live.

Stream identifiers and general hub proxying now enable anybody to transmit data and video to billions of people without uploading more then once. It also saves the better part of all network traffic, as not a single byte has to be sent twice over the same line [120].

The 'Grid' as it's actually being called, formerly the 'Ubicam' (you-be-cam or ubiquitous cam) network, responds to any request for image data by assembling stored and live camera data related to the place, thereby generating an artificial live picture of the right perspective, time of day and even weather, a perfect merger of real and simulated features.

This is not entirely reliable information of course, so it may be used for general survey, travel, ambience simulation and the like, but if I just want to know what's ahead on the road I'd rather rely on some unprocessed live pictures form the car in front of me. Which isn't a contradiction, fortunately, as I can get these pictures in flavors, the older ones browned out by a sepia effect, virtual ones half transparent and so on, so I can immediately figure out how reliable and true any of these impressions really are. When the Grid was first invented, people objected that pictures from personal cams could be abused to trace people and spy after them. Even just being seen live by anyone from anywhere, without even knowing, something that already took place when only stationery webcams were available, was a bit scary and caused sort of upheaval at times. The current Grid cameras are anonymized however, so it is very difficult to find out who's cam's the pictures uploaded are.

The general user has no means for exploiting this data in a way as to trace anybody, as perspectives rendered for him are revealing but a little of the original pictures. Nevertheless at the intermediate servers, somebody could identify someone's personal cam pictures, by the cockpit of the car he's riding for example, and get the position by comparing the landscape seen to the global database. Fortunately, this has been adverted by several other measures, so anybody can now be quite sure about his grid transmissions being safe.

What adds to it: Anybody's own personal recordings are prohibited from being used against the person in trials of any kind, even if they had been opened for real time public access by the Grid, and were recorded or observed by other persons.

The Private Memory Act had long been struggled upon, but in the end the insight prevailed that anything else would have amounted to thought control, forcing people just to avoid certain technologies, an obstacle to progress and an open door towards intellectual enslavement.

Only for this wise decision had it been happening that the global Grid now enables anybody to 'virtually' be everywhere, in a real time reproduction of the entire world, if so desired even including temperature, 3D wind sensing, broadband radio reproduction, smell and more, and all this at no travel costs and no energy expenses.

Virtual travel is also of course much better than 'developing' the coastline with skyscrapers where clueless people can buy condos for exercising their self mummification while staring at the sea.

The other side of the problem, being spied on by being seen from other people's cams, public cams etc, was mended by introducing a mandatory camouflaging scheme:

If you don't want to be seen, the system masks your face, even changes your clothes, or makes you perfectly invisible in any scenery renderings. Private places are also excluded from public view, of course. Only for safety applications like those traffic X-ray and view-ahead features, invisibility is overridden to a certain extent. The system can obey to your wishes by either recognizing you or by responding to a personal 'transponder', a feature of your vision glasses transmitting certain collaborative information to receivers in a limited area.

Current webcams can receive these transmissions and attribute them to the appropriate sender by comparing to personal appearance data as are always used for basic AR device interactions as document exchange etc., in order to identify and locate the correspondents.

There are opt-in as well as opt-out schemes being used for the global real time model (intentionally spying after people or virtually following them, even if they are not anonymized, is against anti stalking and privacy laws of course, and offenders can usually be detected by the picture streams they are requesting).

With our conferences, quite some things have to be taken into account: there is also an option to be seen, for example, as a virtual visitor. You may visit a place and display an avatar of yours (that can of course only be seen by wearers of AR glasses, or by other virtual visitors).

If we have a meeting, we will of course opt to see each other, but not necessarily to be seen by third parties. And in some places, an invasion of avatars would just clutter them if all were visible to all. Imagine if only a few of the million companies around the globe went to have a meeting at Zabriskie Point (including a spectacular virtual blow-up at the end) ...

Well, they can do it, no problem, if they set it up so any of them can only be seen by their own buddies. This kind of events emerging lead to a peculiar consequence: many spectacular places now have 'ghost tables' set aside, where anybody can have a virtual meeting without being bothered by real visitors.

Some have been asking fees for it, but now almost all are relying on ad revenues. They are placing some ad posts around you and get a fortune out of it, because PR companies know that hosts of people will see these ads, inevitably and for quite some time.

In fact, the entire Grid first started from the ad business, as it is easy just to replace signposts from the real world with other, virtual ones and add even some more. It was just a smooth transgression from mere satellite imaging to 3D modeling to linked photos to linked webcams, and then, when the cam density allowed it, to artificial live perspective rendering. People now use it for sightseeing, traveling, meetings, even demonstrations. Many worlds parallel to the real one have been created, with very complicated links to the real one and each other, an entire universe of 'second lives' for just anybody. Social simulations, important for exploring the effects of laws, political decisions and entire society models, could in theory be performed in a brainstorming workshop as well, but the reality aspect proved extremely valuable. Any new 'ideology' that's going to be imposed onto the public will now first be tried in the virtual - down to simplicities as traffic planning. This way, at least some of the many mistakes as there were made in former times can now be avoided. Many people, myself included, are regularly volunteering in these simulation runs. It's a game that makes a lot of sense.

Nevertheless, I personally do like the Grid's travel opportunities above all else. Now you may think I'm a couch potato, too lazy to go out, but this here can actually be a lot more action than just being carried around in a tourist bus.

For example, I like to do virtual traveling on my bicycle trainer, actually riding through alien countries and working out in the course of it. If I'm getting impatient, I turn the bicycle into a pedal plane.

Many people like virtual wandering in a walking machine, or virtual climbing or driving or flying. Maybe next I buy one of these new gym machines that will actually turn me into a bird...

My washing machine

Even the most die-hard computer junkie sometimes needs fresh garment. Guess I have to start my washing machine. This one has a virtual control panel as almost any one you could get these days. I load the machine, then I think it's pretty stupid to bow in front of it to set up the program. I detach the virtual panel and return to my couch, to finish the job right there.

Don't even think I'd use the standard panel. There are numerous guys writing their own fancy controller applications for such a frequent washing machine, so I downloaded one of these that would best fit what I was thinking a washing machine should look like. It has some washing programs that are quite different form those the manufacturer originally built in.

I can even get this very same interface for many different brands of washing machines, so I don't ever have to bother with user manuals again. Most important, it only requires a few clicks to start what I just need it to do. Bingo, click that panel away, can restart it later on to see how far that washing has gone. This machine even has a drum camera. To see if the cat has gotten in, I'd guess.

Plants, lamps and old stuff

Some people have virtual pets, many have virtual plants. Those v-pets I really deem a bit crazy. I'm also not quite so comfortable with virtual plants. They don't have any good influence on air and climate, so I prefer to take the extra work of growing the real ones. Of course I use some gadgets that make it less cumbersome. My watering system is quite handy: little units with a tank and a moisture sensor. They can serve up to 5 flowerpots each, are solar powered from the normal room lighting, and have wireless network. I've configured individual virtual controls at each flowerpot, that are each activated only when I hit a little button (it's the only thing remaining visible when not in use, so this stuff doesn't clutter up the view to the flowers).

So I can give each plant an individual program right in location.

That 'green thumb' software keeps track of the plant's appearances by 3D recording them and lets me literally see them grow by recalling last month's pictures.

I can also access each control remotely everywhere I want, or have them all in a neat list. The same possibilities I have with my window blinds, the heating, the pool, anything. All of the controller units consist of just a chip, no displays, no keys, smallest dimensions, small power consumption. Those far from AC current use little solar units or long lasting batteries.

There's also no lamp in the house that hasn't a virtual control interface, even though it simply duplicates nothing but the power switch. These controller units are made by the millions and are dirt cheap now. Many are nothing but simple infrared or radio receivers. Some carry only a bar or block code that tells my sim how to address them, especially the simple switches. Some I have to program into my sim. Before sims became common, switches were in fashion that had cameras of their own and could 'see' if you looked at them. I still use some of these.

The older hardware stuff standing around here required some setup as well, but in most cases my sim just looked it up in a web database just by its picture, and immediately came up with the right programming codes and even a picture of the original remote that I could operate wherever desired.

One or two needed special treatment, but my sim also works as a learning remote, no problem.

What I like most with it, that no remotes are lying around anymore, and that I can just operate anything here with eye pointing alone. Sort of magic, that is.

Garage job

I think I have to do some car maintenance today. One of the bus operated relays seems to be defective. The controls show that the right high beam doesn't work, but that it's only the relay that doesn't respond, not the lamp. This isn't something you need a central computer for, nowadays. If these cars have any general purpose computers, it's just a recording unit or a tripmaster, noting that interferes with anything that could be safety relevant, and all units are independent of each other, the only concept that can avoid complex and potentially dangerous malfunctions to develop.

When they finally realized that super processors drawing lots of power and being run with complicated operating systems were just not appropriate for relatively simple tasks, car makers managed to standardize a few bus based universal switches and relays. These are now produced by the hundreds of millions and can be purchased at any gas station. As with all technology, once mature it finally becomes reliable.

Cars were mature before electronics (except for the cylinder head gasket), then they became progressively immature when more and more experiments were built in. These were mainly used to secure revenue by hosts of patents and part prices rightout insane. Finally, when car electronics also became of age, things became reasonable once more.

Something I always wondered about was how long they sticked to driving valves with a camshaft. My last fuel engine had electromagnetic ones and could 'drink' almost anything liquid.

Meanwhile they've also standardized things like the motor control unit (actually several modular units for better service) - all simple dedicated chips that are identical for any car and just get teached in with a little program - and several other standard items (no, this car here has none of these combustion engines anymore, all electrical).

None of these modular controllers can just quit with a software error anymore, and they are all autonomous. Together with two power buses (one for backup) and the also redundantly wired fiber bus, these ACME* [28] standard components make cars as reliable and simply maintainable as my son's tricycle.

---

* The Original Illustrated Catalog of ACME Products, by GP Markham. ACME has built a reputation by supplying all kinds of equipment to many well-known comic characters. The product range comprises anything from birdseed to atom rearrangers to cars or jet propelled pogo sticks.

So the switch told me the relay was defective. I've just opened the hood, and now my sim shows me right away where it is.

The maintenance recording unit - also a totally independent device - serves me with detailed 3D drawings and wire plans, projected into the motor cabinet, and lets me see through everything there is.

Maintenance applications like this one had been implemented with simpler display units long ago. Meanwhile it's common and cheap, and car manufacturers have found out that it is a good idea to integrate this knowledge right into the car. Many other hardware products have meanwhile also been equipped with this feature.

This defective relay even flashes, of course the maintenance unit has also noticed it, by listening to the bus communications. So changing it is done in a second, The socket contains a code that tells the relay what to do from now on, and that's it. I didn't even have to go to the next gas station for this. These items are so current that I have some in stock all the time.

Living history

Last year I was in Italy and decided to visit some historic sites for the first time. Twice I had been in Venice before, but never in Rome or Pompeii.

Meanwhile they have installed virtuality transmitters all over. In Venice for example, you can now visit the Arsenal and watch ancient shipwrights producing battleships in series, in a perfect assembly line technique.

Walking through the ancient ruins of Pompeii, you can chose to see the buildings as they are, or with virtual reconstructions added, so the entire city may look exactly as it was before the eruption (or at least as the historians think it had looked).

This is very impressive. One could build such a site entirely virtual, but it's by no means comparable to having the real thing alongside with the enhanced views.

Every two hours the volcano breaks out, pyroclastic flows are rushing down the slopes of mount Vesuvius, ashes are raining (virtually, I really appreciate if this doesn't get too real), and horrified citizens are running through the streets and sometimes right trough you. A really ground shaking sound system supports the volcano eruptions, but they're using it very cautiously because it could damage the ruins.

All pictures and local sound events are provided by a cellular network of image transmitters, each to be received from a short distance only. Any vision simulator can decide which of the virtual objects offered are near enough to reproduce, and build a complete virtual scene combined from these structures.

For a large area, an ancient town for example, this has proven the most efficient method. Transmitting views of thousands of buildings and other things from just one central facility would be too slow in most cases.

You could also see the entire site from a helicopter. It looks a bit as with an ancient flight simulator, with buildings appearing one by one as you approach.

In Rome, in the Coliseum, it's been accomplished with one central cinema transmitter. All of a sudden you find yourself in a blood thirsty crowd, squealing and yelling at the atrocities taking place in the arena. Your fellow visitors also suddenly change, their shorts and t-shirts replaced by togas and the omnipresent Klompen sweat shoes replaced by sandals.

If you're standing in the arena, it's even more thrilling, although I got the impression that the lions always go for the more nutritious guys.

Many historic sites now have their virtuality transmitters. Landmarks also do, some only working similar to virtual signs, but many are like virtual cinemas.

On an ancient battlefield you may suddenly be in for a shock, if you didn't watch for the acceptance levels of your sim. This may also apply to cemeteries, regrettably.

The most impressive makeups may be sea battles. You can charter a boat and watch the battles of Trafalgar, Midway, or Lepanto if you like, at their original sites or at similar locations where special theme parks have been installed. Original sites are the most exclusive, of course.

This is lightyears ahead of the monster cinemas that once dominated theme park assemblies. You can actually get right into the middle of the battle, in case of the sea variety with a real ship, and if you avoid running right trough the virtual ones it will definitely feel quite real. Too real maybe. Will it show people the insanity of these events, or will it just blunt their feelings? Hard to say in any case.

With all virtual landmark sites or theme parks it's advisable to shield the open edges of your sim, so you don't see the nothing beneath the display area, that would disturb the illusion. The sims they offer for short time rent at the sites are all built this way.

Did I mention the dinosaur park ? Real beasts would be more impressive, but I would not like to find myself so close by them.

Lost in space

An exceptional type of theme park application has emerged with the combination of vision simulators with underwater setups long used in astronaut training. You get stuffed into a wetsuit and a helmet with advanced display and oxygen supply. Then they throw you into a water tank, where your position is fixed by jet blowers. It feels weightless, although your stomach still knows it isn't (which is an advantage, as vomiting into the helmet would be horrible). The really important part however is the vision simulation: you can look around and there is no doubt you're floating in free space, 100 miles above the earth, and the image is not only a perfect illusion but also crisp enough to see tiniest detail on the earth's surface. At one side, myriads of stars are twinkling (you'll tell me they aren't, as there is no atmosphere, but it sounds better), on the other side the sun is terribly blinding. Couldn't be more real. Even an entire space suit is simulated when you look at yourself. The ultimate 'kick' comes when all of a sudden you are accelerated towards the moon, fly around it, and then blast off towards mars and Jupiter as with a warp drive.

Feeling no acceleration force here is really SciFi, but who knows-recently the there was an article about magnetic nano particles connected with proteins. An astronaut stuffed up with this should weigh 20 pounds more, but they claimed that in the field of some superconducting magnets, he could stand 20 or 30 g of acceleration. Absolutely weird.

The planets program takes at least an hour, as there is so much to see and you don't want to accelerate sunrises and sunsets on alien planets, nor other spectacular occurrences.

Any picture material available from space missions has been incorporated with the simulation, in ultimate detail, and a sophisticated software merges it into a perfect world model.

Optionally, you can have your own flight controls or even a spacecraft simulated, to conduct your own expedition program. Even researchers like to use these high end simulators, to get a real look and feel of their object of studies.

Something I personally will never do, is to book a vacation especially for these occasions.

I'd prefer some weeks of pure nature, without these glasses...

.....BOONDOCKS OR BUST !!

The following pages have also been found with the historic 'files from the rubble' (early 21st century). Many of the envisioned technologies were in common use a few decades after. It may be of interest to compare the suggested solutions to the partly far more elegant technology of later vision simulators.

part 3: Technical Design

General considerations

The following chapter will present and analyze possible technical solutions for a virtuality interface that seamlessly integrates into everyday environment.

Let's shortly repeat the fundamentals:

Natural objects stick to the environment, not to the user's field of view. This should also be the default option for virtual objects. It keeps sight free and enables the use of many more virtual objects at once. Our entire capability to deal with complex 3D environments can be unleashed this way.
Information interfaces can be reduced to the very basic, they just have to deliver pictures and sound as directly to the user's senses as possible and become so light and small that they go almost unnoticed.

Our most important objective is the creation of virtual devices, virtual 'hardware' objects that are fully integrated into reality, with the default option of being fixed to real objects or locations, just as most real things.
The visualization equipment required must be able to orientate itself in a natural environment, in order to 'know' where it is and how to accommodate visual perspectives.

A special kind of object and scenery recognition is required, three dimensional image analysis (stereo viewing) and other technologies are necessary. I will try to outline a realistic approach to this. Also very important is object handling. The approach to manual or visual steering with virtual keys that I introduced in the first chapter already, needs extremely little computing power. The same applies for combinations of eye pointing with simple voice commands recognition, for example.
The optics necessary will go far beyond current solutions. Anything published so far does not fulfil the objectives according to size, weight, and wearability.

One reason may be that large industrial companies, essentially able to develop the technology, have long regarded AR as a niche application not really worth the effort.

The other reason: while creating 'perfect' optics is not the smartest approach at all, there is hardly any connection between the disciplines of electronics and optics that could lead to intelligent, integrated concepts.

It is quite evident that unconventional ways of construction have to be explored, so this has to be a core thematic in this chapter. Dynamic geometry and focus correction, 'exotic' optical elements like dichroic filters or holographic lenses and mirrors, even non planar displays, have to be considered.

We will be exploring some possible approaches to very light and convenient constructions.

We will further discuss additional components for 'mixed virtuality', wireless interfacing/networking, virtual object handling and security, and more.

Advantages over conventional 3D displays

Many applications anticipated for new display technology are involving 3D. Here, our

All varieties of electronic 3D displays known so far, are forcing the eye to focus to a different distance than the stereo perspective implies. Most also do not care for perspective changes by head movements. Most cannot adjust image perspectives for different viewing distances.

In one or the other way, none so far reproduce all aspects of stereo viewing accurately. This results in a more or less unrealistic impression and considerable eye strain.

With the approach taken here, it should be possible to resolve these problems entirely.

Last but not least, the virtual display area and resolution of really smart display glasses can be orders of magnitude larger than that of any static screen, as only a part of the entire angular range has to be displayed at any given time.

Why it can be done

A good interface must adapt to motion and all sorts of dynamic influences. Dealing with this will make display glasses, a vision simulator as we are calling it here, much more complex but also, in case of optics, more simple.

In principle, there is no other optical part necessary in a vision simulator than a single concave mirror. This way we get a large field of view and considerable enlargement with very little weight. Inevitably we will see image distortion, but this can obviously best be dealt with by software based pre-compensation. We may also try to develop displays with uneven pixel distribution or with a convex surface. Organic LED displays for example could be made this way.

Lenses or prisms, except for small ones, are not as well suited for the purpose, because of weight. A curved mirror is our first choice as the main optical element, because it's not such a good idea just to use a planar glass to mirror images into the eye, as this doesn't only look bad, but also doesn't allow large viewing angles. A mirror will probably be a good choice for a second optical element as well, if necessary.

We may need aspherical optics and other more unusual things. The complexity of the task requires extensive optical calculations (that we won't carry out here but leave to specialists) and a lot of unconventional methods. Mirrors and other elements could also be holographic ones, if we deal with monochromatic light.

Focus and aperture may be critical issues, but it is absolutely necessary anyway, that we provide for dynamic adaptation, based on the input of an eye tracker. This also allows us to do away with special fixtures of the VR device to the head. An acceptable device should always be freely movable, like ordinary glasses, without becoming dysfunctional. With eye tracking and a servo system, we can achieve this.

An eye tracker and dynamic adjustments of focus and geometry, will provide entirely new options for display design.

Given the light weight optics and the possibility to use small displays, the entire vision simulator (except for the computer) can be made almost as light as any modern pair of ordinary plastic glasses.

We also need a perfect position and motion sensor for our device. Key ingredients of position sensing are stereo cameras, attached to the glasses. Usually, sensing positions with such devices is deemed anything but trivial. Yet for our approach, we do not require the cameras to *recognize* anything.

Instead, I will be proposing an approach that relies on simplest image details as lines, angles, etc., normalizes these image 'atoms' to a standard perspective, size, orientation and illumination, then stores them together with geometrical pointers to other 'atoms' and to virtual objects. The atom and pointer data structure enables a description of more complex scenes, and it is rotation and perspective independent.

We do not need any separation or recognition of real objects. It is of absolutely no concern if image atoms or structures describe one object or are distributed between many objects. It is especially unimportant to assign any meaning to any object. We do not try image recognition but image remembering, and only of the very simplest and most prevalent detail.

This somehow resembles the way humans are believed to recognize images. As soon as devices become available that simulate the human visual system [12],[108], these may perhaps greatly accelerate the process.

The data structure would enable us to search for a resemblance of newly seen image structures to stored ones very quickly. As we never need to store any image data from places where we did not place virtual objects, the database remains relatively small. Given the power of modern processors, the search for similarities can therefore be carried out in a very short time.

A GPS or similar device will further reduce the difficulty, by excluding irrelevant places and quickly resolving ambiguities.

Once relevant detail is recognized, even standard video cameras can provide for a millimeter accurate position sensing.

Acceleration sensors will allow to compensate for effects resulting from the limited speed (frame rate) of cameras and displays.
Head movements can be predicted from speed and acceleration at
a given time, quite precisely, due to the relatively big inertia of
the head. Optical flow sensors as in computer mice, can detect
head rotations extremely fast and accurate.

Gesture recognition has always been a challenge. It's also not
even really necessary. I don't appreciate any solutions that require gloves or other special equipment and I don't think
anybody really does. Recognizing human hands or free gestures I
don't consider either, as it has always been difficult and it's even
a bit peculiar: imagine the computer mouse would have been
introduced with no keys, and anything had to be entered with it
by gestures. Queer, isn't it?

Instead, we could let the display project virtual keys or sensitive
areas in objects, and scan the stereo camera's outputs for any
correlated signal change indicating a movement exactly and only
in these areas.

This is very easy and needs very little computing power. Adding
some simple heuristic checks can secure the algorithm against
false triggering. Once a finger is identified in a key area, it can as
well be traced to some extent very easily, in order to enable more
complicated actions (grabbing and positioning an object, or
throwing an object, for example).

Last but not least, we would usually *look* a the key we are pressing. Hence, we could use the eye tracker cameras to implement
eye pointing and this could improve security and also enable
remote key pressing.

It would not be a problem to activate the surface of entire objects
to be 'touched' and switched or dragged by hand or eyes. Indeed,
gestures may only matter if we want to drag objects. In this case
we could implement a 'lock' function and then follow the hand.
It's also possible to exploit accelerated movements in order to
virtually 'throw' objects, in a heuristic context with environment
structure, because this would be one way, for example, to define a
video screen on a wall. This is still way below the difficulty of
mainstream gesture recognition. Dynamic action like this has

already been used long ago with a 3D 'mouse' device, that traces an ultrasound source with 3 microphones attached to a display. A Game application coming with it allowed to throw virtual rings over a stick, by just mimicking the throwing action with the ultrasound emitter. The rings 'thrown into the display' would then appear in there and fly as if they were real. It worked perfectly well, so I have no doubt that this kind of action will be an easy way to handle remote virtual objects. The Wii game console that appeared since the last edition of this book just picks up the thread again.

Eye pointing however will be the most elegant way to deal with remote objects anyway, as it doesn't only deliver an unambiguous direction information, but also a distance information because of eye convergence ('squinting'). Nobody usually peers at anything for more than a second without a reason, and blinking could also be exploited for some actions, so this could all work as a complete way of interfacing. Even dragging things may be done by eyes only, and even in three dimensions if we use active accommodation steering.

Sharing virtual objects with other people would be most natural. Everyone involved should be able to manipulate them. This is another field for research and I will also address it in this chapter. I however do not think it would be desirable to replace all real input devices with virtual ones. A keyboard for example is difficult to implement in virtual. Combining virtual machines with a foldable or rollable *real* keyboard, for example, could be the more convenient. Using an active pen or pointer device could also still be of advantage.

Given all the different tasks to address, bringing the vision simulator into general use will still be a very complex task, and will need considerable research in many different fields.

In this chapter, we will explore possible solutions to many of the tasks mentioned. This will inevitably be far from comprehensive. It is mainly intended as a proof of concept. If vision simulators will have as huge an impact on technology as I am expecting, first implementations will initiate an extraordinarily dynamic development, leading to many surprising new twists anyway.

Hardware assembly

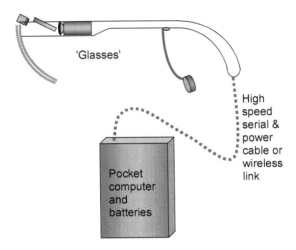

'Glasses'

High
speed
serial &
power
cable or
wireless
link

Pocket
computer
and
batteries

Quite obviously, we want to reduce the weight of the glasses assembly as far as possible.

A powerful CPU may not fit into this part in a foreseeable future. So the glasses should only contain the most necessary hardware. Images, sensor and actuator data could be transported in both directions wireless or by cable. A modern serial bus can transport over 400 Mbit/s on a single wire, that could also be used to carry power. So we need only one very thin cable.

Any computing whatsoever can be performed in a pocket unit that also takes care of all other interfacing, like wireless networking.

In the glasses assembly we only need data compression, serial bus, display driver and camera chips, some actuators, to mention the most obvious. These must be optimized for size and power consumption (the pocket computer as well, of course).

It is by no means physically impossible to reduce the power consumption of the glasses unit far enough as to use separate batteries and wireless data connection. Then we could even drop the pocket computer if we could link to a home or office network. Even real soon now. Read on for details.

Some basic display designs

Let's first have a look at some conventional VR display types:

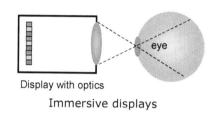

Display with optics

Immersive displays

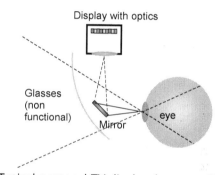

Typical personal TV display (one-eyed)

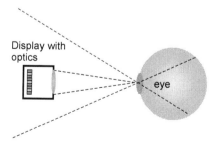

Personal data display (one-eyed). Allows to look around the display by turning the head

Some varieties of see-through displays

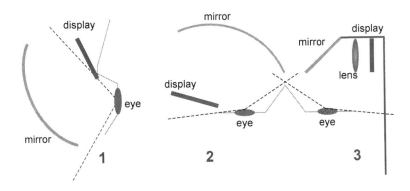

I won't consider any assemblies that don't allow direct sight to the real world, as the eyetap [25] or other approaches that require the user to see everything through cameras. These won't be acceptable for everyday use in a foreseeable future, if at all.

What we need here are see-through displays mirroring additional items into the field of view. The question is what the mirror should look like and where we place the display.

A natural dead angle is at the eyebrow and above. A display positioned there covers almost no direct sight and allows for a relatively wide projection image (1).

The same optical assembly, with a conventional display at the *side* (2), could cause some obstruction and have a smaller projection angle sideways, where humans have a large viewing range, over 180 degrees. Yet with small display assemblies, laser or holographic for example, this could also work quite well.

A typical commercial data display assembly (3) causes even more obstruction, although very light and convenient ones are available.

I will therefore start the design considerations with the display positioned above the eye. All these assemblies could as well be arranged as in example (2).

Some examples of current displays

MicroOptical CV-3 video viewer. monocular, color, 640x480 pixels, 20^0x16^0 35g(viewer) [14] (photo courtesy of MicroOptical Corporation)

Liteye LE-500 [54]; monocular, 800x600 pixel OLED display, see-through optional, 28^0 field of view, 120 grams (photo courtesy of Liteye Systems)

i-glasses theater: 112g, 230000 pixels (photo courtesy of i-O Display Systems, LLC)

i-glasses 3D Pro, 600x800x3 color pixels (photo courtesy of i-O Display Systems, LLC)

Kaiser Proview XL40 ST: 1024x768 green, 45^0 diagonal field of view, see-through, 900g (photo courtesy of Rockwell Collins)

Cybermind Visette 45 XSGA
1280x1024 pixels, 750g,
see-through optional (photo
courtesy of Cybermind BV)

Saab Addvisor 150:
1280x1024 color, 46^0, see-
through (photo courtesy of
Saab Avitronics)

NVIS NVISOR SX [55], bin-
ocular 1280x1024, 1kg, 60^0.
Eye tracker (Arrington Research, [56]) optional
(photo courtesy of NVIS)

Arrington Research Viewpoint
PC-60 eye tracker [56],
mounted on glasses
(photo courtesy of Arrington
Research)

eMagin Z800 3DVisor
[60], 600x800, OLED on
silicon, 40^0 diagonal field
of view, acceleration
tracking. (photo courtesy
of eMagin Corp.)

Mirage LightVu [53] OEM optical module. The glasses unit weighs 40 grams. A 'nanoprism' assembly (non transparent, see-around) creates a virtual 42" screen from a single display (photo courtesy of Mirage Innovations)

Lumus display module using an holographic optical element. See-through, viewing angle are design adjustable. See p.239 for details (photo courtesy of Lumus Inc.)

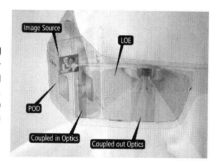

An overview of current products can also for example be found on the websites of EST [29], or Stereo3D.com [50].

In conclusion, there are some products with see-through and high resolution, that would allow to implement some of the new applications we have discussed, but mainly for scientific evaluation, development, and professional applications, as current civil high end augmented reality displays are too bulky and heavy to wear in everyday life (not to mention the costs, but this problem would vanish with mass production). Other products, as the MicroOptical CV3 and the Mirage LightVu are examples how light display units could actually be built, although these models aren't just made for the applications considered here.

The display design coming nearest to our requirements presently is the Lumus (picture above, more at p.239),

Extras like earphones or position sensors are present in certain products as well, but no one has even nearly all features we need. The 1280x1024 pixels resolution and ≈45⁰ diagonal field of view offered by some current products are just a little less than what we would like to have (e.g. 1600x1200 and >60⁰, ideally 3000x2000 at 90⁰ or more; the FOHMD discussed in the first chapter already met or exceeded these specifications).

Typically, current display glasses have no dynamic compensation for position change (fit), no eye trackers (some, optional), no camera based exterior position sensors, no mask displays, and so on. For experimental setups, we could add some of those features. The entire software basis has to be developed as well, and when new markets will emerge, products will certainly be further developed and improved, concurrently with new applications.

We see that it is still quite some challenge to get to a really comfortable vision simulator, one that would seamlessly integrate into everyday life.

A most important task will be the display and the optics. I will therefore give high priority to considerations and suggestions on possible optical and display solutions, including eye tracking and related features.

The future: ACME [28] 'Hairstyle' display. Eye projector and cameras are concentrated in one tiny unit. The user wears a monocle with a totally passive holographic screen coating. The computer unit is contained inside the periwig. Less sudorific products are the hat based 'Stetson' and 'Sherlock' models.

Display technologies

This is a short list of currently available technologies with focus on near eye applications. It can neither be entirely complete or go into much detail. We will have a closer look on some technologies later on.

- LCD (Liquid Crystal Displays) use nematic liquid crystals between two glass plates with polarizer filters each. With electric fields applied, these liquid crystals turn the polarization vector of passing light, so transmission can be varied. Other LCD types allow to modulate refraction index, or phase, and can be used for holographic applications. Standard LCD designs are not so easily adaptable for a glasses display as we need it, because very small pixels are difficult to achieve (the minimum thickness of the LC fluid sets some limits). They may be a first solution for mask displays [13].

- LCOS (Liquid Crystal on Silicon) are LCD displays using a silicon wafer as a driving backplane. They work reflective, allow for smaller pixels (thinner LC layer).

- FLC (Ferroelectric LCD) are liquid crystal displays with 'chiral smectic C phases' that exhibit ferroelectric properties. They are more difficult to make than normal LCD but exhibit very short switching times (<10µs rather than <10ms for typical LCD).

- F-LCOS (Ferroelectric LCOS) displays combine LCOS and FLC technologies. They can be produced with very small pixel sizes (currently 8µm, but 4µm or less said to be possible) and are the technology of choice currently for high resolution VR goggles as well as synthetic holography [33], [51]. These displays are very fast, color is typically produced by sequential illumination, switching the light source rather than working with color filters in the display itself, advantageous especially for reflective displays.

- DMD (DLP) displays consist of microscopic mirrors that are individually tilt by electrostatic forces (more later). DMD projectors are quite current already.
  Contrary to LCD, These displays could actually perform better when pixel get smaller. We could use them - with LED illumination - just like normal displays. New miniature versions for mobile phone projectors offer perspectives for vision glasses.

- PISTON type micro mirror displays, still a research topic, can work as phase modulating holograms, offering many uses from laser beam shaping or deflecting to projection displays to light field generation by Fourier holograms.

- MLM (Moving Liquid Mirror) displays carry a liquid film on a CMOS substrate with an electrode array, undulating the film by electric forces [119]. Can be used for beam shaping by phase modulating (reflection or refraction). Reaction times are way longer than with micro mechanical displays (ms vs. μs).

- GLV (Grating Light Valve) are linear (1D) arrays of microscopic aluminum strips being switched to form an interference grid. Probably not important for our purpose.

- Holographic displays are an *application*, currently e.g. with F-LCOS or piston type moving micro mirror technology, that provides little computer generated holograms. As patterns to be displayed require resolutions in the micrometer range, these displays can only be made in small dimensions and may require enlargement optics [31], [36]. All modes available so far use Fourier holograms, deliver *light field* images.

- CRT (Cathode Ray Tubes): Miniature index color CRTs are available (UV index strips between colors provide for correct addressing of the phosphors). One could think about using a mini CRT backwards, peering through the glass cone from behind. This would also allow to construct a convex screen. Weight and size however would prohibit such an approach.

- LED (Light Emitting Diodes) could be ideal, but in order to produce light, semiconductors need to have threshold voltages (band gaps) corresponding to the energy of the photons we want. Red light photons have 1.5 electron volts, blue about 3, while silicon has a band gap of only 0,7 V (and is not able to emit radiation anyway). We need gallium arsenide or gallium nitrite for example, and combining these materials with a silicon driver chip for a display array is difficult. There is a product, but not yet over 800x600 resolution.

- OLED (organic or plastic Light Emitting Diodes) do work for miniature displays. At the high resolutions we need, passive matrix driving is not an option, so current products use a silicon CMOS driver chip with OLED coatings on top [60]. A fully organic (plastic) design could even provide convex or concave displays. Making blue OLEDs and life expectancy have been problematic with this technology. Nowadays, OLED are even surpassing LED in terms of efficiency.

- Polymer displays are based on organic chemistry, like OLEDs. Formerly, only passive varieties ('electronic newspaper') were summarized here, but now there are also self luminating ones. Reportedly, high resolution versions are in test. Life expectancy is still not so good (1 year for example). There is one variety that switches from transparent to color band absorption [7]; this might be useful for mask displays.

- Electronic Paper: a large variety of technologies. Some don't eve have dedicated names yet. Of little concern here.

- Transparent OLED/Polymer displays are like a glass plate when inactive and pixels are caused to 'glow' when addressed. These displays may be good for some novel design concepts. They are not directly useful for our approach to mixed reality however, because there is always the problem that the display and things behind it can't be focused on at the same time.

- **OLED on CMOS** employs vacuum deployed (not printed, because of small structures) layers of organic LED material on CMOS semiconductor chips, The chip can contain complex driver circuits and, a special advantage, also light sensitive structures allowing to integrate a camera right into a display structure, for a retina tracker maybe (see p.187).

- **Electrowetting** devices use microscopic oil drops that can be concentrated or spread over a pixel area by electrostatic force, to switch it from total reflection to transmission. It could be considered to make such a display with black drops, for masking purposes, yet this would likely have problems with stray light.

- **Dyed Guest Host** displays use microscopic dye disks diluted in liquid crystal fluid for example, that can be tilted by electric fields. Oriented parallel to the light path they hardly influence it, while perpendicular they form a 'solid' wall. It could be an ideal mask display, but contrast is currently only about 1:5 [33].

- **iMoD** displays [61] are working with thin transparent membranes approx. 1 µm over a silicon chip; Light rays reflected from the chip and the membrane interfere, resulting in brightness change and colorizing (the same effect that creates colors on butterfly wings). Applying voltage draws the membrane to the silicon by electrostatic force, changing brightness. As the display elements are bistable (have to be, otherwise color would change), brightness is modulated by pulse width, exploiting the fast switching speed of ≈50 µs.

- **LASER** is very promising but also has difficulties, especially as the beams have to get thicker with high resolution (up to 2mm), and deflection has to become faster at the same time. We will discuss aspects of laser displays later on. We'll see that with an advanced optical design, these may perhaps even be the best solution for our purpose.

Eye physiology

Let us recapitulate some facts about human vision and their impact on display design (color we will mainly address in the media chapter):

1) Our eyes can only see sharp at the center of view. We don't normally notice it, but any time we want to see anything really crisp, we will direct our eyes to it. Larger scenes are perceived by quick eye movements between certain points of interest (saccades). Other detail may simply be overlooked this way.

The resolution in the center of view is 1 arcmin per pixel at most (60 pixels/degree). Interestingly this is just the maximum optical resolution possible at a pupil diameter of 2mm. A perfectly sharp display would need 3600x3600 pixels for 60 degrees of viewing angle. Outsides the very center of view, our eye resolution gets extremely unsharp in comparison. The exact crispness requirements are a complex function of contrast, focus of attention [76] and other factors (see p.204)

The consequences for the design of a near-eye display are tremendous: Focus is necessary at the center of view only.

Anything else can be unsharp. If we could adjust focus dynamically, fast of course, according to viewing direction, we could use a display with 'bad' optics that is really never sharp everywhere.

We need an eye tracker to do this, and we need to dynamically adjust not only focus but geometry as well, yet this effort gives us many degrees of freedom with our display design. A display that is never overall crisp, nor linear, could actually be the smartest design.

Eye movements can be very fast, so we need a fast eye tracker to follow them, faster than a usual camera at last. Eye tracker cameras don't need high resolution, but should always be 5..10 times faster than normal video cameras.

By the way, an eye tracker could also be used to reduce bandwidth in communications, or computing effort with image synthesis as in games, with video, or just with ordinary virtual objects, if only those image parts are rendered or transmitted in full quality that are currently being looked at.

2) An important feature of the human eye is its very large field of view, over 180^0 horizontally (though not for each eye separately, because of the nose). We do not necessarily have to achieve this much, but the general message is, the more the better. For a really good vision simulator, we should target viewing angles of 90^0 or more.

The computing power necessary could be reduced by concentrating most rendering efforts just to the center of view as described above, still providing a very high effective resolution.

3) We can see over a tremendous range of light intensity. It starts from about 1/1000 lux (starlight) and goes up to 100000 lux (Sunlight).

Pupil diameters can vary between 1 mm in bright light and almost 9 mm (at night), but the maximum decreases with age, so for adults the maximum usually is 4 or 5 mm.

A display integrating objects into reality, has to provide them with due brightness. Fortunately the display is small, so power consumption is not a big problem.

Current LED lights can provide huge intensities already. Part of the intensity also depends on the optics. Certain measures like micro lens arrays could further concentrate light towards the eye. The best efficiency is achieved with laser sources, either with scanners or holographic or reflective displays: according to design, nearly 100% of the light produced can be sent into the eye. For this reason, laser displays currently are the technology of choice for combat applications, even though the laser diodes themselves are still relatively bad in terms of efficiency, worse than current LEDs at least.

In any case, the bottom line is that we have to demand very high brightness from any vision simulator design, but it will not require much energy. More details about eye physiology in general, you may e.g. find in [81].

An optical design study

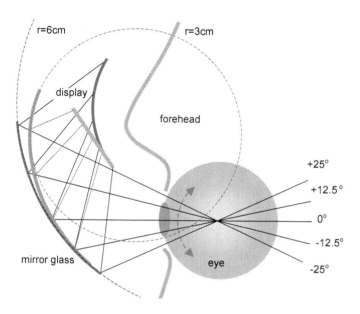

Although the real thing may be laser displays together with holographic mirrors and/or scanners (see later), we may well be stuck with conventional designs for a while. So let's have a look at them.

This obvious design I proposed 15 years ago but it's still current: starting from a very simple layout with a spherical mirror (dark blue, r=6cm, hence focal length=3cm), we can construct some beams (black) and see that the plane of sharpness (dark green) is itself about spherical.

To really show the focusing, we would have had to start from 2 parallel beams from the pupil for each angle, and show that they meet on the plane of sharpness. As the focal length follows from basic optical rules already (r/2), only the reflection angles are shown and the reflected beams are cut at focus length.

We have to take into account that the user will direct his eye to the viewing direction in order to see sharp. The eye is principally a ball that turns around its center. Therefore the different central viewing beams have to meet at its center (I have not shown the pupil for all directions as this would have looked a bit too crowded). I don't consider off axis focus because I assume that this design requires dynamic eye tracker steered focus anyway and the eye can only see sharp at the center.

We see that we get a spherical focus plane, i.e. we need a spherical display or some more optics.

It's quite obvious that by positioning a second shaped mirror before or after the focus point of the first one, we'd get a lot more degrees of freedom for a construction, together with better magnification, which allows for a smaller display and thereby less weight. It is also quite conceivable however, that such a construction will have a smaller exit pupil, causing problems when the user moves his eyes or when the glasses are sitting incorrectly. It also requires a full fledged optical calculation to make this up, so I will not further delve into this here.

We could as well make a single main mirror glass aspherical at the top (here I have shown a gliding change to r=3cm), resulting in a flat focus plane and a smaller display area. Focus length at the top is now 1.5cm, which means 2x stronger magnification, i.e. we have to use a strong geometrical correction in the display image to get an undistorted view for the user. The design will also have to be extended into the 3rd dimension of course, making things a bit more difficult in the end. Nevertheless it has already become pretty clear, that we could provide a big field of view this way (50 degrees vertically here; moving the optic closer to the eye could even yield 60 degrees), and this with a relatively small display and a single mirror.

A mirror can be thin, and plastic is an adequate material, so the entire assembly can be very light. If these glasses move away from the eye just by gliding a bit down the nose, as spectacles tend to do, then we'd get a somewhat smaller field of view, but the image generator - with help from the eye tracker - could keep perspective and focus in order. So we don't need a special fixture to the head. This is an essential advantage compared to many current products. The concave mirror largely resembles typical sunglasses. It combines light weight with strong enlargement and no color aberration. It's geometric image distortions are electronically corrected in the display resp. the display generating computer.

Although this is a very simple and straightforward approach, the first attempt towards a full fledged optical optimization of single mirror designs did not take place before 2008, with references mostly dating about 2007 [103]. It already showed satisfying results even with a flat display and a concave mirror only. The features possible in conjunction with sophisticated electronic distortion and focus compensations still have to be explored.

Once upon a time I broke some Christmas balls, to try out concave mirrors for display glasses

As stated, a second mirror could improve magnification and perhaps give more degrees of freedom for the optical construction.

An interesting approach with 2 optical surfaces (actually three, as there is a surface in front of the display that acts as a lens) has been presented about 2006:

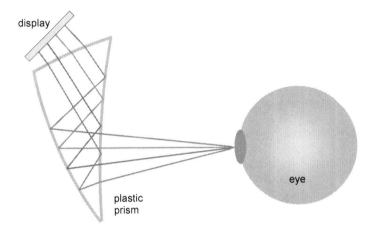

This patented prism based optical system of a commercial product (eMagin,[61]) has strong magnification and a decent viewing angle (not yet quite as much as we'd like to have). The prism is very light (about 11g).

Obviously this doesn't allow see-through, as the prism would heavily distort any direct view, but if we'd replace the front and rear surfaces by thin glasses with mirror coatings, this could work just as well. With 2 surfaces in the line of direct sight, advanced mirrors technology will of course be required, to keep light absorption in an acceptable range.

There are more things we have to consider with display glasses than just the optical path. I'll show these with the simple, single mirror approach, but everything basically applies to more complicated designs as well.

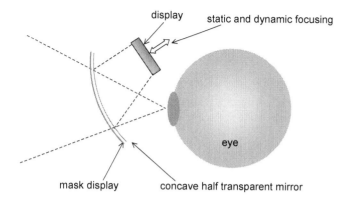

The display could be axially displaceable, which would serve for focusing. A dynamic alteration of focus allows, in conjunction with an eye tracker (not shown here), to simulate the true distance of an imaginary object (later on we'll see that with laser displays, the focusing problem is somewhat reduced but not eliminated at all). A lateral displacement could compensate for incorrect fit of the vision simulator and for image shift due to eye movements, but it may sometimes be more practical to use a larger display and do this by shifting the image electronically, if the exit pupil of the optics is large enough.

The mirror is semi transparent of course and does not shield outside view at all. If the display uses narrow band primary colors, a dichroic mirror coating for example could improve both transparency and reflection to almost 100%.

In order to cut out parts of the real scene for virtual image insertion, a mask display (light valve) is arranged outside the mirror. Preferably it is a curved assembly here, which may be the largest challenge with this approach.

This assembly looks and feels exactly like any pair of normal eyeglasses except for the little add-ons at the edges of the glasses, containing display, eye tracker and perhaps also position sensor cameras. The front glasses can of course still be laid out as sight correction lenses, i.e. also serve as traditional eyeglasses.

Eye tracking

For any acceptable visual interface it is an absolute necessity that the device does not have to be fixed to the head. It should never be any more disturbing than regular glasses. Hence, a certain freedom of movement of the device relative to the eye has to be accepted and dealt with. This can only be accomplished by sensing the device's position, for example with an eye tracker. The eye tracker is also necessary because pupil movements require complex image adaptation in order to avoid dynamically changing optical distortions.

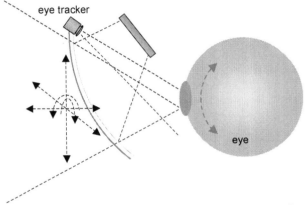

Example assembly with an eye tracker and usual
degrees of freedom for conveniently wearable glasses

The picture illustrates possible position changes of a vision simulator relative to the eye. The eye tracker, possibly some more sensors (measuring distance and tilt), and the image synthesizer software will have to compensate for all of this, dynamically.
The displayed image has to undergo resizing, shifting, tilting, trapezoid distortion etc, in order to constantly appear geometrically perfect to the user. A first work on this type of image compensation can be found in [5].
It is always important to remember that the eye is not steady like a camera but is in permanent motion, centering in on details.

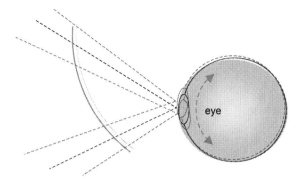

Even by just looking around in a virtual scene, some very subtle perspective changes may occur, that could reveal the artificial nature of the picture and, more important, affect orientation in virtual space. Anything from an unreal impression up to headache or vertigo may result.

For virtual image parts at infinity this is not of major concern, as in this case lateral movements of eyes or display will not change object positions (this also applies to headup displays that we will treat later on). The problem remaining in these cases is that the pupil could leave the exit pupil of the optics. This area is smaller with small display chips (strong enlargement) and very small with laser scanners (more at page 209).

Eye trackers are not anything new [82],[86] but I will consider some design aspects in conjunction with the vision simulator. Afterwards we will also encounter a relatively new variety, the retina tracker.

An eye tracker basically consists of a micro camera and some image analysis software or hardware. Locating the pupil and the iris in an image is just basic image processing (e.g. the Hough transform). The micro camera could use the main mirror as part of its lens, a camera could be integrated into the display, etc.

An eye tracker camera does not require high resolution, but a faster image frequency than the normal video rate of 2x25 or 2x30 half frames is necessary. 800Hz are already available [86].

Sensing eye distance by Iris diameter

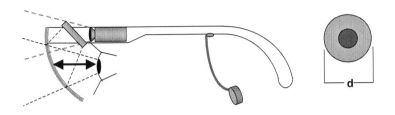

Detecting tilt by width/height comparison of the iris or pupil

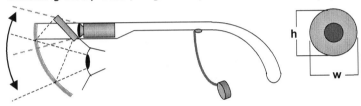

Lateral tilt detection can be achieved by comparing the vertical eye positions.

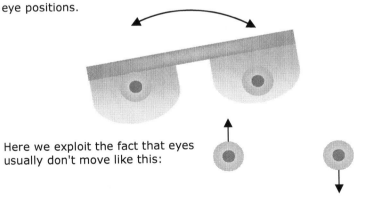

Here we exploit the fact that eyes usually don't move like this:

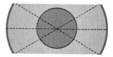

Finding the center of partially occluded iris or pupil
from visible edge arcs.

So eye trackers can do lots of things. But they are not the only
approach we could use.

'One-chip' eye trackers integrating the Hough Transform in a low
power parallel processing CMOS chip are already available. One
could also conceive a completely integrated CMOS light detector
array with an integrated pupil recognition circuit, that would be
ultimately fast. It could even be made just slightly larger than the
pupil image and be moved physically, actually *tracking* the pupil
image this way.

A new method would be the detection of pattern motion ('visual
flow'), as already implemented in optical computer mice. This
would detect iris motion Robust and efficient in milliseconds,
with minimum effort (this is also a powerful scene tracking
method, see p.289).

With help of visual flow, the actual eye tracker could work with a
much lower frame rate, would be much simpler to implement.

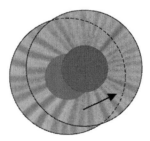

Detecting very fast motion from simple pattern shifting

Eye trackers are not currently usual in display glasses, but will be
indispensable in the future. We are indeed hardly presenting any
applications here that would not include eye tracking.

A DMD display plus eye tracker approach

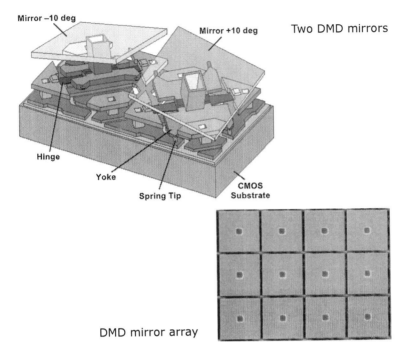

DMD mirror array

Digital Mirror Devices (a technology also referred to as DLP, *Digital Light Projection*) consist of tiny silicon structures, forming a CMOS driver array as well as elastically suspended Aluminum coated mirrors that are moved by electrostatic forces.
The entire structure is etched from a single, solid silicon chip. DMD mirrors can provide deflection frequencies up to 100 kHz and have shown to work reliably for at least 10^{12} cycles. This due to the hyperelasticity pure silicon is showing at these tiny dimensions. One mirror is about 13x13 μm in size. The array is produced from silicon wafers with technologies similar to normal chip production. The mirrors are arranged in a very dense field. Almost 100% of incident light can be reflected (images courtesy of Texas Instruments).

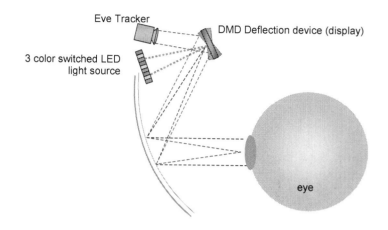

Eve Tracker

DMD Deflection device (display)

3 color switched LED
light source

eye

Principal assembly and focusing scheme for a DMD design

DMD mirrors can tilt by over ± 10⁰, and extremely fast. Images are created by pulse width modulation of single mirrors. The light source is periodically reflected into or out of the projection optics. Color is produced by alternating light sources.

A possible advantage: as DMD elements also deflect light in 'off' position, we could place an eye tracker camera accordingly, so that it would get light from the eye just in this position. This would results in a good eye tracker image with little space required. Rays from the eye will also approach the eye tracker parallel, as required for a camera.

Such an optical assembly could provide an almost undistorted picture of the eye area, good for videophone applications.

The light source shown in this example consists of an interleaved array of LEDs in the 3 basic colors (red, green, blue).

The array is not placed in the focus of the optics (the DMD is), so the colors intermix. These LEDs can be fast switched and eliminate the need for color wheels as in conventional DMD projectors. There are LED-DMD projectors already in production, currently in first micro and cell phone projectors. As the light power even of a matchbox sized device already allows for projected images several ft. wide, there will be no problem using this technology in vision glasses. The DMD chips currently being used there have a low resolution, but larger versions with the small mirror design are announced already.

With vision simulators, one problem often experienced with DMD projectors will not occur: due to the sequential color projection, there are rainbow effects at object borders if we move our eyes. In a glasses design. it is necessary to shift images accordingly to compensate for this motion anyway, so the color components can also be shifted in a way to always hit the same spots on the retina, for a seamless addition.

The light source arrangement always has to take into account that DMDs are basically mirrors, i.e. the light is not strayed, so lighting directions are important.

The drawing is far from being exact. We would have to take into account that current DMDs are tilting diagonally.

Hard to say if with our approach to optical design yet discussed, the viewing angle relative to the display would enable us to move the light source out of the optical path. It would certainly be better for this if the mirrors would indeed tilt up and down as sketched in the drawing.

We would also have to find a curvature for the mirror glass that allows for a still more vertical assembly of the display than in the optical design study shown before.

If we could achieve this, the reflective behavior of the DMD would help us to concentrate most of the light directly to the eye, i.e. we would get very good energy efficiency and a very small leakage of display light to the outside.

Typical DMD's currently have mirrors of 13x13 μm, 1000 pixels = 13mm. Given the display size in the optical assembly we have discussed in detail above – approx. 2 cm high – we would arrive at 1600x2400 pixels for example.

The new Pico projector displays have mirror sizes of 7.56x7.56um, and this may not be the end as silicon process technologies have made immense progress towards smaller structures.

Centered eye trackers for 'normal' displays

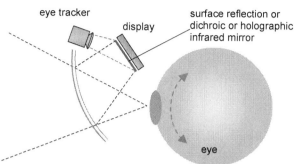

The DMD eye tracker approach may be adapted to other display types as well. As an eye tracker camera needs some light to see, we would probably use infrared light to avoid conflicts with other requirements. Using surface reflection or a dichroic mirror for infrared (one that would have to be transparent to visible light), just at the surface of a LED or similar display, we could have the eye tracker camera looking directly into the optical path.

Vice versa, we could also place the eye tracker first (with a different main mirror curvature) and use it as a reflector to pass the remaining light to additional optics and the display.

Through-the-display eye tracker

The best way for an eye tracker camera would always be to see by the main mirror anyway. We could try to etch or bore (or e.g. with certain organic OLEDs, just leave out) some tiny holes in between the display pixels and let a camera see through this mesh. The picture acquired this way would be a bit foggy (try to look through a piece of cloth), but it could work. Another option would be a 'fly's eye' construction, with little lenses and single camera pixels arranged in between the display pixels. As the camera pixels then have to be very small and we need a supporting matrix for readout, this would work best on a silicon chip, so one would want to combine it with a silicon based display type.

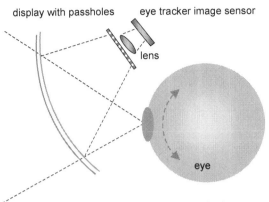

A classical camera chip could be difficult to fit between the display and the eyebrow. Making holes in a display chip would also not be a standard procedure. OLED may be printed on glass or plastic. With silicon chips, holes might be bored with a laser cutter, but this could also destroy adjacent structures.

The lens could be a Fresnel lens directly integrated into the display, saving weight and space.

R	G	R	G	R	G	R	G
B	T	B	T	B	T	B	T
R	G	R	G	R	G	R	G
B	T	B	T	B	T	B	T
R	G	R	G	R	G	R	G
B	T	B	T	B	T	B	T
R	G	R	G	R	G	R	G
B	T	B	T	B	T	B	T

Display with integrated transparent or camera pixels (T)

The retina tracker

Without lenses, camera pixels within the display do not see the pupil, as it is way out of focus. But there is something automatically in focus, which is the retina, seen through the pupil. As the optics and also the user's accommodation will always automatically adapt to render a sharp image of the display on the retina, the same will apply in the opposite direction.

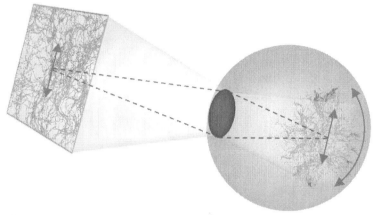

The retina carries a network of capillary blood vessels, characteristic for each individual. Movements of this pattern and even absolute position in it can be determined as easy as that of a pupil. So this can replace conventional eye tracking. Retina tracking is currently used in eye surgery and has also been explored for military applications, but not in connection with AR.
There are some requirements however.
The retina has to be illuminated, and enough light from it has to get to the display/sensor chip. The display will light the retina as well, and also project patterns onto it, but it can also be dark depending on content, and the patterns it projects hardly move with the eye rotation, while the display would have to be following just this rotation, and by means of tracking data. So we will need some extra lighting, probably best an infrared emitter right

inside the display. This may also be required for reducing adverse influences from ambient light.

If we have a small display and optical aperture (an advantage in terms of weight and energy efficiency), our retina sensor will only get a picture if the display and optics are properly following all eye movements. If track is lost, it may be difficult to find the pupil again. If however the tracking mechanism is faster than the eye, this will not happen very often. The focusing of recognition into the pupil area also has its advantages: some people tend to squeeze their eyes a lot, which can be a problem with conventional eye trackers, as there are not enough arc structures left.

Retina patterns can also be used to identify an individual, and therefore replace the iris pattern for this purpose.

The distance between eye and display assembly will change the size of the retina pattern seen. Hence, distance will be detectable.

A retina tracker should however detect intentional accommodation changes as well, to work with ghost objects. Without further measures, willful change of accommodation will just blur the retina picture at the sensor side, without any hint about direction. But there is an option for this to accomplish: the light field camera (see page 392).

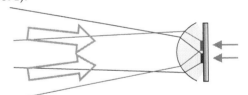

Pixel camera as an angle-to-position converter

This principle is simply explained. Think of a camera having a tiny micro camera instead of each pixel, with some sub pixels of its own. A camera is essentially converting angles of light to positions on its sensor, so each sub pixel selects incoming light rays from a different angle. By selecting different sub pixels from each micro camera and combining them into an image, we can change the characteristics of the main lens to some extent. Change viewing angle, depth of field or even focus, for example.

So we can immediately tell if focus is going forth or back, by simply comparing contrast for several different sub pixel combinations, simultaneously and instantly.

But aren't these tiny sub cameras just too small for a useful angle discrimination ?

A really small display would for example have 2000 pixels on a length of 1 cm. This is 5 micrometers per pixel, or per micro camera. Light can be bundled enough to form pixels 0.5 micrometers small. Silicon technology can provide structures many times smaller. Hence, each micro camera could have 100 sub pixels or be able to discriminate up to 10 angles in each direction. Not even remotely all sub pixels would be needed, as the angles possible for incoming beams are limited. So angular resolution can be managed, an the same applies to complexity.

It could well be that the light field approach is flexible enough also to provide for some hints if tracking is lost, i.e. the optics aperture misses the pupil, which calls for immediate remedy, by pupil localization for example.

Just recently, displays have been built (by FhG-IPMS) that could implement most of the variants described. Their technology is OLED on CMOS. CMOS is ideal and often used for high performance camera chips. It allows to integrate light sensing and signal processing on one chip. Optical mouse chips are CMOS, as are many high end camera chips, or the aforementioned one-chip eye tracker, for example. CMOS chips can also provide signals and back circuitry for OLED driving, of course.

Organic LED material can be printed or vacuum deployed (preferred here) directly onto the chip. An additional (transparent) metal layer can be added on top of the OLED as a counter electrode. Hence, sophisticated chip assemblies are possible, and integrating camera pixels is no problem.

So this in conjunction with an advanced tracking mechanism may make OLED-on-CMOS chips, tiny ones with highly enlarging optics, a strong competition to the laser displays that we are going to explore in the following pages. One disadvantage may be the usually large bandwidth of LED sources, compared to laser, which could make the use of holographic optics quite difficult.

Laser displays

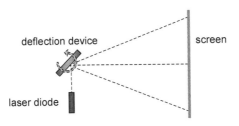

Basic laser projection assembly

An important type of displays for our purpose are laser scanners. Laser scanners use the narrow light beam of a laser diode, modulated for brightness changes and deflected in 'horizontal' and 'vertical' direction, writing an entire image onto a screen or directly into the eye.

The advantages are simplicity of the light source, the ability to generate pictures with extreme brightness (almost 100% of the light produced can be concentrated into the eye), and a little easier focusing. Problems are how to modulate and how to deflect the beam, and also how to get a really crisp image.

Usual laser applications use beam diameters of 0.5...1 mm. This appears quite large. Making it smaller will however cause problems with beam divergence. This is easily understood if we consider that light behaves like waves. With an exit surface smaller than the wavelength, we would quite obviously not even get a beam any more but a spherical wave up to 180 degrees wide. Vice versa, we need to start from a certain beam diameter to be able to focus it to a very small spot. So we actually need an even larger beam if we want high resolution. Indeed for perfect resolution we have to deliver the pupil a 2mm wide beam, and this has to fit, as it is as large as the pupil itself. More about this later.

Color is still a challenge with laser scanners. Making green laser diodes is difficult, but an infrared type with a frequency doubling crystal can be a sufficient while not yet ideal solution. In principle, prerequisites for color laser scanners are available.

Beam deviation

Before discussing laser display design, let's first have a closer look at beam deviation. This is identical to the convergence needed to get to a certain focus diameter. The problem is that a smaller focus point just *requires* a larger convergence (=deviation). It's therefore not simply possible to say „make the beam narrower and we get a crisper picture".

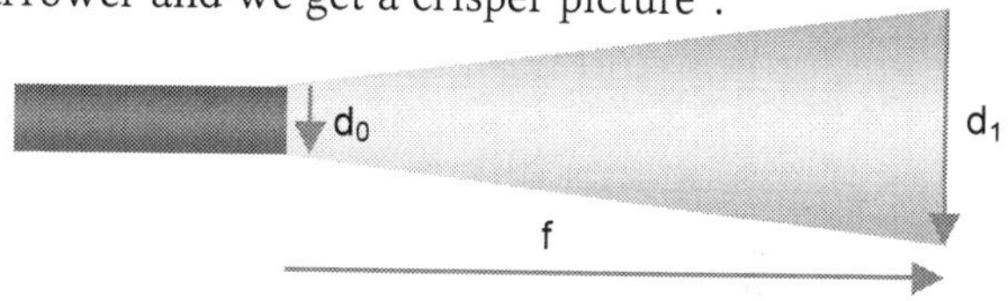

Deviation of a laser beam with given source diameter d_0

The relation for this is very simple (picture above):
$$d_1 \approx \lambda f / d_0$$
You may look up the appendix for a very simple derivation of it, and also for the maximum resolution of a lens (p.376).
An example: λ = 0.5 µm, d_0 = 20 µm, f = 20 mm → $d_1 \approx$ 0.5mm. Hence for a pixel size of 20 µm on the retina we have to deliver a laser beam 0.5mm wide and we would also need a deflection mirror of 0.5mm diameter, if we don't want to destroy beam quality. With a picture area on the retina of about 25x20 mm and this pixel size, we could deliver an image of 1280x1024 pixels, the same as a typical 19" computer screen, but at this image size equaling only ¼ of the eye's resolution. More details at page 376.

Coherence

A property of laser light closely connected with beam deviation is coherence. This is a measure for the cleanliness of the wavefront. A perfectly coherent beam is characterized by a perfectly even wavefront and a zero spread of wavelengths, i.e. bandwidth.
While coherence is useful if we want a projection with high efficiency and high depth of field. it is also often a problem be-

cause it can lead to unwanted interference effects. The speckles around a laser beam hitting a white wall are an example for this. Real laser beams of course are not entirely coherent. So certain measures have been defined telling us how good they actually are.

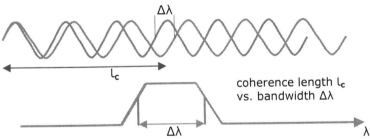

Spatial coherence tells us the evenness of a wavefront. As we have learned that any beam must deviate, the really useful parameter is something different: imagine a lens focusing a beam to a point. The better the evenness of the wavefront, the smaller the point can be. Hence the size of the best achievable focus point is a measure for beam evenness. Hence, spatial coherence is simply given by the size of a real or imagined light source. The smaller the light source, the better it is. This is independent of wavelength or bandwidth, hence it can also be applied to white light. See page 383 for an extremely simple derivation of some formulas.

$\Delta\lambda$

l_c

coherence length l_c
vs. bandwidth $\Delta\lambda$

$\Delta\lambda$

λ

The other parameter is the so called timely coherence. It can be represent in several ways. Most known is the so called coherence length. This is the length for which a beam stays in phase. Some meters at best for real beams. Of course, going out of phase can be interpreted as a change in frequency. Hence, timely coherence is also another measure for bandwidth. So we can as well use the bandwidth (color spread) of a source to tell its timely coherence. The picture illustrates the direct link between coherence length and bandwidth (bandwidth here shown in wavelength instead of frequency to make things clearer). A little more at page 381.

Effects of too good a coherence, as speckle noise and interference can be dealt with in several ways, and this is an important topic for laser displays of course.

A dispersive element for example, enlarging the source diameter, can adjust spatial coherence. Vice versa, a pinhole blind is normally used in holographic assembly for making the beam cleaner, as in the above picture (so called *collimation*).

Timely coherence can be reduced by modulating the beam with a high frequency. Pulsing it, for example. This directly reduces coherence length. From a signal theoretical view, we could also argue that any modulation produces side band frequencies. In the extreme case, it is e.g. possible to turn a red laser into a white one, just by pulse modulation.

Spatial coherence, or light source diameter, is of importance in any projection assembly, as it determines aperture, effectiveness and depth of field. As any glasses display is sort of a projection assembly, this is also of interest to us.

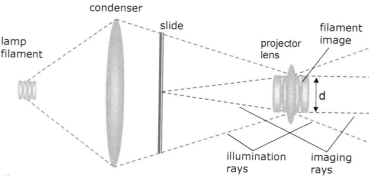

The picture illustrates how the lamp filament is depicted into the projector lens, determining the beam diameter and hence the effective aperture. Hence, the depth of field of a near eye display (also a projector) depends on the size, i.e. *spatial coherence* of the light source, no matter if laser scanner or, e.g., DLP display.

A classical laser design

We will first review an early laser design, that has been analyzed in [27]. It serves as a see-through data display, monochrome red at 640x480 resolution. Data are displayed in a constant position in the user's field of view. The brightness, typical for a laser display, allows its use in bright sunlight, e.g. in military applications.

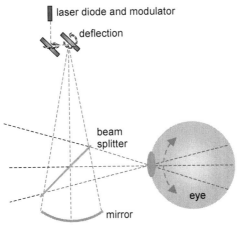

This design comprises a laser source, horizontal and vertical deflection mirrors in MEMS (micro electro-mechanical systems) technology, and a beam splitter/mirror assembly. This is a simple optical arrangement with hardly any geometry errors. Yet it's not the small convenient design that one would like for general use.

Later designs have the optics over the forehead and only an half transparent mirror in front of the eye. Informations about current products and new developments can be found at [15].

This example illustrates a typical problem with laser displays: if the user moves his eyes, the laser beam may miss the pupil, especially when the latter is very small, adapted to bright sunlight for example. The design reviewed uses a special assembly that allows to split the laser beam resp. to displace it sideways in steps. If the pupil moves, at least one ray bundle is always there to enter the eye. For details of this tricky technique, see [27].

Beam deflection modes

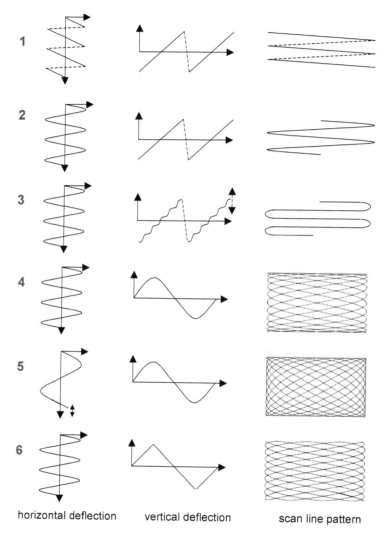

horizontal deflection   vertical deflection   scan line pattern

Laser scanners draw pictures line by line, just as a classic TV picture tube. In a TV, a saw-tooth like voltage is used to deflect the electron beam from side to side with nearly constant velocity, then bringing it back even much faster, to draw the next line instantly (picture,1). Moving a mirror this way would incur very violent accelerations even though such mirrors are very tiny devices. For the vertical (slow) deflection this could still work, but with the horizontal (fast) deflector we already operate at the edge of feasibility anyway.

The smoothest way to move a mass forth and back is in a sine wave like motion. Yet this results in an uneven line and brightness distribution (2). Brightness could be compensated for, but we see line patterns at the image edges that would only disappear at very high resolutions. A new method to address this problem would be modulating the deflection mirror with a small high frequency sine wave also in the vertical, that would keep the lines about horizontal over most of the display area (3). The edges could then simply be dimmed out and we get a fairly even line pattern with smoothly moving mirrors.

Current laser scanners most often use the Lissajous mode, deflecting both directions by a sine wave. (4) shows an example with 2 sine waves of similar frequency, drawing a tumbling ellipse inside a square area. Obviously the lines get denser at the edges. This also applies for sine waves of very different frequencies. The useful area in this mode is about 80% of the deflection angle, and even then we have to compensate for non linearities and, more important, for different brightness and resolution.

A new solution I am suggesting here is number 6: a triangle for the low and a sine for the high frequency axis deliver an almost even line density while reducing accelerations to a minimum.

A laser design approach

Let's now have a look at an approach starting from the basic design for classical displays as considered before.

If the laser source would emit an ideal, very narrow and coherent beam, the eye's lens would influence geometry but not focus (the narrower the beam, the less), making the design much simpler. We could make the image originate at a single point.

Distortion could be compensated by just modulating the deflection unit. Yet it isn't all that simple.

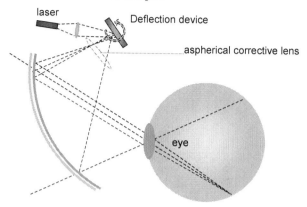

Basic adaptation of a laser unit

In this drawing, the pupil and the deflector are positioned at about 1.5...2x the focus length of the mirror. The pre-shaping of the laser beam is only hinted (we could also for instance conceive a concave deflector mirror).

For a crisp spot at the retina with the eye focused to infinity, the beam would have to arrive parallel, so in turn it should converge at about focus length before approaching the deflector, where it would perhaps again have to be as wide as at the pupil. We could try to bring the deflector closer to the main mirror, in order to catch the laser beam at a smaller cross section, but this would also mean the deflector would have to deliver a larger angular range.

Deflecting a laser beam from a narrow spot would also spoil the wave front, the deflected beam could not be properly focused anymore.

A mirror as large as the beam diameter at the pupil would at least be 0.25mm even for VGA resolution (640x480), and almost 1mm for some good resolution ($\geq$1600x1200), sufficient to generate virtual computer or HDTV screens with some reserve for surroundings and perspective.

At this resolution, we need ≈100 kHz deflection frequency for an acceptable frame rate. Moving a mirror so fast is really difficult, to say the least.

Compensating focus errors of the main mirror could be easier than with the conventional displays: with a small corrective lens (picture), whose focal length changes over its surface.

The laser beam, although not entirely parallel, is usually less sensitive to focus changes than a classical assembly, as the effective pupil opening is no larger than the beam diameter. With low resolution displays, this could e.g. mean 0.4mm vs. 3mm, giving 8 times the focus tolerance of a classical display. At the highest useful resolution of 1/60 degree however, the beam diameter has to be 1.5-2mm, so in bright light the advantage then becomes zero. Let us consider some more properties of laser projectors, or scanners as one could also call them.

Good news first: Laser scanners can be very small. Laser diodes are tiny, so the entire laser unit, including deflection, could almost be shrunk to the size of a sand grain, so it would be the smallest and lightest display one could think of. But here are also some problems that we have to address.

Laser diodes are very non linear and do only work above a certain power threshold. It is therefore not possible to simply modulate them by changes of supply current. They can however be operated with very short pulses, so a digital pulse width or frequency modulation is usual.

The second challenge is concerning deflection. Measures have to be taken for the protection of the eye. The beam should never be allowed to rest, as it would burn holes into the retina if all its small but extremely concentrated power remains on a single spot.

The deflection unit itself incurs major difficulties if we need 100 kHz or more for horizontal deflection. Achieving these frequencies is in principle possible with very small mirrors like those in DMD's. They have a resonance frequency of about 100 kHz and can endure this speed for years. Their size however is only 13 μm, way too small. Apart from the fact that DMD mirrors are designed to operate bistable, it is quite obvious that there is a huge difference between a 13 μm mirror and the absolute minimum we would need for a useful display resolution, 0.5mm.

Anyway, we only need a single mirror and do not have to use the extremely complicated manufacturing process of DMD. Hyper-elasticity and small size are allowing to create a super fast and reliable MEMS element from silicon or other materials by etching, laser cutting, or other methods.

In order to achieve large deflection angles, we have to fully de-couple both axes with an intermediate frame and independent hinges (h) for horizontal and vertical guidance (picture).

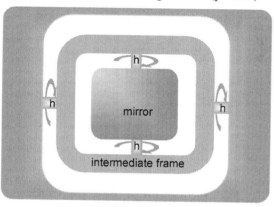

Such a structure might use electrostatic or electromagnetic drive, for example. Electrostatic forces are getting stronger with smaller dimensions, so they are usually always the method of choice.

Unwanted resonances and parametric effects have to be ad-dressed by proper driver design and damping. Heating of the mirror may cause geometrical errors that are difficult to address. High frequencies and very large deflection angles are principally possible with silicon based MEMS elements, but the mirror size required remains a problem.

Projects about scanning mirrors be found at [8] or [15], and the most current information is at [92]. Not anything published so far concurrently delivers the resolution and the deflection angles we require, but results are promising, resolutions of up to 800x600 yet with a single mirror.

The Laser dilemma

Beam deviation dictates the minimum size for a scanner mirror to define a focus spot small enough.

- High resolution requires a
- larger mirror, but also
- faster mirror movements.

One solution would be a low resolution, large scale picture with high resolution dynamic inlays following the eye's center of view.

Picture: only the center area is crisp.
Stare firmly at it, and the edge blur goes unnoticed.

With laser scanners, this is less difficult to achieve than with other display types. We could perhaps place two small MEMS deflectors side by side, so near that all rays still enter the pupil. One deflector would act the usual way, the other would perform a quasi static offset deflection overlaid with a raster deflection of

½ or even less the angle of the other. Aligning both images precisely is a bit difficult, but not so much if we dim the inlay area in the large picture. We could even use three deflectors and provide an inlay inside the inlay.

The human pupil however can get very small, down to 1mm, and we may have to use some special optics to merge two or three beams in a proper way. A 3-way beam splitter element can be manufactured by simply photographing 3 beam sources. The holographic optical element (HOE) we get works similar to a hologram depicting just 3 points. Re-aligning the beams could possibly also be done by an HOE.

Diving into more construction details here would be beyond the scope of this book, and there is a problem with these HOE's: Making them work for more than one color at once is pretty difficult. It's a pity, because the usual and probably best way to deal with color in laser scanners is to merge three (red, green and blue) laser beams by some dichroic mirror assembly and to deflect this 3-color beam as one.

Another method would be abandoning the rectangular raster scheme, deflecting the beam in a circular spiral movement: Only harmonic, sinusoidal movements would be necessary for this (two sinus motions with 90 degrees phase shift result in a circle being drawn). If the spiral starts at the center of vision, it can be made progressively wider towards the outside, naturally and smoothly adapting to the decreasing crispness of vision.

Varying the spot size and brightness of the scanner accordingly, an evenly illuminated, continuous image can be generated. Moreover, drawing a denser pattern at the center would imply faster movements but at a smaller amplitude, hence would be easier to achieve.

The spiral approach however has one difficulty:

Either we need a scanner with two axes of about equally high resonance frequency, or if we would have a fast rotating mirror device combined with a slow in/out motion, we would have to deal with large gyro effects (like those known from the 'magic suitcase' in physics lectures). So even though spiral deflection may be a fascinating idea, it also has it's difficulties.

Rectangular raster scanners have the advantage that they can operate at constant frequencies and if their suspension is designed to have its resonance there, at very little driving power. With the hyper-elasticity typical for certain micro mechanical suspensions, both friction and wear would be close to zero.

Generating multiple inlays with only one mirror, as mentioned before, also suffers from off-resonance operation most of the time. But there is another way combining differently sized mirrors, that can avoid most of the problems: assembling them concentrically.

Similar techniques are also known from loudspeakers, for similar reasons.

These concentrical ring mirrors could of course be etched in one process, as a single device.

Rings would have an additional advantage. As with lens resolution (p.376), the inner parts of a lens just contribute to more blur at the focus point. Hence, if we omit the center, we could possibly make the lens smaller. For a laser beam as well, a ring mirror may require a slightly smaller diameter for the same focus spot size.

In order to say more about such a concept, we need to know what resolution(s) we should actually go for.

From the lens resolution derived before, we can instantly tell the theoretical resolution of the human eye.

We have a system with a lens diameter of between 1 and 9 mm and a focus length of about 20mm. The larger lens diameters are quite rare and do only occur with young people still having a very flexible iris tissue. Most people have upper lens diameters of 4...6mm. Under fairly good lighting conditions, we can assume about 2 mm or less.

At 2 mm, we get a retinal focus spot of about 6 μm. This equals an angular resolution ($\tan\varphi$) of about 1 arcmin ($\frac{1}{60}$ degree). Although this is a theoretical value from the optical constraints only, it is by no means surprising that the really measured crispness values of human eyes are just this good: Evolution tends to optimize anything to the extreme.

At larger pupil diameters, resolution could theoretically be better, but the density and size of retinal receptors are setting a limit to this. Lager pupil diameters also only occur at low light levels, where resolution has to be traded off for sensitivity.

At bright sunlight, the pupil shrinks to about 1mm, and eye resolution therefore to 2 arcmin. This is still perceived as entirely crisp. It equals a 19" computer screen at 1280x1024 and 40cm distance, that also looks utterly crisp with no single pixels becoming visible.

Classic TV standards however are based on 1 arcmin. This equals a resolution of about 500 pixels on a screen having a height of 1/5 the viewing distance. The actual line number used is 480 for NTSC (US standard) and 576 for PAL (European standard).

This should actually be a little too sharp. If the program sources used really were crisp, like digital images on a PC screen, the TV should look good at half the usual viewing distance already.

A perfect source seen on a PC screen proves this really to be the case. With an old tube TV however, if you approach it, lines begin to show up very early. This is due to the fact that most TV standards use interlacing, which means that odd and even lines of a picture are drawn separately, in two subsequent *half frames*.

Even tiny eye movements cause these separate line patterns to be displaced and eventually to merge. A typical flat panel screen does not show this effect but this doesn't mean it is better, as it's signal processing replaces interlacing by all sorts of nasty artifacts and loss of crispness.

Hence, classic TV standards have defined an overly crisp angular resolution because of interlacing effects, while in fact the programming material hardly ever approached the crispness possible. Using interlacing for a laser scanner does not have to result in merging scan lines, as the scanning could follow eye movements immediately. So this is a much better situation.

---

*note that the resolution in display lines or just pixels could be mixed up with the definition of resolution in 'lines' origination from photography, where it actually means pairs of white and black lines, a definition also still used in video technology to characterize horizontal resolution. This often leads to confusion.

With scanners, we could also change the image content while the image is being written, allowing to follow eye or head movements without any delay.

What we will have to consider when using inlays, is that all beams produced should be able to enter the eye in any situation. In bright sunlight, the pupil can get 1mm small. This also limits the size of the laser mirror to about 1mm: in case of a solid mirror larger than 1mm, we would lose light just when it's most needed, and in case of a ring mirror the outer rings would be occluded. A 1mm mirror can only draw retinal focus spots equaling 2 arcmin. Hence, 2 arcmin is the adequate resolution here.

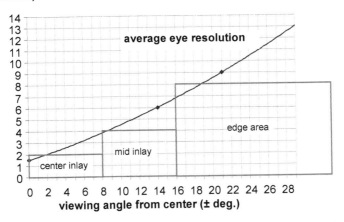

We also need to know something about the eye resolution off center. The above diagram shows some average results from experiments I did. It also shows the resolution ranges of three mirrors producing a picture with ½ and ¼ sized inlays, designed for a center resolution of 2 arcmin. and off center resolutions almost always better than the eye.

Each mirror would deliver about VGA resolution (640x480) to get a total resolution of 2560x1920, way beyond HDTV. At 2 arcmin. per pixel for the center display, the total field of view served could be more than 60x90 degrees (most people's ordinary glasses have less).

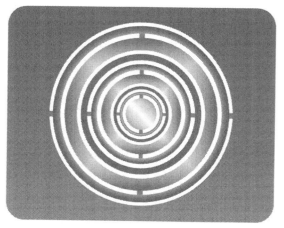

Hypothetical coaxial 3-way beam deflector chip
(size approx. 1.5 mm or 1/16")

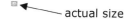 actual size

An outer ring mirror only 1mm in diameter (look at the picture legend above, to see how tiny this is) could draw the innermost picture inlay, with its small viewing angle and hence very small excitations.

The eye is less flicker sensitive at its center of view, so this mirror could be relatively slow. With interlacing, the deflection rate necessary is less than 10 kHz.

The next ring would be about 0.5 mm 'large', and the center mirror about 0.25 mm, delivering the larger focus spot and better agility needed for the outer picture areas.

A bit critical could be the deflection angle required, for the outer ring first place. Just for the inner inlay, with it's ±5 degree viewing angle, this mirror would have to tilt by ±2.5 degrees, that is only about ±30 μm at the edge of a 1mm mirror. Very convenient to handle, but if we also want to move this inlay over all the viewing range, we would require nine times as much. Here we could use a trick. We could let the outer mirror do its ±2.5 deg. only, and move the entire mirror assembly, following the eye movements. This is a relatively wide angle movement but substantially slow, so it could be done with separate actors, like piezo elements for example. The inner mirrors would then have to move contradictory, but these small mirrors could produce these angles at a much smaller excitation.

All this put together, an ultra high resolution, ultra small, ultra light virtual retina scanner is perfectly conceivable.

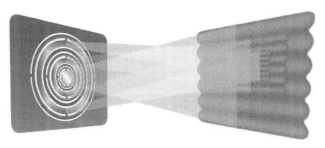

Line scanning scheme for 3 mirrors
producing staged inlays 1:2:4 in size

Existing products are not yet this complicated, but development goes on.

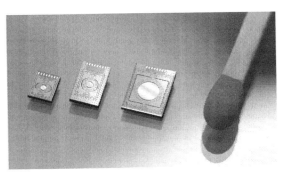

Various MEMS scanning mirrors (photo courtesy of FhG-IPMS)

Optics for an eye-operated cell phone

Cell phones may be the first mass market product implementing essential parts of augmented reality technology, especially eye tracking and eye steering, probably with simplified glasses, monocular maybe and without mask displays. But imagine dialing and web link clicking just by gazing, hands-free.

A large virtual display screen would be a great advantage, and it could be provided by very simple and very light optics. The eye tracker system is meanwhile available as a single chip [86], cheap and tiny, so we can start constructing a device as light as a bauble:

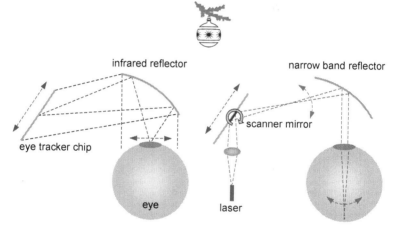

We combine an eye tracker (left, shown bigger than real) and a laser unit (right) in the same optical path. The tiny laser scanner mirror is integrated in the center of the eye tracker chip (hardly affecting its function). Just a single, small dichroic or holographic mirror (we will address this later in the book), over 90% transparent, brings the picture into the eye. We will also need something that makes the laser beam always hit the pupil, compensating for eye motion. For simple applications it could be sufficient or even better to see the display in only one fixed direction, but even then we sometimes want to use eye pointing at large angles. This and the probably always imperfect fit of the device makes motion compensation always important.

In this application, we may move the entire tracker/scanner unit, which would also allow to use a very small tracker camera chip, hardly bigger than the pupil. This would of course contribute to weight and power drain (in the grams or milliwatts range, but anything counts here).

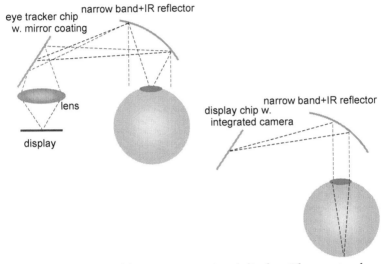

Other varieties would use a conventional display. The eye tracker (shown enlarged) uses infrared light, which enables the two different light paths to be integrated.

A display chip with integrated light sensitive pixels could work as a retina tracker (right).

Just a single, small dichroic or holographic, over 90% transparent mirror is necessary in front of the eye. All focusing here is done by mirrors, that today can be manufactured on plastics in very high quality. With a totally integrated eye tracker chip, this could all be cheap and simple, weigh milligrams and draw just a few milliwatts of power.

The simple goggle phone can deliver a lot of functionality without a mask display already. At least the text of web pages, for example, could well be displayed as luminating characters floating in free space, hardly occluding the real environment. Only some dimming in case of bright sunlight would be desirable to support it, maybe a very simple solution with anisotropic glass or LCD.

Even depth sensitive eye pointing and ghost objects would be possible, with a little camera viewing the retina through the pupil and measuring the eye's lens focus. An exotic variety hereof is proposed beginning at page 392.

Exit pupils

One major problem with building the ideal AR spectacles is concerning the exit pupil of the optics. This is the area where actually light leaves the system at the place where the user's eyes are located.

This is so important because if the user moves his eyes. or the display moves relative to the eyes, his pupils may easily get out of this area and the picture may vanish.

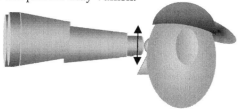

With classic optics, large magnifications are resulting in a small exit pupil, also calling for mechanical compensation of eye motion. We all know this from binoculars. The larger the magnification (and the cheaper the make), the more difficult it gets to hold them, so that both eyes will see anything at all.

As we will anyway need an eye tracker in order to show virtual objects correctly, we could compensate for eye movements by just moving the projection unit with the pupil (also suggested in [27]). A curved motion scheme could be of advantage, as it would help to keep deflection angles within the best range.

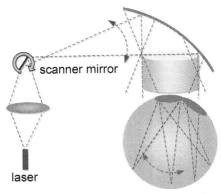

With laser scanners, a wide beam aperture can be designed if so desired. It would result in a wide range of tolerable eye movement, but would also incur significant loss of light.

Moving the entire laser unit - as shown below - is much better.

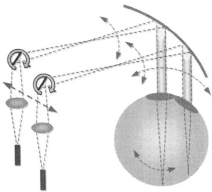

With narrow beams, all light can enter the eye, but eye motion is calling for a compensation. Like with almost all other adaptation problems, this can be solved mechanically.

With an additional electronic displacement and distortion compensation, as in any other case, this would work perfectly well, and it could save a lot more power than would be needed for the microscopic servo motors, at least if the scanner unit could also be made as small as physics allow.

Piezo electric micro motors

Piezo motors made rapid progress recently, and are now a technology promising to provide all kinds of perfect static and dynamic adaptation for the optics of display glasses, at stunningly low weight and power consumption.

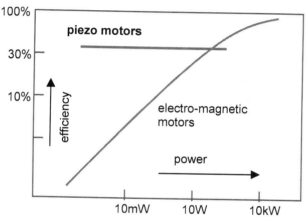

Electro magnetic motors are good at high power applications, several kilowatts that is, where they can almost be 100% efficient, making possible train drives or car engines of magnificent performance. At low power however their effectiveness drops, literally borderless.

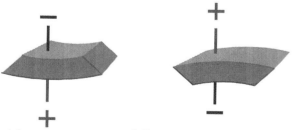

Piezo electric motors are quite different. They are relying on the piezo electric effect, the phenomenon that some kinds of ceramics are bending if electric voltage is applied to them.

If a piezo crystal is excited by external force, it delivers lots of voltage. The first electric gramophone pickups were crystal type, for example. As piezo elements usually are hard materials or crystals, they do only deliver small movements. Making a motor with this principle is a bit difficult, but we can get thousands of small movements per second and the only challenge is to add them to one big motion.

Unlike electro magnetic motors, piezo motors do not lose efficiency at low power. They don't deliver the almost 100% of big dynamo machines, only about 1/3 of that, but they also do this if we get down to milliwatts or even microwatts.

My first electronics kit when I was a boy contained a piezo electric headphone that was so sensitive that by just holding it to the next heating radiator in series with a simple Germanium pin diode, I could clearly hear the local AM radio station. A stunning display of efficiency.

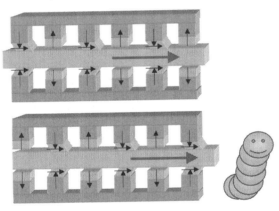

Caterpillar type piezo motor [115], principle

The most obvious way of building a piezo motor is creating something acting like a caterpillar. Climbing micro step by micro step but at several thousands of them per second, it can move by many millimeters per second, quickly enough for mechanical adjustments of display glasses, even following eye movements.

A somewhat less obvious principle works like a nut on a thread, the nut being bent in two axles, so that it moves along the thread (or, the thread through it), in a snake like motion (picture below). The simpler a structure is, of course, the easier to miniaturize.

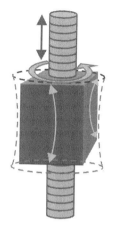
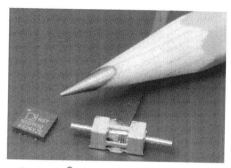

Squiggle® piezo electric motor [91]: principle (left), motor and driver chip compared to a pencil point (right). Photo courtesy of New Scale Technologies

Piezo motors like this one are already being used in auto focus systems of many pocket cameras right now, nothing confined to laboratories anymore, but technology readily available.

It may be a little confusing to think of a glasses' display unit wiggling around all the time, compensating for eye motion, right-out primitive it may appear at a first glance, even wasting energy. But realize that this display unit itself could be as small and fragile as a fly's wing, and how fast, violently and enduring such a wing can move with how little energy. Nature has long solved the problem of fast enduring agitation, and all the 'battery' is contained in that tiny animal.

Moreover, the tinier it gets, the more enduring mechanics can be. Think about micro mirror displays, whose tiny mirror elements can do thousands of movements per second, for decades without tiring, because of an effect called hyper elasticity.

Hence, mechanics aren't necessary what they used to be - wear and tear - as soon as we are entering the world of micro and nano systems.

Holographic displays

Holography works with interference patterns. These occur when coherent waves (e.g. laser light) from different origins add or annihilate according to their phase and position. Recording a hologram is done by letting a direct laser ('reference') wavefront interfere with one reflected by objects, and 'freezing' the resulting pattern on a photographic film. If later on a single laser wavefront equal to the reference passes the photographed pattern, interference between the passed parts of the wavefront results in identical wavefronts as were previously emitted by the recorded objects. The principle works with reflective and engraved patterns as well.

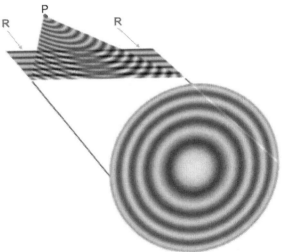

In order to illustrate this, we regard the very simplest of all holographic setups. Consider a point source of (coherent) light, e.g. one pixel P of a scene illuminated with a laser. In addition, we consider a totally planar wavefront R derived from the same laser source (i.e. entirely synchronous).

If we place a receptor (e.g. a photographic plate) in front of this, we get an interference pattern of concentric circles. These are not equidistant; their distances are a function of the distance from the scene pixel to the receptor. If we now place the developed photo plate in front of a planar wavefront as with the recording assembly, the concentric wavefront from the image pixel will also be synthesized, because the rings themselves act as wave origins and their addition just does the trick. Such a basic pattern of concentric rings is also called a zone plate and works like a lens.

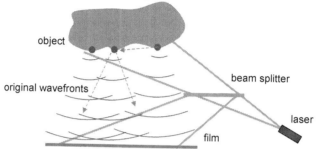

A simplified hologram photography assembly: a single laser delivers a reference beam to the film and illuminates an object. The wavefronts from three points on the object are shown as an example. Wavefronts from all points of the object interfere with the reference beam and form the hologram on the film. Note that self interference (dashed lines) causes noise with natural hologram recording.

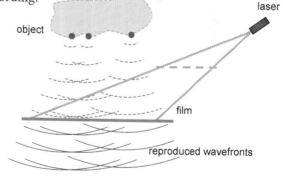

If later on another laser of the same wavelength and position reproduces the reference beam and illuminates the holographic pattern on the developed film, the hologram pattern converts it into the same wavefronts as if the object points were still there. A front illuminated reflective hologram would do the same trick.

Superimposing many patterns, allows to reproduce many pixels simultaneously, together with their proper distance, hence the entirety of light waves from the original scene. We see that holography in essence is a very simple thing.

It's quite natural however, that any tiny part of the pattern doesn't know if to deflect the beam left or right, so we get two exit wavefronts, one producing a 'conjugated' virtual image before the plane (we will see more of this a little later). Therefore, the actual recording assembly shown uses slanted beams. If so desired, an hologram appearing before the plane could still be generated.

Keyhole Holograms

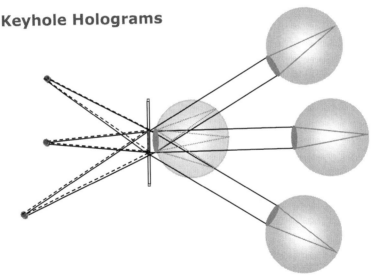

With a hologram, the same fringe pattern has to deliver the information for many viewing angles at once, even for the entire image, as it can also be regarded from any different angles.

This imposes high demands on image quality, especially dynamic range, resolution and graininess (noise). More important, it also implies that the entire hologram scene can be seen through an arbitrary small area of the hologram ('*keyhole hologram*', picture). The picture very simply shows the most famous property of holograms, still showing the entire picture even if broken up into pieces. The selection of perspectives of course is diminished in this case.

Interference patterns as on a photographic film can also be simulated with computers and reproduced with a display. We should note that with physical hologram recording, we can't exclude the above mentioned self interference from indirect lighting. With synthetic holograms, this and other adverse effects can easily be avoided by proper pattern generation.

So far we have simplified one thing: interference patterns are not standing still in space. Their maxima and minima are traveling, depending on the angles of the constructing beams, slower or faster, even with an apparently superluminal „phase speed" in certain cases. What causes a photo emulsion to blacken, are the electromagnetic maxima of light waves that are consecutively transgressing it at certain locations. The minima of the interference pattern are alternately occurring on the same path.

At the locations between the maxima and minima paths, no exposure is caused.

What we observe here are three dimensional traces or 'fringes' in space, somehow resembling onion shells. In case of a flat hologram, the fringes recorded on the plate are just cross sections of these 3D structures. If the photo plate is thicker (in practice, this is nearly always the case), a certain three dimensional layer section of the fringe pattern is recorded. This structure is called a volume hologram (more from p.232 on).

For direct display applications, volume holograms are less interesting, as it would be utterly difficult to modulate an entire volume in terms of absorption or refraction index.

Volume holograms are however important as static, recorded patterns, forming so called holographic optical elements, that may become very important for near-eye displays and that we will examine later on.

We will first have a look at some more hologram properties as can be understood by the simple 2D zone plate approach.

The ambiguous zone plate

As any combination of light origins can cause a 'solid' wavefront as long as their light beams towards a certain direction are all in phase (or shifted by multiples of the wavelength λ) usually there are several possible exit angles for a laser beam hitting line patterns like a zone plate or a diffraction grating.

So at least in the case of a zone plate seen from its center line, there will be some more virtual images appearing, spoiling its optical usefulness.

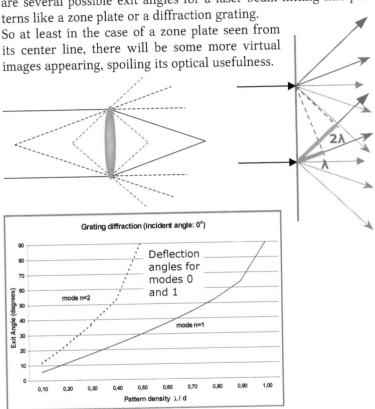

In this case, the plain vanilla zone plate even is a collecting and diverting lens in one. For practical applications it is therefore better if we use slanted setups, canceling unwanted beams out into uncritical areas, as we have seen already with our simplified hologram photography setup. At page 386, you may find a calculation retrieving all possible angles (grating equation).

Resolution requirements

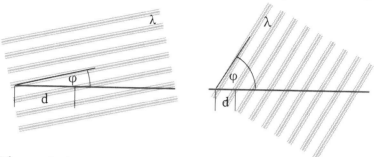

The resolution necessary for a hologram film or an holographic display depends on the angle of the incident light: the larger the viewing angle we want to reproduce, the better the resolution required (picture). The gray values of the pattern constitute sine waves (wavelength=λ). According to the sampling theorem [34], these can already be reproduced with at least 2 pixels per wave, i.e. we need pixel sizes of about d/2, or a little less, because pixels are squares and resolution therefore is lower in diagonal direction. In any case, reproducing exact gray values is an absolute necessity, as holograms are superpositions of many wave patterns and each of these faint additions is equally important.

If the display is illuminated almost perpendicular, φ is just the angle between illumination and resulting waves, so the pattern resolution just depends on the degree of deflection, or the viewing angle required. For our reference beam, we are not confined to a planar wavefront of course. This was only chosen for an example. In practice, the reference 'beam' would be a concentric wavefront, originating from one point.

As wavelengths of visible light can be as low as 0.4 µm (blue light), we will need pixel sizes between about 0.2 and 20 µm, depending on the illumination and deflection angles desired.

For big screens, this would normally not require megapixels of resolution - as with classical displays - but *terapixels (trillions)*. This simply forfeits attempts to implement it with current technology. With very small displays however, it's not quite so difficult. There even are first applications of such a technology.

Index holograms

Simple gray tone holograms will inevitably absorb *at least* 50% of
the light, just by their gray levels. Moreover, light is distributed
into several exit beams, hence diminished, even in cases where
these beams are not seen due to their extreme angle. We also have
to consider that light power is amplitude squared, so if we regard
the power effectiveness, the picture gets even worse, resulting in
efficiencies significantly below 10%. One way improving this is
utilizing the light from the 'black' areas as well as from the transparent or reflecting ones. Analogous to the gray value grating, we
can think of a hologram where the 'black' areas also reflect light,
but with a phase delay of $\lambda/2$. These waves would then *add* to the
total amplitude. This can be achieved with a hologram of a certain
thickness and a varying refraction index. Higher refraction index
just causes a decrease in light speed. So if light has to pass
through such a layer, parts of it are delayed against others, resulting in a phase shift. Varying this phase shift continuously and
periodically between hologram lines, a 100% output contribution
can be achieved from any location in the hologram, resulting in
efficiencies that can e.g. be about 30% for a single mode. Indeed,
certain plastic materials or photographic film can record light
intensities and turn them into variations of refraction index.

Such *index* holograms can also be much thicker than a wavelength, allowing for 3-dimensional patterns that do cannot only
cause refraction or reflection but are selective to certain incident
angles and colors and define exit angles with an effectiveness of
up to 100% (holographic optical elements, see p.232)
There are also at least 3 current display technologies generating
(flat) phase shift holograms.

Some liquid crystals are changing their refraction index when voltage is applied. This kind of LCD displays needs no polarizers and is therefore very efficient, but it can only work with coherent light and phase effects. The usual implementation of this principle are LCOS displays, where the LC fluid is layered on a silicon chip containing driver circuits coated with a metallic mirror surface. These displays are working reflective and are available in LCOS and FLCOS (ferroelectric) varieties, mainly used for laser beam shaping [84], but also dedicated for projection and near-eye displays [110]. The FLCOS variants have the advantage of very short switching times (a few microseconds).

LCOS display with 1920x1200 pixels, pixel size of 8 μm
(under the magnifier, Aurora Systems Co.,Ltd. [84],
picture courtesy of Holoeye Photonics AG [51])

If we get further down with pixel size (below 1μm), holographic displays could also be a solution for vision simulators. Alas, even with F-LCOS this is not so easy to accomplish, as the liquid crystals need some thickness to provide an effect.

Embossed holograms

Phase shifts can as well be achieved with simple printed holograms, using a mirror surface with engraved patterns that really cause varying light path lengths. For example, a photo resist lacquer on a substrate can be exposed with a hologram and then developed, leaving a landscape of higher and lower lines. The engraved pattern can either be galvanized with a mirror surface, or replicated by appropriate processes, e.g. making a metal stamp that can imprint the pattern into simple plastic. This type of hologram is widely used for authenticity seals on products, credit cards etc., as it is cheaply replicated but difficult to forge.

A new type of phase shifting display type uses micro mirrors that are suspended for parallel up/down movement, like little pistons. Phase shifting is again achieved here by path length. These displays are already available for evaluation.

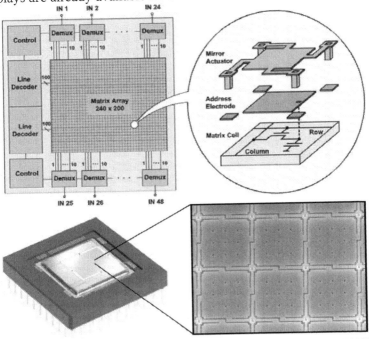

240x200 piston micro mirror array (image courtesy of FhG-IPMS)

An holographic scanner

What we have seen so far can also be utilized for the laser scanner approach: imagine we would just use the hologram simply to *deflect beams*. It could then be much smaller and would have to change images much faster, but in the extreme, it could work exactly like the moving mirror reflector, yet with a larger surface and at almost any speed.

Feeding an entire hologram into the display, for any tiny change in deflection angle, is of course not possible. The according holograms should already be stored or calculated within the chip.

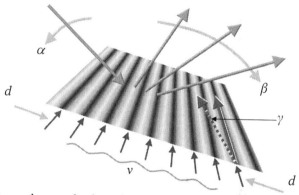

So if we change the line distances *d*, we get different deflection angles β. If we actually calculate this, we see that an angle of 50^0 or 60^0 for the incoming beam for example would theoretically allow to alter the angle of the departing beam from about 10^0 to $>80^0$, without any unwanted modes (n>1) showing up. The conjugated beam can simply be absorbed by a light trap. Limitations are efficiency, the inferior definition for small angles due to large d values, and the smaller apparent mirror area for large angles (that can be partly compensated by a larger mirror area).

The straight line pattern could be generated by providing a sine pattern (for gray values) in just one dimension and feed the values *v* into the chip from the side, steering all pixel elements in a line at once. 'Exact' phase values can be approximated with pixels smaller than wavelength and fine tuned pixel gray or phase values (as with any digital system, such as a digital amplifier reproducing sound waves, for example). One could also try to approximate the ideally continuous pattern with *binary* sub wavelength pixels and sort of a dithering mechanism. In any case, it should already have become obvious that this is really achievable.

By changing the line angle γ as well, we could deflect in two dimensions at once. Generating such slanted line patterns is pretty complicated, as the lines have to appear in very precise angles. With some dedicated calculation circuitry however, excellent phase accuracy can in principle be achieved for any pixel in a raster display. So this is only a matter of finding an appropriate design. As the chip will essentially be 1...2 mm small, we could also just tilt or rotate it for the slower deflection axis. There we won't need more than about 100 Hz, and this is not too difficult.

Several other operation modes are possible, for holographic elements. A small hologram could produce parts of the viewing area sequentially, serving each with its own partial image, staggered inlays for example with resolution progressing towards the center of view, as we have yet discussed with laser displays.

The deflection chip could even write a picture with different resolution parts in just one sweep, switching line frequencies even within lines, with no alignment errors. It could also address the edges more often, where the eyes are more flicker sensitive.

Some digital holography approaches are using DMD devices [36]. It is quite obvious that DMD pixels could be made even smaller than F-LCOS. DMD should be getting the faster the smaller they are. Sufficiently small structures don't even have to be exact mirrors, because a sub wavelength mirror will reflect anything as a spherical wavefront anyway. For a hologram without artifacts though, we need to produce patterns with gray levels, and pulse width modulation won't work here (interference of photons emitted at different times can't realistically be expected).

So the existing attempts to produce even simple Fourier holograms with these devices are yielding unacceptably noisy results. What could be working are structures way below light wavelength, using the dithering approach. With silicon chip structures of 45 nm ($^1/_{10}$ of blue light wavelength) in mass manufacturing already, this is not unrealistic at all, and it could be an entirely different and much simpler construction than current DMD.

The piston approach or index modulated LCOS however are looking much better so far, as they are analog and natively produce phase shifts (hence, good efficiency). A problem will be mechanical constraints of pixel size vs. required phase shift.

A piston display may well need excitations of ±80nm at pixel sizes below 1 μm, which is difficult indeed. We can also expect effects from pixel boundaries etc.

LCOS displays will have crosstalk effects between very small pixels, which may be an advantage though, as is smoothes pixel boundaries. Yet phase shift requirements may dictate an LC layer too thick for comfort even then.

Another solution could be based on an old principle: a thin liquid film on a surface can form ripples when electric charge is applied locally. This is known for the ancient but powerful Eidophor video projectors, where the liquid is an oil film in a vacuum tube and charges are applied by an electron beam. Spread some liquid over a CMOS chip, and you may apply charges by electrodes on the chip surface, driven by circuitry inside. Microscopic ripples arising may just be right for holographic purposes, and light may be modulated either by phase modulated reflection as with an embossed hologram, or by different delays from the varying thickness and the refraction index of the film. Current implementations are known as MLM (Moving Liquid Mirror displays) [119]. Mounted in a housing with a glass window for protection, such a display can be quite rugged and enduring. In any case, this would just be a chip with some liquid applied, hence as cheap as it gets, and the resulting smooth ripples would be very friendly for light shaping. The culprit currently is modulation speed, some milliseconds typically, making this technology interesting for holographic displays maybe, but not for holographic scanner mirrors.

In principle, holographic modulators and laser scanners are just extreme varieties of a general wave function modulator for laser beams. No wonder that the development of high resolution displays with extremely small pixel sizes was not actually stimulated by display glasses but by laboratory applications as laser beam shaping, and that they are usually known as 'spatial light modulators'. What should be aimed at for the future, are display chips with extremely small pixel sizes. Integrating not only driver but also signal processing structures into an holographic display chip could make sense if a real time synthesis of patterns is required. Achieving full fledged Synthetic holography in real time however, may take 10..15 more years of chip technology development. Fourier holograms may nevertheless be accomplished quite soon. We will learn about Fourier holograms a little later, as they are best derived from light field displays (pp.243,248).

Could holographic displays be useful for display glasses anyway? Maybe yes. With a 'normal' hologram, thousands of different viewing angles are contained in the wavefront. The larger the display area, the more there are. Hence, a large hologram contains a lot of partly redundant information. If we closely look at a small hologram piece like through a keyhole, as we have discussed already, we get almost a 2D image, except that it still may have different focusing for different objects, a little remainder of 3D. If it gets even smaller, it works like a hole camera and focus is the same over the entire image as well, i.e. then it's really 2D. Clipping out still smaller pieces, the image would get more and more blurred as there won't remain enough fringes to sufficiently define a pixel. From the standpoint of information theory, the issue looks as follows: we deliver any information the little hologram has, just completely to the eye. No other perspectives etc. have to be generated. Hence, the number of pixels theoretically wouldn't need to be much larger than with a conventional display. As pattern line sizes are always dictated by wavelength, a very small display will not need an astronomical number of pixels even for holographic purposes. Its image has to be enlarged by optics anyway, e.g. we could look at it with magnifying glasses. We only have to accordingly generate the displayed objects, to appear in their real size after the magnification.

With the vision simulator optics reviewed so far, we have seen that it is very difficult to get large magnification together with overall good focus and low distortion. Yet with a display chip showing a hologram, we have the option to add some 3D properties. In other words, we could assign any virtual distance to any pixel displayed. This behaves a bit as if we were simulating lenses. Lenses recorded in a hologram look and behave like real lenses, and with a synthetic hologram, we could simulate not only lenses but fairly complex and dynamic optical behavior. So the image pixels just don't have to stick to the display plane. In a hologram they usually don't anyway. We could also do this according to where the user just looks at, i.e. to the virtual distance desired for each object. The approach works with some real 3D information, hence it will require more computing effort than a Fourier hologram. With a fairly small holographic display always seen from a very limited angular range however, the only real benefit would be a possibility to simulate focus. From the standpoint of hologram calculation, this may well be possible without too much effort, as focus could probably be synthesized by adding a pre-defined holographic optical element function to a simple Fourier hologram of the picture projected. Given the fact that a dynamic display adaptation is probably necessary here as well, the advantages of holographic focusing are however questionable.

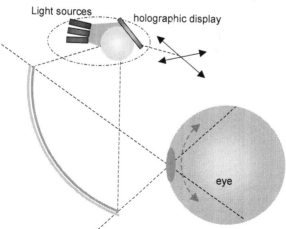

Raw scheme with synthetic holography display (imaginary pixel positions visualized by sphere)

I won't delve into more possible constructive details and variants like geometry, illumination etc., as this technology is still somewhat speculative and the issue would get very complex. Let me only mention that holograms are good for a lot of other tricks.

For example, we might even be able to overlay or switch holograms to let the display also serve as optics for an eye tracker camera (something very important that we have to keep in mind with all designs), similar to our DMD design example.

Display technologies: a summary

Laser displays allow for very light constructions, yet there is the problem that higher resolutions require a wider source beam and a faster deflection unit at the same time. Maybe the holographic scanner principle or multi resolution inlays can help resolving this. Focus independence isn't an advantage at least against other displays using small light sources, and we won't need it anyway. An important point for laser displays could be their pixel sequential image buildup, allowing the beam to follow eye motion, to use interlacing without problems, even to change image content while the image is written.

Conventional displays are available in many varieties. Building an optical assembly with a large magnification and a large viewing angle is nevertheless a challenge. Conventional displays also suffer from a one frame delay following motion, that can only be fully compensated by moving the display mechanically (but any display may need this anyway). Yet achieving high resolution should be easy, and in case of bi-directional displays (with camera pixels), retina tracking can be integrated quite elegantly.

Fully holographic displays could in theory combine many advantages, and it may be possible to build appropriate display chips, but holograms are so computing intensive that it will take decades until they may be considered.

Fourier holograms (p. 248) or light field displays (p. 243) may be offering some unique options, especially for focusing, and should be considered now and again.

'Half transparent' mirrors

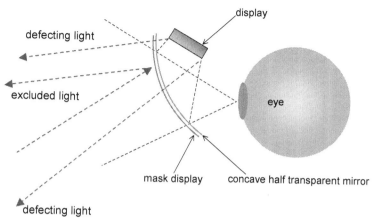

defecting light

excluded light

display

eye

mask display   concave half transparent mirror

defecting light

Let's now have a closer look on the 'half transparent' mirror that we need for the glasses, to combine the real with the virtual.

Just using thin silver coatings that allow half of the light to pass through while reflecting the remainder, is an approach still used but far from being optimal.

With spectrally selective (dichroic) or spectrally as well as directionally selective (holographic) mirrors, nearly 100% of the display light could be utilized, while ambient light would be attenuated by only a few percent. Here we would exploit the fact that a perfect color picture can be produced in the eye by only 3 very narrow banded color sources.

Dichroic mirrors

Dichroic filters/mirrors are produced by deploying very thin coatings (usually 20...40 layers) on glass. The resulting filters can have a very narrow bandwidth, down to about 1 nm, compared to the entire about 300 nm of the visible spectrum. Contrary to dye filters, they do not absorb (transmissivity >90%), but selectively reflect parts of the spectrum. There are high pass, low pass, band pass and notch filters. Basically for our purpose we need notch filters, that reflect just one color, i.e. band pass mirrors.

There is no problem (except for costs) to use multiple filters stacked upon each other, in order to reflect several narrow color bands concurrently.

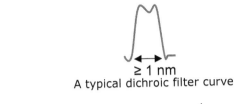

≥ 1 nm
A typical dichroic filter curve

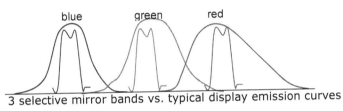

3 selective mirror bands vs. typical display emission curves

Dichroic filters/mirrors have extreme frequency selectivity but unlike HOE's, they have no directional component,.

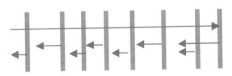

Fine tuned vacuum deployed layers of different refraction index, each reflecting part of the light.

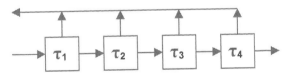

Simplified filter equivalent (multiple back reflections excluded)

The principle will work the better, the narrower the original emission bands of the display colors are: in this case, more of the light produced will be reflected to the user's eye and shielded from the outside. We could therefore achieve an almost 100% effectiveness if we use laser displays. With broader emission curves, a dichroic multi band mirror would at least improve color definition.

As the filter characteristics are defined by the thickness of coating layers, they also vary with the angle of incident light.

With our typical vision simulator construction, light does not hit the mirror vertically. Therefore the filter frequencies would deviate. Yet it is no problem to adjust the coatings for this, even to produce coatings with a gliding change in thickness.

Some manufactures for example offer narrow band pass filters with a center frequency that varies from blue to red over the length of the filter, and with high precision. With a linear photo detector array, this makes a simple but good spectral analyzer.

With a laser projector display, reflection angles vary only a little, and the light is perfectly monochrome, so we could use very narrow banded mirrors, resulting in an almost 100% transparency of the glasses. This would not be a 'half transparent' mirror anymore, it would not visually absorb anything at all.

Likewise, hardly any of the laser light would get outside the mirror.

Dichroic mirrors may be relatively expensive to manufacture, but the advantages are convincing. In mass production, they could certainly be affordable.

It is meanwhile possible to deploy vacuum coatings, and therefore produce dichroic mirrors, on plastic glasses as well.

Holographic mirrors however, can be produced spectrally as well as directionally selective, and they may perhaps even be cheaper to manufacture. Let's have a look at this.

Holographic optical elements (HOE's)

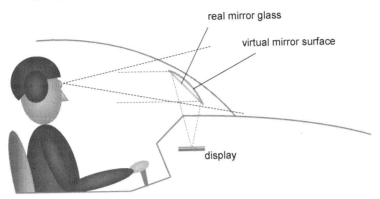

real mirror glass

virtual mirror surface

display

Headup display (HUD) in a fighter jet plane (principle)

Holographic patterns cannot only represent images, but also optical elements like lenses and mirrors. So called volume holograms, recording a wavefront in a thick film layer (several wavelengths thick) exhibit even more interesting properties. Usually such holograms are recorded in plastic film, and the pattern after development is not represented in gray values but in zones of different diffraction index. They can be transparent to ordinary light and show their special behavior for light of a certain wavelength only, coming in at a certain angle only (constructive interference here has to comply with level and vertical patterns concurrently, which leaves only a few results).

A virtual mirror as in the picture above is not defined by the substrate plane, so a planar glass plate can exhibit the properties of a concave mirror, without any lens effects appearing.

This technology has been established decades ago [94], with headup and helmet displays in fighter jets, recently also with headup displays in civil airplanes. It's advance into other areas is actually a bit overdue.

The virtual image in a headup display appears at infinity, so eye adaptation changes are avoided and the image is position stable against the horizon even if the pilot moves his head.

Construction of an HOE (overhead display)

As we have seen with volume holograms already, beams constructing the hologram and resulting beams - if only one of the constructing beams is afterwards applied to the resulting hologram - are identical.

Hence for constructing a certain HOE, we just have to apply the exactly same beams as we wish to appear during its use later on.

A 'reflected' beam has to approach the substrate from the opposite side during construction.

What is important to notice: There is always a certain angular range where the resulting HOE will work for. Otherwise, it would only be good for light sources coming from a single point.

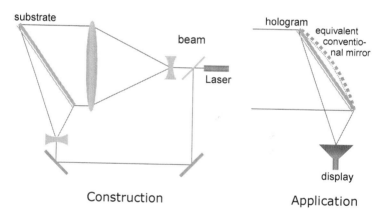

Construction   Application

- Construction: Shaped beams from the same Laser source are forming volume patterns in a light sensitive substrate.

- Application: The pattern has been developed into a volumetric refraction index hologram that will convert parallel into concentric beams and vice versa, just like a parabolic mirror.

For a more precise description on making these Hoe's, see p.390.

Volume holograms in detail

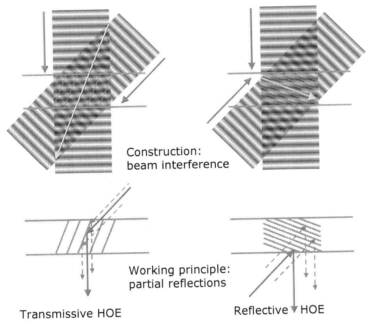

Construction:
beam interference

Working principle:
partial reflections

Transmissive HOE   Reflective ▼ HOE

A volume hologram contains interference patterns of light waves as regions of different gray level or refraction index.

The most important fact here to consider: the light fronts are not standing still, so the interference patterns will also travel, in a direction being just the average of the light front directions (marked by arrows). As it is practically impossible to perfectly show this in a still picture, you will find an animation of it at the book's website (see back cover). There you can observe an interesting effect arising in the right picture: The interference pattern seems to travel faster than light (just illusion, as these patterns themselves are not electromagnetic waves).

Note that the left and right cases are essentially identical, if we just modify the angle between the two wavefronts and turn them both around. The only remarkable difference resulting is that this causes the beams to come from the same or from opposite sides of the substrate. For calculations on fringe patterns, see p.387.

Black and white in this picture mean negative and positive maxima of the light waves, and these are both exposing the film. Spots of plus and minus amplitude travel through the photo emulsion, exposing it along certain lines, while between these lines, only zero transitions occur, and these are not exposing the film. So this is not just about 'freezing' the interference patterns in the film. The actual interference pattern even needs some (very short) time to be properly recorded.

The really fascinating part of this however is that even with volume holograms, and despite of the quite indirect pattern forming process, the resulting 3D diffraction grating causes light to be refracted or reflected with the same angular proportions as the constructing beams. Beams coming from the same side will produce a refractive hologram, while beams coming from opposite sides will produce a reflective hologram. With these index, or *phase* holograms, the effects of multiple layers add up.

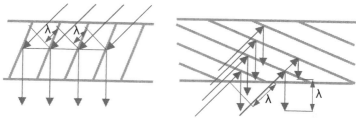

It works like this: at surfaces where the refraction index changes, some light gets reflected in almost any case (more at p. 385). Even when only a small part gets reflected, reflections from the multiple surfaces within a volume hologram can add up to almost 100%, if in phase. For example, planes parallel to the film surface, with $\lambda/2$ spacing, will reflect waves with delays of λ, $2 \cdot \lambda$, $3 \cdot \lambda$..., hence all with the same phase, so they will all add up.

For the particular wavelength(s) it works with, such a mirror, also called a Distributed Bragg Reflector, can be better than a silver mirror. Distributed Bragg Reflectors have applications of their own, for example as reflecting surfaces in wave guides (optical fibers), or as super efficient reflectors in lasers and laser diodes, With sufficient thickness of the film, there is only one possibility for constructive interference, for direction and wavelength of the output as well as the input beam. In practice, there is always a certain range, depending on the thickness of the medium.

Note that we are neglecting refraction at the medium border in all pictures here. What we also do not consider for simplicity is polarization, that occurs with refracted and reflected beams. This doesn't change the general principle however.

Interestingly, almost any hologram films are several wavelengths thick, so they expose properties of a volume hologram. Ghost and conjugate images are therefore much weaker than expected, and even white light illumination can be possible.

We should note however, that when working with a large range of wavelengths, we may get multiple and therefore also unwanted operating ranges. The same holographic mirror reflecting light at wavelength λ could also deliver effects with $2\cdot\lambda$ or $3\cdot\lambda$, as it will find some surfaces with the right distance.

As the human visual range is only about 400...700 nm, a range less than 1:2, this is usually not a big problem. Nevertheless dealing with color, especially combining holograms for full color reproduction in the same volume, is not a trivial task.

Usually, three separate layers of volume holograms for red, green and blue basic colors are combined. This is simpler to achieve and has less unwanted effects.

Characteristics of holographic mirrors

Some figures: an HOE with 15 layers could approximately have a frequency bandwidth of 15 nm, allowing for a 3-color glasses' display mirror with about 85% efficiency. The directional range would still be >10 degrees, enough for optical applications. Interestingly, if this was a photo hologram, these figures would be good enough for sufficiently coherent light selection from a white source, and for a decent viewing range as well. For some calculation hints, see page 388.

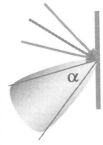

Basic holographic combiners for glasses

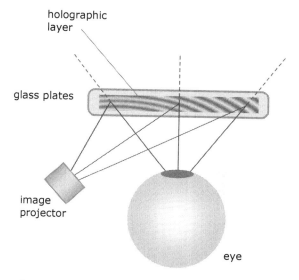

holographic layer

glass plates

image projector

eye

The principle is now obvious, and as simple as it gets: many layers of faint refraction index changes are forming partial reflecting mirrors inside the holographic element, and if we are using light of the right wavelength, and within a certain angular range, all reflections from these layers will add up as if they came from a single solid mirror surface.

Light of the 'wrong' wave length or angle is scattered a little bit, but apart from a faint coloring effect, the holographic layer is almost entirely transparent to it.

Color mirrors are simply achieved by stacking three layers for different, monochromatic light sources: red, green and blue (right).

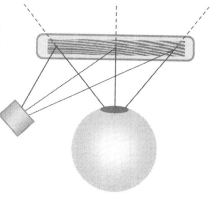

Although extreme reflection angles are possible with holographic mirrors, this may result in some difficulties with surface reflections of the carrier glass. These could in principle be reduced if curved substrates are used. Manufacturing HOE's on these is not a problem. Planar HOE mirrors however would also allow for planar mask displays, simplifying their construction a lot.

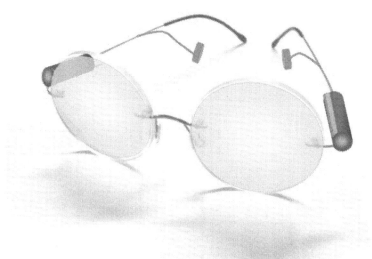

Impression of an ultra light advanced vision simulator

The picture shows a future vision simulator that would have advanced mask displays - in this case perhaps planar ones - and holographic mirrors. The optical assemblies with position cameras, image projectors and eye trackers are built into compact units in the handles. Also shown are the earpiece/microphone units. Alternatively, the glasses of such a device could as well each consist of two plastic glass domes, between them some yet unspecified mask display technology whereof we may only assume that a transparent driver circuit is deployed on the inner side of the outer glass dome for example, and a counter electrode on the opposite surface.

An holographic mirror would be integrated into the inner side of the assembly. This holographic optical element could also be more complicated than just a mirror, using the many design degrees of freedom of HOE's for sophisticated optical tricks.

The display of choice would most likely be a modular laser scanner. Hence, the entire display hardware for one eye (the part included in the glasses, not the computer that would currently go with a pocket unit), eye tracker included, would essentially consist of two silicon chips, an holographic foil, a thin mask display foil and a laser source the size of a sand grain, all together weighing less than 1g.

A new, advanced HOE design

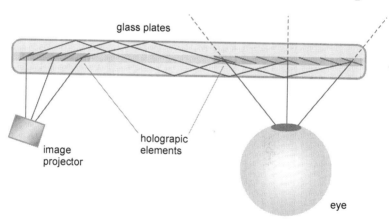

glass plates

image projector

holograpic elements

eye

The extremal characteristics possible with holographic elements are enabling very unconventional designs. In a recently launched product by Lumus Inc., light beams from a display are first turned into an almost flat bundle, then total-reflected several times from the very edges of the HOE carrier glasses, then reflected into the eye in a totally controlled manner, allowing for design freedom with both the display and eye beam angle, aperture and focus length.

HOE's vs. conventional optics

HOE's can work similar but are never identical to conventional lenses or mirrors. In fact, they are made up of many partly reflecting surfaces within their substrate. Taking this into account, we can instantly visualize their behavior in certain configurations:

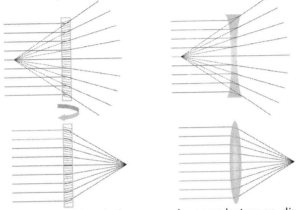

Flipping transmission holograms changes between diverting and collecting lens behavior

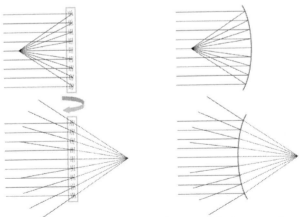

Flipping reflection holograms changes between diverting and collecting mirror behavior

Materials for volume holograms

The most used material for volume holograms is light sensitive dichromatic gelatin on glass, that after development is laminated with a second glass layer. Appropriately processed and sealed, these HOE's stand 20 service years even in fighter jets, under intense stress from temperature and sunlight [108-112].

Normal photographic emulsions can also be developed into index holograms. By a process called bleaching, black silver halide is turned into transparent silver bromide, exhibiting strong refractive properties and index changes.

Practically all photographic holograms that we are used to are made this way, and they are indeed volume holograms, with directional as well as spectral selectivity, enabling illumination by simple halogen lamps, and even images containing multiple colors as well. If you are interested in more, a comprehensive guide to photographic holography is [116].

HOE (optical volume hologram) from photographic film:

Film   Exposure   Developing: Silver halide (black)   Bleaching: Silver Bromine (refractive)

HOE from dichromatic gelatin (the usual material):

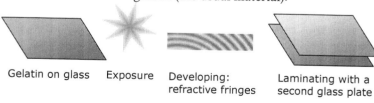

Gelatin on glass   Exposure   Developing: refractive fringes   Laminating with a second glass plate

Holographic canvas

Regarding the versatility of Hoe's, it may be interesting that not only mirrors can be represented in a volume hologram, but as they essentially still are holograms with full imaging abilities, objects like canvas screens, for example, are possible as well.

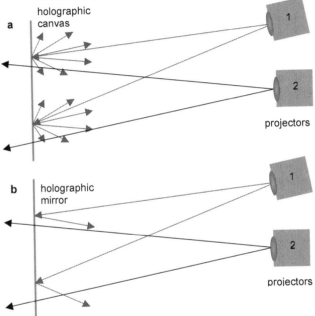

A virtual canvas screen in the hologram shows up in the projector light, with a decisive difference to the usually homogenous lighting: according to the image in the projector, any part of screen gets different intensities, forming the image on it as if it was a real screen. With carefully chosen exposure arrangements for the screen recording, it can be designed so that it can only be lit from the angle of the original reference source (1) [42].

So any other ambient light cannot spoil the image. The light from the lower projectors passes the screen untouched (2). The reflection characteristics are still those of the photographed material, so we have all options from canvas (a) to mirror (b).

Light field displays

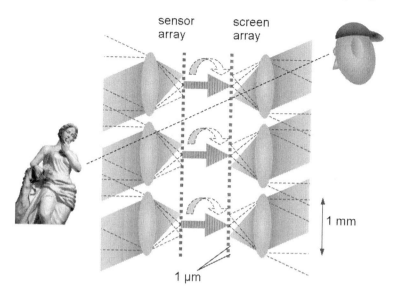

A dense array of micro cameras could record all light beams going through an area in space (e.g. a window that we or the cameras are looking through). They would take up all information about angle, position and intensity of all beams, hence all information to reconstruct them. This is called a light field. As a description of natural views, an alternative to holography.

Each camera converts angle to position on its image sensor. An equivalent array of micro projectors could reproduce all beams with high accuracy.

Another very simple explanation for the principle; Each camera/projector pair here acts like a camera obscura, hence a small hole, and many small holes simply are forming a window!

Signal transmission in this case could use raw data (but this are n^4 pixels!), compressed light field data, or synthetic holographic data. From the view of fundamental physics, such an approach would be conceivable (1mm camera size, 1µm pixel size are in the possible range and well fit for large screens).

In practice, one would of course not use myriads of micro cameras just to record 3D movies, for example. There one would of course use fewer cameras, and fill the perspective gaps at encoding (more in the media chapter).

The major step towards realistically conceivable light field displays however would be to concentrate on the horizontal perspective and to generate at least the vertical perspective viewer specific only. But let us first look into some fundamentals, before presenting a realistic approach.

Micro lens guide

Projects involving lenticular arrays have usually always been, trying to achieve a perfect light field representation by nothing but beam shaping. In the real world, it is almost impossible this way to avoid transition effects when viewers change position.

The answer is adaptive displays, dynamically generating user specific beams (and here we are not referring to the many single viewer approaches simply shifting around grids of stereo display stripes).

Before getting into this, one has to comprehend, again, that lenses can be described as position to angle converters. For micro lenses of a lenticular array, we can make the following assumptions:

Micro lenses can deliver a very large depth of field. Overlapping beams can be achieved by slight blurring or defocus. Optical perfection is not necessary and stripe positioning is absolutely uncritical if adaptive display techniques (calibration and user tracking) are employed.

A micro lens projection assembly is simply the opposite of a camera with a tiny lens: As anybody knows, a dirt cheap camera with only a millimeter wide lens can record an HD picture, hence have the necessary angular resolution. Vice versa, the micro projector can also resolve hundreds of different angles at ease.

Using micro lens arrays in connection with micro pixel displays could as well deliver light field effects for display glasses, for example enabling focus simulation just as mentioned with holographic displays already.

This however is an unlikely development for the same reasons mentioned there already. Nevertheless, light field technology has many links to display glasses and in order to understand it, large display are a good vehicle.

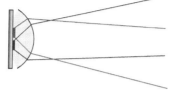

Simple 2-stripe assembly for a stereo parallax display

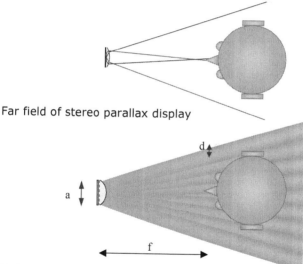

Far field of stereo parallax display

Multi stripe assembly of a light field display and light beam bundle, drawing separate pictures to a viewer's separate eyes.

The maximum angular resolution simply is (p.376):

$$a/f \approx \lambda/d$$

Example: a=0.5mm, f=3m, λ=0,5 μm, $\rightarrow$ d ≈3mm. Fairly enough for a stripe width of e.g. 3 cm, separating views for both eyes!

Simple but efficient: **dynamic beam shaping**

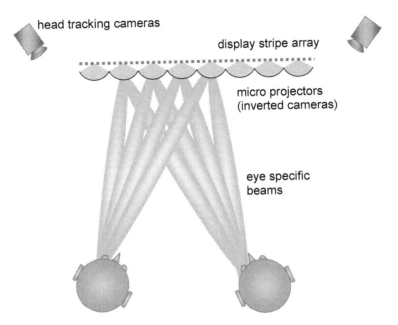

Here we have such a special lenticular display, the inverse of a camera array [105].

We use display and lens stripes. It is horizontal stereo only, but vertical perspective (or even the entire picture), can also be viewer specific.

Each lens forms a micro projector (inverted camera) with extreme depth of field. Stripe position is converted into angle. High angular resolution is possible.

In viewer adaptive mode, only stripes corresponding to a user's eye would be activated, and tolerances could be compensated:

The display would be pre-calibrated once before use, by displaying test patterns and analyzing the signals from the tracking cameras. Hence, high precision is not necessary here, neither concerning lens geometry nor stripe positioning.

Such a display is nowadays in reach, it could be manufactured as a high resolution OLED display, in future maybe even as a wallpaper (roll-to-roll printing and lens stripe engraving) display.

The lenslets will need an anti reflection coating (remember the many reflections with those stereo postcards), but just a look at some modern plastic glasses reveals this to be state of the art.

Hence, this will be quite a cheap approach, and this is very important, as there already is no big market for expensive displays anymore, and even the less so in the future, when they will have to compete with display glasses.

It can't be pointed out strong enough how entirely different this is from the numerous auto stereoscopic approaches that have been unsuccessfully resuscitated during the last decades over and over again [109]. While these were trying to deliver more and more perspectives simultaneously, boosting complexity and complications, causing switching effects when viewers moved from one perspective to another, here we generate a specific perspective for a specific user at a time, the perspective changes when the user moves, even if he is still in the area of the same display stripe, it even changes when he moves vertically, generating a perfect 3D impression in all directions, and when he has moved far enough in the horizontal direction to enter the area covered by the next display stripe, this stripe will show exactly the same perspective during the transition, delivering a smooth and seamless handover.

At larger distances, we could introduce a smooth transition to monoscopic but still perspective corrected view.

The only disadvantage of the approach: perspectives for one viewer may sometimes interfere with others. Only if two viewers are at the same horizontal position however, which is not so likely in typical TV viewing situations.

The major advantages however: 'only' about 10 times the active pixel count of normal displays are required, and only perspectives for really present viewers have to be generated and displayed.

There is also a huge energy saving, as only display stripes for actual viewers have to be activated, pointing the light exclusively into their directions.

Holographic light field rendering
(Fourier Holograms)

Now that we have learned about light field displays, we can use this to understand the very core of current holographic display technology.

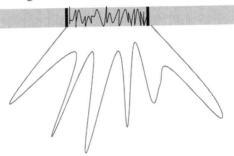

A laser beam hitting a line pattern at an angle is deflected according to the pattern frequency (grating equation, p.386). Overlaying several patterns of different frequencies results in several exit beams at different angles.

An entire line spectrum results in a complete angle/intensity distribution, hence a light field. As frequency translates into angle, the angular distribution can be calculated by the *Fourier transform* of this spectrum (hence, Fourier Hologram). A display stripe containing such a spectrum is the perfect equivalent of a micro lens with micro display stripes behind it. Simplified holographic displays have been built like this, as early as 1994 [65].
Quite obviously, the lenticular array approach shown before is equivalent and easier to accomplish, also with fewer problems e.g. from coherence effects.

A Fourier Hologram Projector

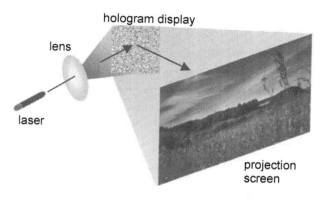

Holographic 2D projector (Light Blue Optics, [31])

The above picture shows the principle of an holography based projection display, generating 2D projection pictures on a remote screen.

A *2D Fourier transform* renders an angle/intensity pattern, i.e. a light field causing the projected image. With the small angles involved, an LCOS display of 13 μm pixel size (CRLO Displays Ltd., [33]) is already adequate here.

The display works with a special processor chip able to generate the interference patterns in real time. The special algorithms are the most important innovation in this case.
Practical implementations are meanwhile including 3 display chips for full color reproduction.

This technique so far can be expected to work for a deflection angle of about 10 degrees total, already enough for a projector if we add some optics. F-LCOS pixels could be made even smaller, enabling larger angles as well. The structural size of the driver patterns itself is not the limit, as silicon structures can meanwhile be manufactured way below 0.1 μm.

Contact lens displays ?

The quest for the most minimized near-eye display hardware already brought up some speculations about building displays into contact lenses. Even research projects have been started in this direction, sponsored by defense funds.

Given the many problems contact lenses already have in everyday applications however, it is hardly conceivable how this could work in the battlefield. First, they aren't supposed to be worn more than 12 hours for various reasons. Then, even though you may even swim with contacts, even with open eyes at least in freshwater, this is delicate as long as the contact lens is still in tear liquid, as a sudden splash could then wash them out.

If you drink too little, you dehydrate and the contacts may simply fall out of your eyes. Imagine a soldier fumbling around with liquid trying to clean and reinsert his contact lens. Dust and sand a also create problems. Dirt in the eye is much more difficult to get rid of if contacts are involved.

Apart from this, it is not only a technical but also a major physical problem to design anything that generates an image in the eye while sitting right on the pupil.

This doesn't seem to bother some people, there is even a patent from 1995 about a contact lens display (US5682210, [96]), that carefully avoids even the slightest remark about how to form an image with this device. Imagine someone in 1700 A.D., applying for a patent for a car, without even mentioning that it would need a motor...

Meanwhile, actual 'contact lenses' with some electronics inside have been reported. The wording of the newsflash („with micro scale components that automatically bond to predetermined receptor sites") however implies that his is rather a misunderstanding about what is actually a retinal implant [97],[98].

The LED array contained in it could never form an image if it was really a contact lens..

Nevertheless, let's have a hopefully more reasonable look at the options we have.

The most straightforward approach would be sort of a display, with many little light sources. But in order or form an image on the retina, the light has to come in approximately parallel, as it gets focused by the eye's lens. Small light sources however do not emit anything parallel. Any single source, the smaller it gets, is emitting a more or less spherical wave. This way we wouldn't get anything like a picture inside the eye, or at best it would just be a very blurred agglomerate of a few pixels.

Remember: anything being able to focus a light beam sufficiently as to form a crisp pixel has to be 1...2mm in diameter, at least. 2mm would be very crisp (1 arcmin of resolution) but probably not so useful as the pupil may become as small as 1mm in sunlight and then this would be wasted effort.

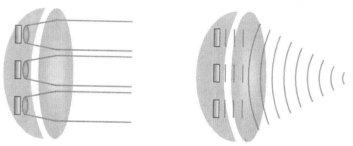

Nonsense (left) and SciFi approach (right)

The result would be a lot different, if all light sources were in phase. Then they could all together form a beam that could create an image by scanning (with the light sources working as a so called phased array, known from radar or satellite antennas), or they could form a light field that would create a complete pro-jected image at once.

Just using many tiny laser diodes however, would not deliver any global phase relation. What we need would be a single laser light source, whose light is then modulated by many single elements distributed right in front of the pupil.

For a first try we could think about forming a Fourier hologram, only delivering images appearing at infinite, but affordable to calculate. Modifying this for different image distances would still be possible with limited effort, and if we would implement a dynamic focusing with this approach, it could work just like in the 'classical' vision simulator, adapting to the actual items the user looks at. So full fledged holograms, possible but computing intensive, would not be necessary in any case.

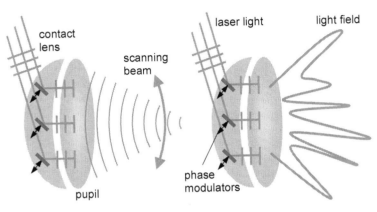

Moving mirror phased array scanner (left) and Fourier Hologram (right) using a single coherent light source

The modulation we would want is phase modulation, which could for example be accomplished by liquid crystals changing their refractive index according to voltage as in some existing LCOS displays, or by movable micro mirrors modulating the length of the optical path.

Apart from the difficulties of miniaturizing something like this far enough to fit into a thin and hopefully still flexible contact lens, the modulating elements would also affect direct sight, which is of course not intended.

One way of retrieving direct sight is inserting large gaps between the light forming elements. This may work quite acceptable, even if some moiré effects could occur within the projected image.

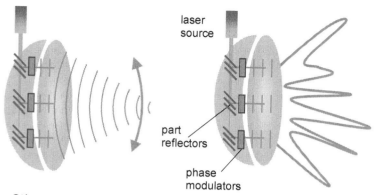

laser
source

part
reflectors

phase
modulators

Other varieties, with partial reflecting or holographic mirror
elements and phase modulator cells, e.g. LCD

Shaping of light is not the only challenge with a contact lens
display. A major problem is providing energy. Nobody would
want a wire going to the lens.

One alternative would be solar cells, powered by environmental
light or by infrared emitters close to the eye, or by an external
laser source that could concurrently deliver the in-phase-
illumination for our image forming elements.

Even with the latter approaches, we would still need some frame,
helmet, or glasses construction to hold the energy source. It may
be questioned where the advantage against 'classical' display
glasses would then really be.

The external laser source variant somehow recalls the wig display joke at page 166. These display variants aren't confined to
contact lenses anyway, they could also be integrated into glasses.

The problems don't end here: We also have to provide signal
processing for the display, and this can be quite heavy (pun
intended). Providing a scanned beam would be rather simple and
would also have the known advantage of scanners, being able to
follow the eye motion without delay. The other method, creating
a full parallel light field, would need a lot more computing power,
even though we could mostly limit this to creating a Fourier
hologram.

It's obvious that for any foreseeable future, most of the signal processing would have to occur outside the lens.

The next point is signal transmission: the display has to be provided with an image of whatsoever kind. This could be modulated onto the energy transmission for example, hence on light, which would deliver the best signal bandwidth anyway.

Still then we need eye trackers to know where the lens bearer looks at. In theory, microscopic cameras inside the contact lens could do this, by looking just where the eye looks, and they could also concurrently deliver orientational data. Nevertheless it would have to be decided which signal processing should or could occur inside the lens, or which should be done outside. Finally, a contact lens could rotate, or be displaced a little, so its position against the iris would have to be known, detectable perhaps by tiny cameras or light sensors inside the lens border, looking towards the retina...

By now it's getting pretty obvious that for a realistic approach, a lot of components and processing would still have to remain outside the contact lens, hence the question about realistically conceivable advantages of this approach over display glasses remains wide open.

Completely missing here is the necessary mask display, currently still requiring glasses in any variety.

Which doesn't exclude that this could lead to something useful in the future, and trying to develop the apparently impossible may always lead to some useful results unforeseen.

In a more remote future, we might well be able to build a volume hologram display that could be fully modulated in three dimensions, perhaps consisting of transparent electrode layers with liquid crystal fluid in between, perhaps offering the possibility of regrouping light beams and forming virtual images right out of the incoming light. This would also eliminate the need for a mask display. We have to take into consideration however, that environmental light is not coherent and not monochromatic at all. We know holograms forming 3D color images just under the illumination of a halogen lamp, but they still depend on a small light source and still do exhibit some blur.

In principle, the regrouping of light beams necessary to form a new virtual image from incoming light of another, is however conceivable. If HOE's can split beams, they can also merge them. The problem is, ghost images will also arise, resulting in both false images and loss of efficiency. More promising could be an approach that first reflects certain beams, constituting a mask display, and then forms new image parts from an additional light source.

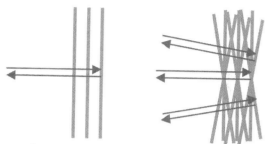

Holographic mirror structure (left), several overlayed (right)

Reflecting a certain light beam of a certain color and direction is simply done with some straight layers of different refraction index, perpendicular to the beam. We could overlay many such structures, one for each direction, into a complete HOE structure. With the very high directional selectivity we need, these elements would also exhibit an extreme color selectivity. We would have to stack many of them, one for each wavelength, to complete the job. And all of this would have to be a dynamic three dimensional structure of several thousand pixels in each direction.

We also have to consider that such a display, in order to modulate all of the incoming light, would have to be as large as the pupil can get, hence up to 9mm in extreme cases (a diaphragm could be used to limit this a bit, of course, but how much degrading of natural sight would we want to accept?).

Hard to say which will be 'easier' to accomplish: this one, or a futuristic neural interface together with a full fledged brain chip...

About eyetaps

Just for completeness, let's have a look at a display variety that replaces the entire sight by artificial images from cameras. This is not what I think to be acceptable, but it's the currently most frequent approach to fully integrated virtual objects. This approach does not use (or need) a mask display, obviously. Its other disadvantages are however severe.

An eyetap is defined as a visual interface that intercepts the optical path to the eye, places a camera in the altered lightpath instead, and synthesizes the very same visual impression from a display, where also additional (virtual) image elements can be inserted.

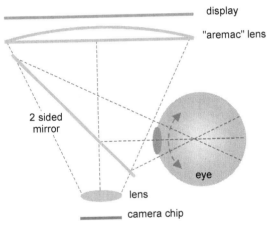

The classical eyetap assembly uses a 'beam splitter' (actually rather a 2-sided mirror) that delivers to a camera the same perspective that the eye would get. Indeed this isn't really true already, as the eye will always move to center in on the point of interest while a camera stays static.

The other part of the assembly should reproduce exactly the same rays that the camera has stolen away, by a display that obviously needs a concentrating lens to produce this reverse light bundle. The assembly is called an 'aremac' (camera spelled backwards).

It's obvious that the example shown here collides with anatomy, as there is no sufficient space for the 'aremac'. Actually working designs of this type can only deliver a much smaller viewing angle.

A wide angle eyetap attempt

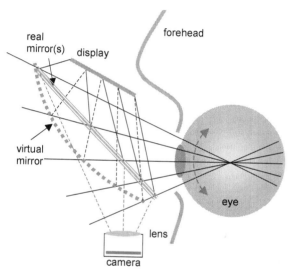

A design study for an advanced eyetap. The real mirror plate is 100% reflective on the outside and carries an holographic mirror on the eye side. The outside mirror reflects all incoming light, and the camera gets the same perspective the eye would have.

The holographic mirror is curved and focuses the display image towards the eye.

Like any eyetap, this assembly has the apparent advantage that it needs no mask display. This here also has a larger viewing angle than other constructions. Nevertheless, it is not only as undesirable for everyday use as any indirect viewing device, it also looks quite awful because of the large flat mirrors and the cameras hanging from them.

Apart from the problems of specific optical designs and the capabilities of current cameras and displays, the eyetap idea has several other difficulties as well:

1) We need to move our eyes to see sharp in more than one direction. Therefore we can't just replace the eye with a camera and expect to get an identical optical behavior.

2) Replacing the entire view with an artificial one requires to reproduce a viewing angle of >180 degrees. The only alternative would be to have a display that leaves the outer skirts of our field of view open for direct vision. This requires 100% contrast and brightness identity of the display and the natural picture, a lot more difficult than with our approach.

Another approach could be, bringing some optics before the eye to create an intermediate crispness plane, where either a transparent-, or a mirror-, or a combined display could be placed. In case of a mirror display, a DMD could, for example, switch between the original picture and a projection of virtual objects.

If this was possible, it would have the advantage that (almost) no active elements are in the way of natural sight, but still the optics we would need are hardly conceivable at all, because they should deliver 180 degrees field of view (or at least seamlessly insert into the natural viewing range), shouldn't distort the picture and also shouldn't be heavy. Nothing like this is in sight.

Enough reasons to concentrate on the entirely different approach of just adding pictures to natural sight.

In order to insert objects without appearing transparent, this obviously requires a *mask display*, also not an entirely simple way, but one that's likely to work.

The 'unsharp' mask display

In the introduction we have already seen that a mask close to the eye will work, even though it can't be sharp. Maybe holographic technology could even lead to something better, but the simple black mask approach is already good enough, the example pictures in the introduction weren't exaggerated at all, and as you can simply test with a black piece of cardboard anytime, the boarder around a masked object is far smaller than anticipated. Let's try to calculate this, and find out why.

First, we need to know where the boarder actually comes from. Edge diffraction would have an effect in an area beneath the mask that is in the order of a few wavelengths at most, hence less than 10 μm. Consider a mask 3 cm before the eye, covering an object 3 m away. The diffraction area, projected to the distant object, would then be 1mm wide, hard to perceive indeed. So border diffraction should be negligible in typical cases.

Most of the edge border just results from the size of the pupil. The mask covers an object entirely, if its shape is big enough to cover it from any point on the pupil. It covers its border just partially, if parts of the pupil area can still see around the mask border.

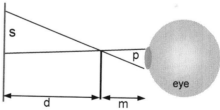

The pupil diameter (usually 2-3 mm) can be thought of as being projected onto objects, turning the pupil diameter p into a maximum edge shadow width s (left). The relation obviously is $s=pd/m$. The mask display must cover the object shape plus pupil diameter projected to the mask (right).

The coverage function is therefore just a simple integral over the pupil area, from one side to the projected mask edge line.

But we are not yet ready here: our eye has by no means a linear perception of brightness. In order to include this, we proceed from the fact that a gray card as photographers use for calibration purposes, has an actual reflection factor of only 20% but is perceived as 50% gray.

This leads to a logarithmic brightness perception law of the form:

perceived brightness $\quad B_p = 1 - A^{\ln 2 / \ln 5}$ $\qquad$ (A=attenuation)

This taken into account, we get the following diagram, showing the calculated and the perceived background shadowing around an object in terms of maximum shadow width.

Mask Display Edge Occlusion

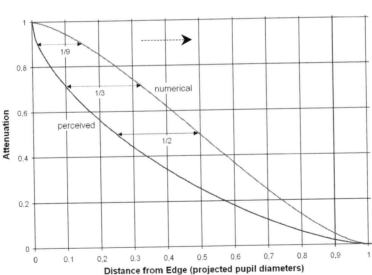

The difference is really huge: at 80% occlusion, the perceived mask shadow is 5 times smaller than the numerical one. At 50% occlusion it is still 2 times smaller.

Examples:

- pupil 1.5mm, mask distance 30 mm, object distance 30 cm (e.g. a PC screen), mask shadow 25% of 15 mm or just less than 4 mm.
- Same pupil and mask, object distance 3m (virtual TV), mask shadow for 50% occlusion 40 mm, for 80%= 8mm.

Close to the object, the perceived background light shining through the mask shadow rises extremely fast. This explains why the simple cardboard experiment reveals a very sudden and crisp, 100% coverage as soon as we arrive at a certain point, the point where the pupil is covered entirely.

Quite obviously, our 'unsharp' mask display works way better than one would first anticipate.

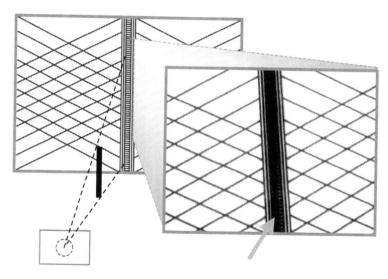

The above picture shows a test pattern (left) and and enlargement of a real experiment masking the central area with a toothpick sized black stripe. Even though this picture suffers from the somewhat makeshift character of the experiment, it shows how easy it is to mask even small objects and areas quite selectively.

Technologies for the mask display

In the introduction we have already seen that a mask close to the eye will work, even though it can't be sharp. The bad news is that there isn't yet an ideal candidate for the mask display.

It is mandatory that such a display could switch from black to transparent (not opaque). It may be quite desirable that the mask display could be built in a concave shape. Otherwise it could be suboptimal or perhaps look bad in front of a concave mirror.

There is no need for a very high resolution, as this display will always be seen unsharp, but we have just seen that the mask is still much crisper than we would anticipate from simple calculus, so we still need a resolution that can only be achieved with active matrix driven displays. Which is a challenge, as the, pixels should be completely adjacent to each other, being able to cover an area entirely, but not leaving a non transparent grid when not activated. Hence we need a transparent driver circuit, something yet available but only since very recently.

Last but not least, the mask display should be light and rugged, e.g. best built from plastic.

LCDs could do it, but have a significant light loss due to polarization filters:

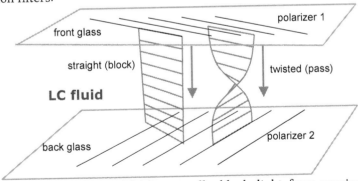

Two polarizer filters (1),(2), normally block light from passing. Depending on the voltage applied between the two glass surfaces carrying a transparent metallization, the LC fluid can turn the polarization of passing light, making the device transparent again.

Obviously, an LCD panel always absorbs at least half of the light. Nevertheless, it would not look worse than some fairly weak sunglasses (you may check this with one of those fancy desktop watches that seem to consist of nothing but a free standing glass plate, and these aren't even optimal). It could even be much better if one could make a polarizer that turns everything to one direction instead of just absorbing one part.

By the way, there is a patent [13] that deals with all kinds of LCD shutters and may be interesting to read, but there is no word about using them as a mask to cover up or release selected image areas.

LCDs are not easily manufactured other than planar. Yet in principle, an LCD shutter could be built with plastic glass, if spacers between cells keep cell thickness constant or if we use domes, which are more rigid. Life expectance would be a problem with this, because of vapor diffusion through the plastic. We would also need a transparent structure to drive the LC fluid. Conductive metal layers, thin enough to be transparent, can already be evaporated on plastic. Passive matrix drivers however will hardly be able to deliver enough resolution.

Active driver structures would provide more resolution and speed, but first transparent semiconductor circuits have been demonstrated just very recently, with vacuum deployed layers based on tin- or zinc oxide, and also with organic materials (plastic) in context with OLED displays. One interesting fact is that Very small additions of carbon nanotube dust as in industrial production already, can make polymers conductive and also allow for conductive lacquer layers with almost perfect transparency.

If the driver structures were flexible, the display could be manufactured in a planar process and blown to the spherical shape later on. It should also be possible to vacuum deploy driver structures onto curved substrates directly.

Technologies based all on plastic, like polymer displays, are another option for a mask display. Electrochromic polymers that switch between transparent and selective color band absorption, may be a candidate. There are red and green transparent colors currently available (each generated by absorbing the rest of the spectrum). Current research has led to a green variety that has 2 absorption bands [7] (3 layers could even allow subtractive full color mixing). For our purpose, it could still be necessary to use two absorber layers to cover the entire spectrum, and transmissivity is not yet ideal. Switching speed is good. A prevalent problem is durability.

Dyed Guest Host displays and similar technologies work with microscopic disks diluted in liquid crystal fluid for example, that can be tilted by electric fields.

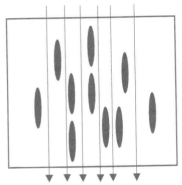 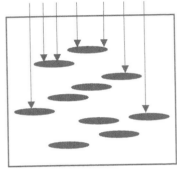

Oriented parallel to the light path they hardly influence it, while perpendicular they form a 'solid' wall. It could be an ideal mask display, but contrast is only about 1:5 with current samples [33].

We could of course speculate about many other technologies:
Nano particles smaller than light wavelength, could perhaps be caused to agglomerate into larger particles to absorb light.

Electrowetting displays with dark drops could also be considered but aren't really likely to work here.
The solution could as well come from techniques similar to phototropic glasses. These use silver halides that provide silver particles when lighted, just resembling a photographic film. We need something fast and electrically operated, but maybe this principle could lead us somewhere.

Another approach could originate from display principles usually employed for electronic paper. Some chemicals, certain liquid crystals or polymers for example, change their refraction index if voltage is applied [101]. If patches of these materials are embedded in others, that for one state have the same refraction index, the entire volume is either homogenous and lets light pass unaffected, or light rays are repeatedly refracted and reflected, letting the entire material appear blurry or opaque, depending on the size of the patches.

From the incident side the material gets to look brighter, from the other side it gets darker, even maybe very dark if the material has a certain basic attenuation, that increases when the light has to travel further. Hence while the currently usual application is electronic paper, this principle may also be useful for a mask display.

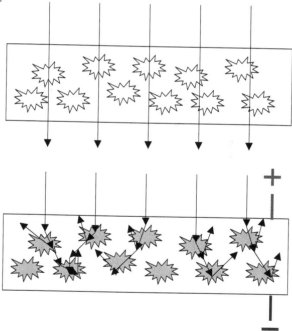

Principle of an 'electronic paper' variety

Power consumption

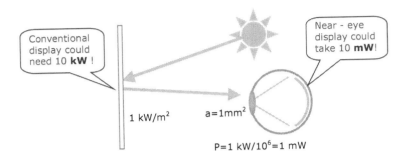

Viewing a totally white scene in bright sunlight, only 1 mW of the light enters the eye. Practical viewing situations require much less energy.

Dynamically adaptive displays can guide almost 100% of light into the pupil. Piezo electric motors for example, enabling this in a perfect manner, have efficiencies up to 30% and would only have to move micrograms in this application.

Hence, near eye displays need very little energy for illumination. Mask displays, sound add-ons etc. will only need a few milliwatts.

The *light power* we need follows straightforwardly from the fact that bright sunlight has about 1 kW/m^2 and that our pupil has less than 2mm of diameter in this situation, hence an area of approx. 1mm^2. In an evenly illuminated scene, this obviously casts about 1mW of light power into the eye.

The brightness with this is up to 100000 lux. Given the fact that virtual objects cover only part of the viewing area, we need between 0.05mW and 0,5mW of actual light power entering the eye. In bright sunlight, that is.

Trying to do this with a large flat panel screen, even if we succeeded, we would need *kilowatts*. Indoors, we have 100 or 1000 times lower brightness, reducing power requirements a lot.

The ratio between electrical power and light output can vary between 5 and 30%, and depending on display type, between 10 and >50% of the light would then actually enter the eye. Which gives a wide variation of possible results.

We could therefore conclude that something around 1mW average *electrical* power would be sufficient for the display, even in relatively bright environments.

As we are obviously dealing with portable units, power requirements should be as low as possible.

The display is not the only energy consumer in the vision simulator, but it's a good point to start at.

In case of the DMD version we have seen, it's already obvious that we only need to give the LED illuminator a certain beam focusing, in order to concentrate most of its light on the DMD and thus towards the eye.

The optics always have to be focused in a way that parallel rays at the eye would converge at the display, hence parallel rays at the display (from a directed light source) would as well converge at the eye.

The same will apply to any optical assembly with a small exit pupil. A large part of all light produced will enter the eye in these cases. This also applies for Holographic or light field displays that could also concentrate light energy to the eye in a very flexible way.

With laser displays, effectiveness can even be up to 100% starting from the light output of the laser diodes. The effectiveness of these diodes themselves is not ideal, but still acceptable.

The sound system is really modest. Good button headphones can produce a tremendously loud sound just out of some mW (milliwatts) of electrical input.

In Summary, at some point in the future we may see a glasses assembly with an average power consumption of about 10 mW.

In comparison: there are optical glasses that weigh 100g with their large normal glass lenses and that people still wear.

An accumulator for a mobile phone can be as light as 10g and run the device for days. We could integrate 2 of these (perhaps in the handles for better balance), and the entire glasses could weigh less than 50g even today.

Hence, display glasses without power cable will emerge far earlier than one would first guess.

When very low power versions finally arrive, even tiny solar cells on top of the glasses could be sufficient in many cases.

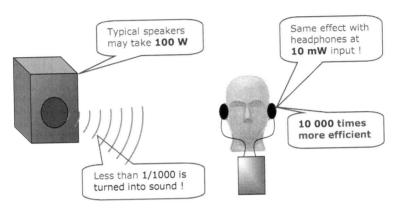

Another power drain will result from communications, if we use wireless. As the distance to span would only be about 50 cm, a radio frequency output in the range of some milliwatts should be sufficient, even though we need so much bandwidth.

The computing power we need is much more critical. It is obvious that we have to externalize most of it. Even then we still need a communication link with the computing device that can carry several TV channels, 2 channels in high resolution.

We could use some compression in order to save bandwidth, but that needs more power, which could only be kept in an acceptable range maybe, if we use dedicated chips for compression and decompression (note that CRL Opto announced to develop F-LCOS displays with integrated MPEG decompression, see [33]).

We may conclude that of the power consumption of near eye displays will go into signal processing.

Dynamic image generation

Obviously we cannot realistically expect anybody to accept a device that is somehow 'fixed' to the head, like those gruesome makeshift VR displays that dominated the early days.

As an acceptable device cannot stick to the head more than some ordinary glasses, we have to detect the position of the glasses as well as the viewing direction and predistort pictures accordingly. This all adds to the basic requirement to generate dynamic 3D perspectives according to head position.

Head position can be detected by (without claim of completeness)
- Cameras registering real objects and their relative distance and angle to calculate their own position
- Optical flow sensors, detecting average motion in the picture of a fast scene camera to detect angle changes
- Tilt sensors using gravity to determine the vertical
- Acceleration sensors and rotation sensors, exploiting inertia
- Magnetic compass sensor
- GPS (Global Positioning System) and local varieties

Tilt, acceleration and optical flow sensors are fast and have high resolution. They are necessary to do any image compensations precisely and in real time. They are also necessary to do predictive position calculation, because image generation and usually the display as well, will have a delay of at least 1 frame (e.g. 20ms), which would result in a significant displacement with fast movements.

Displays writing the image pixel by pixel, like CRT and (laser) scanners, offer the possibility at least to change their beam deflection in real time, hence they could react to acceleration sensor input directly, within microseconds. This would allow for a really rock stable image impression. Other displays like LCD build up an entire picture at a time and often have slow switching times. It's inevitable that with these displays, fast movements could result in sort of a stroboscope effects. A fast frame rate (75 Hz or more, like with computer monitors) can help to avoid this.

With a very small display and a huge enlargement factor of the optics, we could end up with a small exit pupil, that would cause the image to vanish if the eye moves sideways. Compensating for this would require to shift the entire display.

Moving the display to provide exact focus just for the image part currently being looked at, is another important ability as it provides for a realistic distance impression as well as it lowers the requirements for optical precision.

As it is absolutely mandatory to create a steady optical impression, any mechanical or electronic movements have to be accompanied by an electronic image pre-compensation.

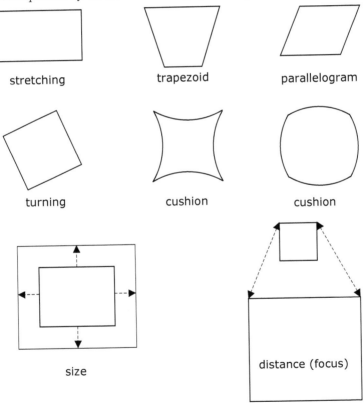

stretching   trapezoid   parallelogram

turning   cushion   cushion

size   distance (focus)

Types of distortion pre-compensation in the main display

Position and scene identification

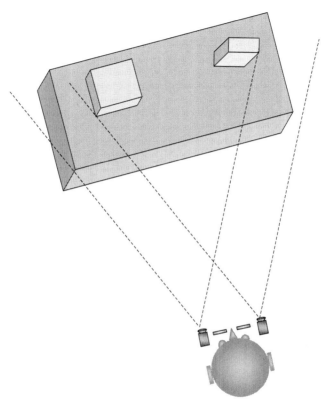

Apart from GPS and acceleration sensors that are also considered here, the 'right' way to built a position sensor for a universal augmented reality display – what I here call vision simulator – is to use cameras that recognize the environment and calculate their own position from the relative perspective. It is the best approach because it works like our own visual orientation.

This method has some difficulties that we will now have a look at. Note that in [22], advances in this area have been reported, and there is another thesis just finished [41].

Position camera assemblies

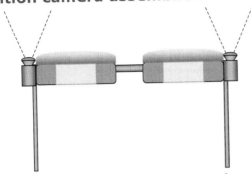

Side cameras have a larger stereo basis, maybe an advantage, but more deviation from the user's own perspective, and bad perspective matching if used for stereo camera recordings or teleworking.

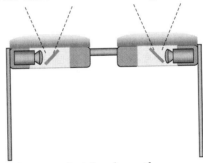

Smaller cameras could be moved right above the eyes, or mirrors could be used to bring the camera lens locations as close to the eye centers as possible, achieving a closely similar perspective. Everything including displays, if small enough, could just be integrated in the upper section of the glasses. With laser projection displays, the cameras could even be positioned more freely.

We could also use holographic or dichroic mirrors or holographic prisms or lenses to steal away some light from the direct path to the eye and get a camera picture from the very own perspective of the user's eye. This would not work well in dark environments though, and the parallactic corrections we need with the simpler assemblies are not really a reason to accept these and other difficulties.

Ignorance required:
Solving the orientation puzzle

Let us first state that it is absolutely unnecessary for the system to know what it sees, not even to separate objects (it does not need to know that some edges define a desk, or a chair, or a sideboard). We do require nothing but to re-recognize edge structures later on.

This already is not so easy, as these structures look differently from each perspective. So the biggest challenge for our task is to develop a 3D structural search and recognition algorithm that is ignorant to perspective related variance of this structural data.

Could we achieve this, the comparison of the 3D variations (perspectives) would also yield very accurate position information about the viewer, enabling us to correctly restore any virtual objects that were previously defined in a certain place.

The system would know to have seen this room or scenery before, could also determine its exact position relative to it now, and could correctly display any virtual additions desired.

I will now outline some possible data structures and algorithms for visual position sensing in arbitrary scenes.

As said before, one difficulty can be avoided: we will never need to isolate real objects (like chairs, cars, etc..), not even to mention assigning to them any meaning, even not to find directly adjacent detail, but it is still not simple, because in practice, there are many influences obstructing and distorting image detail.

What we first have to achieve is simply to be able to compare a *detail* that we have seen with a *detail* that we see now, then their geometrical relations with other *details*, and this in the fastest way possible.

It's obvious and always supposed in the following contemplations that in practice we will deal with many subsequent pictures from varying perspectives that allow to assemble an omnidirectional view and even to link objects in different directions or rooms.

Perspective invariant structural identification

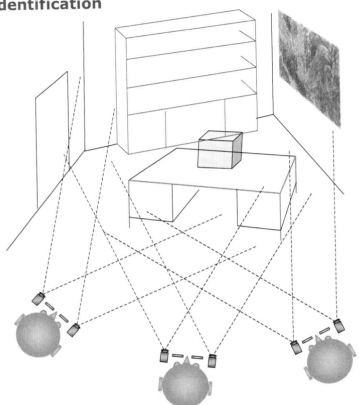

This picture shows several vision simulator users, viewing the same simple office scenario from different perspectives. (Also depicted is a virtual object on the desk, how this is dealt with we will discuss later). Real environments, like this office (concededly one of the simpler cases) exhibit some basic structural data that can be picked up by the stereo cameras of a vision simulator.

Easy to detect are edges of solid 3D objects, because these can be separated by stereo cross correlation, and the data gathered is already 3D. We also see an image at the wall; we will have to define special treatments for its 'surface patterns'.

Basic examples of structural data variations

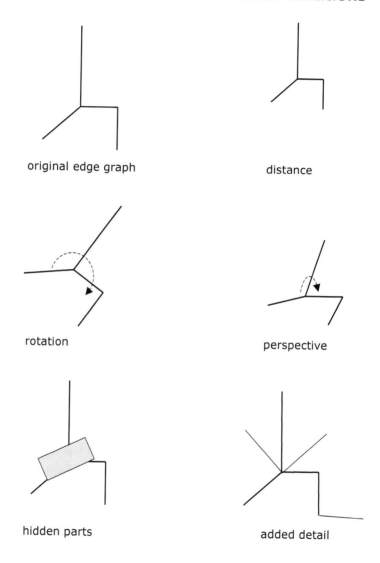

original edge graph

distance

rotation

perspective

hidden parts

added detail

The approach shown here is that of normalization : If we could define some rules that certain structure shall always be stored in a certain orientation and in their original size, we would later on be able to search for them in our database with a good chance of success.

Obviously, a single angle, tripod or rectangle (to name some basic elements), is absolutely insufficient for a recognition. Yet we could store more complex structures starting from the detail, defining adjacent edges, angles, surfaces in a tree like data structure.

This could look as follows:

- Use simple cross correlation to match lines and edges between the images of the stereo cameras.
- Use this data together with gravity sensors to bring everything to the vertical and to its actual size.
- Use some heuristic algorithm to determine color and brightness in order to normalize these values for object surfaces seen.
- Store the geometrical relation between basic details, linked with the details themselves, so that they form a mesh that could define a certain scene just starting from some arbitrary detail without having to care for any other structures between them. This may be quite similar to our own way of orientation: We remember some details very accurate, but many others not at all.

The real size of detail objects ('atoms') can be obtained by simple calculations using stereo perspective. Orientation needs standards that have to be defined, for example a flat object will obviously be stored in a normal perspective just up front. If we store every detail object this way, and its orientational data relative to the real world and to virtual objects separately, we only need to apply the same normalization (that is, simple coordinate transformation) to any detail we want to compare to the database later on.

A picture at a wall (as a simple example) can be identified as a single and simple detail object and its real size and orientation can be obtained from the stereo vision by correlation and triangulation. The image can then be normalized to its real size and normal view. Storing images in order to compare them, could be done by storing coefficients of a discrete cosine transform, like with JPEG encoding, as one of the possible methods. Coefficients could be compared hierarchically from coarse to fine, enabling a search among thousands of pictures without much effort.

Surfaces of any rectangular objects are fully identical to images, which allows for a generalization of the approach. In case of irregular objects, e.g., a plant or a tree, one approach would be to store them just like pictures, from different sides (always keep in mind that we are really considering apparently adjoint structures, rather than really distinct real world objects). What we always need is a reproducible algorithm to define the directions. If we don't want to store their entire structure, we could store perpendicular views, for example. If there are straight sides, it pays to normalize relative to the most prevalent features.

We will always have to store the angles for the real orientation towards a standard (usually North), in order to bring this data together with orientation coordinates. In a human made environment, we will usually be able to find some simple structures for orientation, and this may already suffice for many applications.

Nevertheless, even orientation in very irregular environments (outdoors, wilderness) has recently been approached in [22]. It would generally be very helpful – or even required – for the methods discussed, to have some additional position sensors in the vision simulator, at least for perpendicularity and also for North direction. Even in simple and inexpensive varieties, a GPS would be a very natural extension. What could also be envisioned are local setups of time stamped transmitters, that could do for a building for example, what GPS is doing for the entire planet. We could also send signals from the vision glasses and account for their arrival times at different receivers in order to provide position information. These local varieties could require less power or smaller antennas that real GPS, would also be more accurate and have less reception problems, so they could really be an alternative for local applications.

Searching structural graph isomorphisms (remembering locations)

As any scene has many elementary details, we will have to store the same scene from many starting points and use interlinked pointers to keep the data structure from becoming too redundant. Developing the best data structure is one of the main challenges we are facing here. This is very different from the classical image recognition approach, that tries to find separate real world objects. Although we also start from elementary structures, we do not care for real objects at all. What we care for is meaningless structure. A structure can consist of a square at one wall, a corner at the other and a circle that's really part of a lamp, for example, these linked by pointers noting their relation and distance values noting their relative position. It's absolutely irrelevant if these details belong physically or logically together in any way. Anything we care for is geometry, and maybe the pattern or color in a basic circle, triangle or square, or directly adjacent to a point, line or corner.

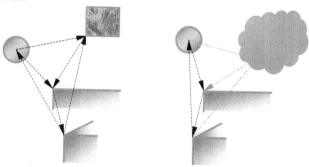

To the left, several primitives ('atoms') of a scene have been normalized and linked with pointers. To the right, although one of the primitives is occluded, the others together with their relating distances and orientation coefficients etc. (not shown) provide good confidence that we are indeed dealing with the same scene

If later on a first scan for a certain detail remembered delivers a million hits (not much for a current computer), we can subsequently exclude all false matches by looking at linked detail. This will rapidly close in on matches that are likely. Some more 'intelligent' tests could also be added, to get to a firm conclusion.

The original relations between our 'atoms' are vectors in 3D space. If we would try to actually compare two vector graphs we would end up with the same problem we already had with the 'atoms', but here it's not done with the normalization approach, as this would only work if we could implement it according to some precise global reference.

We don't however need to bother with this at all, we simply use the length of the vectors instead. Distances alone can define a structure, also in 3D, but not its orientation. So we have a simple way to match 3D structures by just matching distances, and this is inherently indifferent against rotation! Mirror symmetric structures aren't distinguished this way, but that's negligible.

The entire process again seems to resemble our own methods of orientation: it is obvious that we use heuristic selections of detail, rather than complete data sets, to recognize things and locations. Just look at a scene for some seconds and then try to remember any detail. Most probably, you won't even remember 10% of anything that could be relevant. Even in spite of this, you may still be able to recognize the picture many years after.

What we will have to deal with as well, image detail could be moved or covered by other objects. Multiple pointer paths in the data structure ensure that if any object is missing, the others are still interlinked around it. We need a heuristic approach to determine if the scene is still the same, despite of changes.

The approach in conclusion works like this:

- Identify a simple detail (corner, rectangle, circle etc...)
- Normalize the detail, including its surface pattern, to upright, facing, actual size, using position, direction sensors and stereo view. Normalize illumination.
- Store normalized data (patterns as coefficients of discrete cosine transforms e.g.) and its original position data (from comparisons, GPS data etc.). If there are several normal views possible, store them all.
- Link detail objects by pointers and relative position data (vectors) to represent entire scenes. There is no need to have a complete set of all details of a scene, nor even any directly adjacent detail.
- We only have to store data from locations where we install virtual devices. This leads to an extreme reduction in storage capacity.

For later orientation, do this:

- Identify and normalize details as stated above.
- Search database for single details
- Follow links to see if related details are stored
- See if enough related details are in appropriate distance in actual scene. Continue search until a sufficiently large structure is found.
- Use the stored and the perceived distances and angles to determine own position.
- If available, simplify the process with GPS or other data.

A global orientation database *

With an efficient object cataloging and search algorithm, a global object database may be possible, accessible by the web, offering the opportunity to re-recognize even objects and scenes that have never been stored locally.

We all know that we are able to instantly remember places where we had been even only once.

A vision simulator could even identify locations where it had never been before, just by matching its actual visual data with a global database. This would somehow make the GPS superfluous, or add to its functionality. At least, differential GPS would not be necessary anymore, and we would be able to measure location to an inch or better.

The approach is especially interesting as GPS very often has reception problems, especially within buildings.

To achieve this, we would require a much faster database search capability than with our basic approach, where we only need to know places where virtual devices were installed.

Actual searches would always have to be carried out by the remote database server, obviously.

An approach towards utilizing image data as an aid for orientation has also been described in [3]. There, image data was just stored by a web connection, to be reviewed by human beings later on, in order to re-identify locations. Because of the perspective problem, this does not yield an appropriate algorithm for machine based orientation.

The current difficulties in image processing are mainly speed and recognition problems that could perhaps be alleviated by hardware that emulates structures of the human brain [12].

Up to the publication of this 3rd book edition, several advances in optical orientation could be noticed. For example, a cell phone based orientation approach a bit resembling the 'atoms' principle has been implemented [113].

---

*The question mark behind the headline has been removed since the last edition. Meanwhile, there is research and companies trying to implement similar features already, e.g. [108].

Manual interaction – mastering virtual keys

Cameras attached to a display could not only give a direct means of virtual/real scene fitting. They might also be utilized to monitor the user's hand movements and gestures, allowing direct interaction with virtual objects, such as pressing imaginary keys, moving objects or defining new objects out of virtual menus projected into space. As people can hardly ever be convinced to always wear datagloves, this is a fairly important issue. Tactile feedback is not possible with this approach, but is also not necessary in most cases. A key pressing animation or a beep is usually sufficient.

Many research projects have already tried to implement gesture recognition. Common to all is the relatively high difficulty to recognize the hand and interpret the commands in complex environments. It has also been tried to recognize hand actions towards real or projected keyboards.

Much easier is the approach with Virtual Keys:

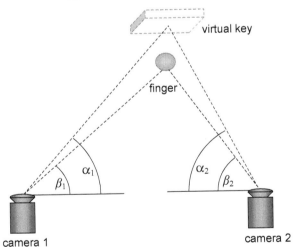

Consider we use the glasses assembly discussed above. A virtual key is displayed in the vision simulator. The position of the key is given by the relative angles α_1 and α_2. If the user tries to operate this key, a finger must appear at approx. some slightly smaller angles β_1 and β_2 in each of the stereo cameras. It must then stay there for a short moment and move towards the virtual button, increasing β_1 and β_2 to about α_1 and α_2.

With a simple correlation operation, a recognition of flesh tones and perhaps a simple shape recognition (finger shape), we can easily determine if something relevant happens.

When trying to press the key, the user must move his finger towards it. The x,y coordinates where it would appear in the stereo camera pictures (close before the key) are also known.

The principle advantage here lies in the fact that we only watch one certain point of interest, if a thing like a finger appears in the camera picture. Hence, the entire complexity of this approach is decisively lower than with the usual hand recognition schemes.

This setup could be further secured against accidental wrong inputs by some checks if this is really the finger of the user, or by requiring some special action like a 'double click' or others to trigger the virtual button. We could further reduce the effort by regarding only keys that the user looks at. This way we could also include keys that are out of direct reach.

The most powerful addition to this interaction scheme would perhaps be eye tracking, as we have already outlined as 'squint-and-touch' in the first chapter. We don not necessarily look at a key when pressing it, but mostly we do. Looking at, can define the area of action in a very precise and unambiguous way, even within a volume, even if we fill an entire three dimensional space with densely packed virtual keys or objects. Eye steering could also increase the selection of actions available in this case, not just clicking but marking, dragging an so on.

We have to keep in mind that we must program the mask display to shape an optical path for any real objects positioned in front of virtual objects. This also applies to the user's hand when he moves it towards a virtual object. This has nothing to do with hand recognition. Any near objects may be sorted out by stereo distance measurement.

A lot of other things concerning virtual keys has been covered in [26].

Cluttered spaces

We have to consider that the position cameras could see fingers touch an object that for the user is hidden behind a more proximate object. This has to be excluded from interaction, so the user couldn't accidentally cause unwanted actions on objects he can't see.

This is even an issue with eye pointing, although it isn't quite likely that a user's eye parallaxes would correlate with a far object that's hidden behind a near one.

Program windows however could sometimes be hidden behind others, so we have to make sure that an eye pointing action is assigned to the right, the proximate one.

Eye switching

A great way of interacting would just simply require *looking* at a key to be pressed. The eye tracker data always allow to determine viewing directions. People also don't usually stare at things without a reason. Normally, our eyes are moving restlessly, fixating different points in quick sequences named 'saccades'.

So if we stare at a virtual key for more than a second, it should certainly mean that we want to operate it.

There are more secure options as well. We could use additional hints like lifting our eyebrows, or, as within a recent, especially remarkable paper, 'half blinking', to unambiguously signal that we are meaning to operate something [104]. Indeed, the research cited showed that simply staring alone is a bit slow and can cause a problem called the 'Midas touch', causing everything we look at to start doing things unintended.

Our very center of view is extremely narrow. Hence it would only depend on the exactness of the eye tracker to discriminate even small distant buttons from each other.

An eye tracker could be self calibrating, by learning from the user apparently looking slightly beneath a virtual object and intelligently interpreting this as alignment errors.

It is therefore possible to start actions with eye pointing alone, or we could use it in conjunction with voice commands, or with pressing a key at the simulator itself. So we could reliably act on keys or icons too far away to be touched.

We could use eye pointing to activate cells in a spreadsheet, to move a cursor, to drag windows, and so on. Together with a mouse or mouse pen, it would become incredibly versatile.

Another application could be with situations where we use our hands otherwise, riding a bicycle, a car or an airplane for example or operating complex machinery; it would be necessary of course to design this in a way avoiding any hazards resulting from occasionally looking away from more important things.

Eye pointing is not entirely new, as you probably know:

- A camcorder model once came with an eye tracker in the viewfinder, and it focused to the part of the picture being looked at.
- An experimental display screen once allowed the user to erase any parts of the image just by looking at them (ingenious nonsense, in a way).
- World famous physicist Stephen Hawking uses an eye pointing device to select words from a computer screen.
- Current commercial products can be found at [52], for example. Military applications have been reported [57], and the new Eurofighter actually has an eye operated head up display.

With vision simulators getting into mainstream use, everybody will be able to use eye pointing for many things that we might not even be aware of right now, and it will really be one of the most attractive features of this technology.

Even the problems with cluttered spaces could be alleviated if we use eye pointing together with active distance selection by squint and/or focus, as we have already learned from the 'ghost objects' section.

Additional components ('Mixed Virtuality')
Virtual writing with a real pen

A special pen with a modulated 'position light' could be used for an easy detection of the user's hand movements by the position sensor cameras. Virtual lines would be drawn when the pen is moved inside the virtual paper plane (this plane would normally better be chosen to fit to a real desktop's surface, or at least to a drawing board, to provide a tactile surface).

Adding a ball to the tip of the pen would allow to write very realistically on any hard surface. The ball could also provide signals about its movements. For example, it could have a surface structure that is detected by sensors, so it could work like an inverted optical mouse.

We could also use a fixed tip with a high resolution optical sensor as in a normal optical or laser mouse. If we add a pressure sensor and transmit its output and the ball movements by wireless link, the pen could also work without being seen by the position cameras at all. It would then behave quite similar to a mouse, its pointer being displayed in the virtual window of an application or on the surface of a virtual object.

The virtual surface to operate on would first have to be 'activated', by a virtual key action, or just by looking at, for example.

Another interesting add-on to the pen would be acceleration sensors. They could be used to carry out ballistic actions towards distant objects, without the difficulty of following hand or finger movements optically. They could as well be used to enhance the camera based detection in the basic 'into the air' writing example above.
There are many other possibilities for 'mixed virtuality', necessitating other dedicated hardware perhaps, that I will here leave to your imagination.

A laser pen

A pen could become an even more universal input device for a vision simulator: it could be extended with a laser pointer in order to provide a means of interaction with remote objects.

Arranging wall screens for example would be easy and accurate with it. Modulated light could be used to visually identify the pen and its beam with the position sensor cameras. Radio or infrared communications could be used to transmit pressing of the keys that the pen should certainly have.

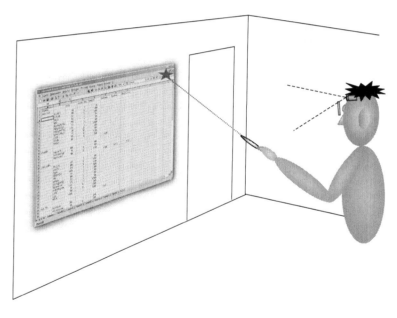

We could use a pen to click on the handle of a virtual window and enter drag mode. Then, by pointing to a wall and activating the laser, the window would automatically be mapped onto the wall. The laser pointer could now be used to manipulate the window from distance. Like a magic wand.

The laser pen works quite accurate and helps the vision simulator by directly showing a light spot at the desired place, revealing its accurate distance even on an unstructured surface.
We could as well use finger pointing of course: this would only require first to recognize the finger, by pressing a virtual key for example (if we want to avoid the difficulties of full gesture recognition). Accuracy is a bit low with this approach.

Nevertheless, the most exciting alternative for remote control still remains Eye pointing, not quite as exact as a laser perhaps, but absolutely elegant.

The ultimate pen

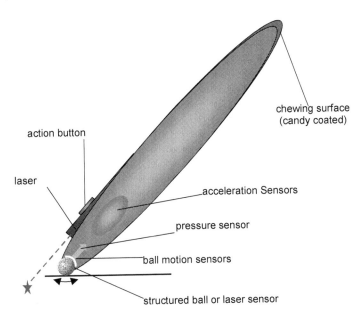

Full featured pen mouse for use with a vision simulator

If we use a laser mouse sensor instead of the structured mouse ball, it's clear that it should not glide on its lens, as this would get scratched and blind. We should use a passive ball or round tip or ring with the sensor beneath or in the middle.

It is quite likely that such a pen could replace mice in almost all mobile applications even right now, as it doesn't even need a straight surface. You could 'write' with it on an armrest, on your leg, into your palm of your hand, just anything.

Maybe we should add an eraser...

Camera mice

Camera based position sensing is one key ingredient of full featured display glasses. A somewhat related technological approach uses a camera as a sensor for a hand held 3D input device [89]. The visual flow sensor of an optical mouse detects motion over a micro structured surface. It can as well be used in connection with a photo lens, to detect the shifting of images recorded, hinting the movements of the device itself. An additional zoom detection could add 3D capabilities.

Strangely enough, not one such product has appeared so far, not even for 2D, even though the sensors of any optical mouse would already do this, a zero development task, and demand would be tremendous because this would make couch computing a cinch (just the next best thing to eye tracking here, for operating a cursor).

Nevertheless, some papers have recently been published, about using visual flow (there usually called optical flow) as an high-speed ingredient for the visual, camera based orientation in augmented reality displays. One problem assessed was concerning multiple reference systems (inside a car and out).

Light Swords

I've mentioned light swords in the fiction part, so you may have asked yourself „how should I grip it?".
Obviously, there has to be some dedicated real handle, for the virtual light sword. This isn't the actual object concerned in a game, but some universal hardware gadget, like a joystick.
It should have position and acceleration sensors and force feedback. The latter needs some thinking about. We could perhaps use some pulse magnets to kick around weights in the handle in order to simulate impacts.

What would work even better, if we use some rotating weights. These would work like gyros, creating a counteracting force to any rotation. This way, that the grip would feel heavy, just as if a real sword was attached to it, and these fast spinning weights could also generate a quite violent kickback if stopped instantly, simulating hits with the virtual sword (we need two counter rotating weights for each axis, only one is shown in the picture).
Some batteries would also be necessary of course, but such a handle shouldn't be too light anyway.

This handle could also be used for virtual guns, and even some decent applications like virtual gulf clubs, baseball bats, tools.
It could as well be attached to a real desktop with a little suction pad and used as a joystick, force feedback included.
Occasional gamers could of course use the 'ultimate pen' instead of a specialized device, for many kinds of games and more serious applications.

The 1st implant...

Have you ever looked into your USB stick? Maybe it has a transparent housing, then you already know that this many-gigabytes-chip is smaller than your fingernail. It can keep data without energy supply, needs very little to write them, and actually the real chip is even smaller than the case around it and does not have to be thicker than a few microns. Every 2 years (any single year recently), the storage capacity of these chips doubles, with hardly any end in sight. Soon we will be able to buy Terabyte chips this small.

What if we use this as the 'harddrive' of our vision simulator, and what if we make it external, a removable device holding all of the sim's data and programs (except for it's basic operating system maybe, that provides the hardware drivers)?

Such a concept has appeared with notebooks, and it could be the future there.

Such a tiny chip would not have to go to our key bundle. It could as well be slipped under the skin, near the sim, and it could be supplied with energy and communicate only by radio waves.

A weird idea at a first glance maybe, wouldn't we become androids this way, couldn't someone pervert this gadget into a surveillance instrument, even an electronic ankle bracelet?

And how could this thing gets its energy, how could it communicate, and wouldn't it be inconvenient anyway?

Lets start with convenience: Silicon chips do only need to be microns thin, and then they become extremely flexible. Something like this could be embedded into some tissue friendly material, it could also for example have a comb like structure instead of a square, being very flexible and able to slip under the skin without disrupting nerves or other structures.

Next, energy and communications could be solved for with technology already thought out for RFID: a little antenna on the chip could be switched on and off by a transistor, making it absorb more or less energy. The device would not need to have any circuit capable of processing the actual radio frequency used. It would just modulate the backscatter from a nearby transmitter. In the course of this, it could also draw energy from there: a simple Schottky diode could rectify the excess RF and supply it to the memory circuit. Schottky diodes are known since decades and can be made of silicon. Hence, even if we use way over ten gigahertz for the RF transmission (which would be of advantage as we would need only very small antennas: a dipole antenna for 24 GHz would be about ¼"), no exotic semiconductor materials would be necessary for our storage chip.

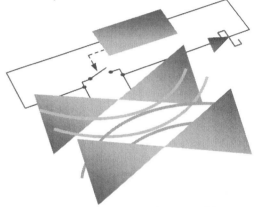

The RF energy could be modulated at gigabits per second with almost zero power consumption on sides of the storage chip. The small energy drawn from the RF could even be sufficient to operate the storage device itself.

Next question: electronic slavery. But this here is just a storage device. We decide what to write onto it and we can control if anyone else has or has tried to write onto it. Just as with a simple USB stick or with an external harddrive.

But what about detectability?

As said, this gadget could only operate when getting a strong RF field. It could hardly be detected from a distance of more than a few inches. Moreover, we could program it to react to certain coded transmissions only. Finally, we would of course always use strong encryption for any data we write onto it (or would we - most people these days are absolutely negligent about these issues with their sticks and notebooks already).

The data as well as the transmissions would never be accessible to third parties. Against force, we could provide fake data sets that would appear with one password while the real ones would appear with another (a strategy present with personal encryption systems already, e.g. Truecrypt, but much more efficient here as nobody could actually know about the real storage capacity of our device). So this thing would be strictly personal.

Could it perhaps be stolen? Yes, of course, but much less so than with conventional devices, as it had to be operated out, also had to be found first place, and we could as well wear two of them, for redundancy. If someone snatched our vision glasses, we'd just take another pair, that's it.

Personal passwords our sim would only know temporarily, in volatile memory, and it would actively 'forget' and wipe them of course, as soon as it loses eye contact, i.e. doesn't see our iris or retina pattern for more than a second. It would of course stop to work at all, when taken on by another person.

We could of course integrate more functions in such a chip, use it for identification, payment, as a passport. Then, more complicated questions about personal security and privacy might arise.

The simple memory chip however could teach some people a lesson. It becomes part of the body. The data in it also becomes part of the body. Retrieving such a chip it physically would violate the bodily integrity of people and hence human rights. Retrieving the data wirelessly may be seen as a different case, by morons that is.

But what if the data is encrypted? In a state of law, nobody can be forced to testify against himself, regardless if there is anything to hide or not, so in any case, forcing the password out of him is a crime.

Even if they wouldn't concede, certain governments have already violated human rights by legislation allowing to arrest somebody for not revealing a computer password (arresting is violence and with this purpose even fulfils the definition of torture). Maybe the simple memory chip implant will finally help recognizing these things.

Brainstorms

The ultimate user interface might be reading thoughts, directly. While there is hardly any chance of decoding anything intellectually meaningful from our brain's electromagnetic smog, quite recently success had been reported using the electrical potentials from multiple points on the head skin for basic actions like moving cursors etc. It requires two things however, a significant 'teach in' procedure, and sort of a hairnet connecting the sensor electrodes. While glasses are acceptable to most people, wearing a hairnet with electrodes would be for freaks.

The implant we have considered before may lead us to some thoughts if it might not be possible to use several little chips under the head skin.

The problem however, apart from the energy supply (that might use radio power from a sim as with our implant, or fuel cells living on blood sugar, or whatsoever), the electrical potentials we are talking about are typically tiny and of low frequency. Hence, physical wires between the sensors seem unavoidable. Not a really good prospect, but never say never...

Wireless interfaces

Generally we have to consider that the entire computing power of the visual interface cannot be integrated into the glasses assembly in the near future.

We may need some pocket computer, or in some cases external computer power of a company, campus or home network.

If we want to externalize computing power from the display interface, we have to transport 2 HDTV channels for the display, 4 normal TV channels for position sensor and eye tracker cameras, possibly 2 more TV channels for mask displays, audio in/output channels, and several sensor channels. It should be possible to transport all signals over some serial digital channel like Firewire or USB2. In this case the question is if any TV or HDTV channels should be compressed.

Encoding and decoding as well as compression/decompression and the interface protocol chips, will add some complexity and power consumption to the display interface, but less than if we add a processor.

Then we could also much easier use a wireless connection. With some current varieties like Bluetooth however, bandwidth limitations are still severe. A single TV channel, if we use a low power consumption approach for compression, like MJPEG or DV, needs up to 35 Mbps, HDTV up to 200, so the only current option for this is wireless LAN, and an advanced one.

We could optimize compression a bit further, and wireless interfaces are evolving quickly, so this will surely become an option when any of the basic devices envisioned will be accomplished.

The bottom line currently is, that we may need a power connection from a pocket device for the very first implementations, so connecting to this device for data is straightforwardly done with a serial bus, sharing with power one single thin cable.

As soon as we can include low power compression chips, with glasses assemblies then probably being in the 50...100g range, the batteries for wireless communications would easily fit in.

Wireless communications need an emission power proportional to the square of the distance spanned, and proportional to the bandwidth required. So the high data rates we need will certainly contribute to power consumption, while the small distances to a pocket computer require much less power than with most other applications. Only the unsteady conditions of wave propagation near to the body may spoil this picture a bit.

Remote computing

In certain environments, we could run the vision simulator entirely without a pocket computer.

We could use a local computer network to run everything, including the real time adaptation algorithms and video processing of the vision simulator. This could be done in office or home networks, where the distance to the next wireless node is small (limiting the necessary radio power) and sufficient dedicated computer capacity is available.

We would need some more radio power for this variety, but it's still in a reasonable range.

It is obvious that we need secure encryption for any communications. With external computing, many other security questions arise. Materials contributing to this kind of applications can be found in [3].

Security

A portable device carrying most of the user's private data in order to be useful in all situations, is very vulnerable to theft.

Notebooks are easily secured by fully encrypting their harddisks, although this is rarely used because most users are plainly unaware of the possibility. Data on such a machine is only accessible as long as the user is logged in and power is on.

There is still a problem if a notebook is stolen while the owner is working on it, as the thief could get at everything currently accessible.

With the vision simulator, there may be two items that could be stolen: the glasses and a pocket computing unit. The glasses may not carry their own data storage, in this case their theft is of monetary concern only, but we could use them to secure the pocket unit or a memory chip.

We would totally encrypt a pocket unit anyway, as far as it holds data. Apart from quantum computers that won't be available so soon, there is no known method to crack a really good encryption. So this is really secure.

An even better option would be the chip implant, as stealing this one would be difficult and getting at its data can be forfeited by several means. The implant would also take any permanent data storage over from a pocket unit, if there is one.

We would also encrypt the communications between the pocket unit and the glasses. It is no problem to make this really secure as well.

The algorithm of choice would be working like the well known https* protocol. The only way to crack this is to fully break up the communications and insert a 3rd party device that processes every byte of it before transmitting it to the original destination. This way, encryption keys could be faked and the whole communications could be eavesdropped, but this is not so easy in our case. If we use wireless links between the pocket computer and the glasses, the distance is very small.

An eavesdropper would have to get very close, receive the signal of one part while jamming the other, and retransmit the packets modified afterwards, i.e. with a delay. It is quite obvious that this whole interference scheme is something that would work on a wire, but is utterly difficult to achieve with a wireless link. The unit would only need to watch for delays, radio interference and other anomalies.

We would also use encryption keys that are exchanged in a secure environment only. As this is not a communication with an alien partner as with arbitrary connections in the Internet, we would only use an automated key exchange if we establish the communication for the first time, for example if we replace a broken pair of glasses.

Afterwards, we need not touch the key at all. Once the keys are established, an attacker has no chance to get anything meaningful out of the data transfers [48], [70], [71].

Now if someone stole a pocket unit, he/she could not access it because he/she has no device that could communicate with it. It's like a notebook with no one logged on anytime.

---

* The secure internet protocol. Active if your browser shows the padlock icon. Uses public key encryption. This is a method working with key pairs, a public key that can be freely distributed for anyone to encrypt with it, and a private key that also allows to decrypt and that only the originator of the keys possesses. The mail encryption program PGP for example uses this method. With https, machine 1 crates a temporary key pair with a random number generator and sends the public part to machine 2. Machine 2 does likewise and sends its public key to machine 1. Now they can communicate safely in both directions.

If the thief would steal both a pocket unit holding data, and the glasses, he could readily access the owner's data as long as the unit is powered. There is a lot of possible damage conceivable, that I won't discuss here in detail.

We could also imagine a thief just taking the glasses and using them while threatening the owner with a gun.

What we now want to have is something that prohibits the glasses to be used by unauthorized people, and also if they or the pocket unit are taken away.

There is one very elegant possibility to do this: Using the eye tracker for an iris or retina analysis. This could work continuously and safe. As soon as the glasses are taken off, or taken by someone else, they stop working.

Another possibility to achieve this is with the chip implant mentioned. This is obviously a most secure option.

Hence, the glasses could protect themselves from displacement.

Other types of attack may be more promising: If we know the inner workings of the display (quite probable if they are once produced by the millions), we could try to tune a radio receiver to some harmonics of the line frequency and exploit the modulations that are probably occuring.

The difficulty of such an attack can be increased by optimizing the wiring, lowering the power dissipation of the circuitry (useful anyway), shielding the device (a weight problem), randomly modulating the display line rate, or by actively producing interference noise to make the signals unusable.

With LED like displays, some form of eavesdropping could be just to look at somebody's glasses. Inevitably, some light would leak out, and the display could be quite 'large', some cm in cases.

So one could eventually catch a glimpse of what's going on in the display of their encounter, but that's not really a big issue.

With laser displays, one could eventually see a large projection of leaking light on the floor, even though very dim. In case we use color selective mirrors, that leakage would be so low that one couldn't likely exploit this.

The projector could theoretically be powerful enough to provide a good picture on a sheet of paper in a dark room, but normally the intensity would always be tuned to match the brightness of the environment, so this wouldn't work in practice.

The usual appearance of a laser display for other people would be a dim and very tiny dot of light from the projection mirror.

With dirty glasses, one could probably see an image right in them. It's hard to figure out how large this problem could actually turn out to be, as it is also very dependent on the technology used.

With holographic projection at last, there's a good chance that this would be very safe. Eavesdropping several GHz of holographic data going to the display would be very difficult. Seeing something in the tiny displays from outside would as well be close to impossible, even more so if we also use holographic mirror glasses.

Secure private realm technology

For data security, we would use a pocket device for all processing but do dynamic backups on a remote server, and a chip implant perhaps. In this case it's advisable to encrypt anything before it goes out. Incremental backups save bandwidth and can be done fully encrypted if all files are encrypted separately. The external service should not do anything but to provide storage. All control over it should remain in the glasses. The algorithm should enable restoration of all data by knowledge of password and possession of the appropriate software only.

This approach would remain unbreakable if the password is long and secure enough and always kept safely.

A secure remote data storage facility as envisioned is not fiction anymore. First applications of this kind have recently become available, for use with portable computers [6].

I therefore do not consider this a technology specific to vision simulators. Some special problems may have to be addressed, but in general, current developments will certainly cover most of our special requirements.

We have discussed a possible attack scheme for communications between glasses and pocket unit. There a protection was given by the fact that it would be difficult to interfere with a very narrow and low power communication link. With the backup scheme one might think an interference could get easier, because of the larger distance between links, and because of the many network nodes possibly involved. Yet this isn't the case, as the data never need to be decrypted. The backup server needs no key. The key entirely remains with the user, and anything entering the web is useless without it. So the remote backup unit remains nothing but a storage, and there simply is no attack scheme for this protocol, other than hijacking the user's computer. Even if someone would alter the data stored, the result could be nothing but garbage, annoying but not a security threat.

If someone would set up a treacherous hotspot that appeared as if it was a trustworthy outlet but in fact would be the spider web of some cybercrooks, they could possibly interfere with a https session and do any kind of damage, but that's a quite common threat to everybody just walking around with a conventional notebook and a WLAN card, it has nothing to do with the dynamic backup scheme discussed above, and cannot affect it's security.

Public objects

To provide publicly visible objects, it is necessary to announce their position and nature in a way that nearby computers can receive these announcements. A viable solution would be to use a radio channel and transmit data packets with the basic informations continuously with a CSMA or CSMA-CD* protocol.

---

* Carrier Sense Multiple Access with Collision Detection: A node 'listens' if the channel is free, then starts to send a message packet. Collision detection means that if 2 nodes started simultaneously, they can detect it from signal interference. In this case they stop and 'back up' (delay for a random time) before retrying. Many nodes can share such a channel without much administration. Ethernet (your computer's network card) works this way [39]. Wireless varieties often don't detect collisions [43]. They detect problems by missing receipt messages or the like, then randomly retry to send.

These transmissions need only provide position and nature of the objects. 'Nature' means type, basic information about size, importance, relation to real things, and their appearance. If any nearby receiver decides that an object could be of interest, it should transmit a request, causing the originating machine to send further information (if the request is accepted), containing the image data of the object as well as shape and imaging information about nearby visible structures relative to which the object should be located. This precision locator information is necessary because GPS alone would not allow for a precise positioning.

Objects that should integrate and relate to real environment need to be positioned with an accuracy of millimeters that couldn't even be provided by differential GPS or other radio based methods.

The process somehow resembles web browsing, where the initial packet selection would equal the use of a search engine. The search in our case is also refined physically, just by the proximity of radio sources that can be received. In the next step, a http or similar connection to the web server, being the public node, is established, and the page, being the virtual object, is requested. The browser window in this case is the real environment.

Content, as in the web example, can be static or animated, also interactive. The user could perhaps be allowed to manipulate it by hand, eyes, laser pointer, voice, virtual keyboards, or others.

With such a networking approach, where nodes randomly appear and disappear, only a probabilistic access algorithm would be appropriate of course. Contrary to a general misconception, these approaches are more reliable than deterministic ones even in real time environments, due to their inherent robustness [39],[43], [78],[79] (the delusion that only deterministic protocols could ensure reliable real time behavior, hitherto led to many peculiar developments, e.g. with industrial and car networks).

Another interesting approach are binary codes, e.g. block codes, that by general convention could be interpreted as web links. Seeing such a code, a vision simulator could surf to the web address specified (by WLAN) and get according information from there. The advantage here is that no local web transmitters are necessary, at least not any provides by the originator of the virtual objects, and there is an instant and unambiguous relation between object hinting and desired location. Schemes like this have recently been created and are in use already, in experimental museum guiding systems involving additional information delivery to mobile phones, for example. The camera of a mobile phone can also serve for block code recognition. A disadvantage here is nasty block codes spilling the scene, and it won't work well in some situations, for example if we want to set up signposts that can be seen from a car.

Shared objects

The same way public sources can create and distribute Objects, any vision simulator can provide for this as well.
Such objects could be abstract things like hard disk files, or they could be currently displayed objects or windows. We could as well envision that somebody lets his computer generate an animated replacement for his own person, a feature that could be used for gaming or virtual theatre play. Shared objects also comprise any kind of virtual devices belonging to real machinery, like the control panel of a washing machine, the instrument board of a car or a plane, input panels for home or office installations, virtual ambience objects like virtual window views, decorations or even virtual wallpapers belonging to certain rooms. Virtual Christmas decorations, or any kind of signs also belong to the category of privately published virtual objects.
Access rights to such objects have to be defined, as even objects in outdoor areas are not necessarily meant for everybody (a sign pointing to a phone switchbox for example could be confined to service people), and inner room decorations should not be accessible to people outside, even if theoretically they could configure their vision sims to see them right trough the wall. Object descriptions should therefore use encrypted protocols in many cases. What can be different is the way keys are handed out.

Interior objects could for example use printed block codes or an infrared link to distribute a key, hence anybody in the room would always have access, and these objects would behave just exactly like real ones, i.e. could be seen through windows but not through the walls.

Restricted objects

Public objects could easily clutter up public areas for anybody using a vision simulator. Some should necessarily be seen by anybody, like temporary traffic signs. Some could be considered harmless and therefore allowed for public distribution, like window dressings or posters. As virtual objects could have some disturbing properties, like being heavily animated, being too bright, sticking out from the wall (in case of 3D placards for example), even those usually harmless objects should comply to certain restrictions. Much worse would be the generation of virtual objects right on the road, the display of creatures attacking persons, and so on. Hard even to imagine all possible types of hazards that could arise from public virtual objects. They could not physically attack anybody, but nevertheless distract so much as to cause serious accidents. Any public object must therefore either comply to certain restrictive rules about its position and nature, or have a publicly controlled certificate, or the digital signature of a public authority, to be present in security relevant areas. Individual vision sims also have to be programmed in a way to reject objects if they would have the potential to seriously distract the user. A useful virtual object on a road for example could be a virtual road sign marking a recently occurred accident. It could even be allowed for private people to generate these, for example in conjunction with a car's hazard lights (where the object could just be automatically generated by the car itself).
Another handy possibility would be cars transmitting their position data like with the airplane virtual radar mentioned, so they could be 'seen' behind bends. These applications of course need a very secure structure of certificates to defy abuse.

Sound

A non immersive display should of course be accompanied by 'open' headphones, that allow outside sounds to enter without much attenuation.

Button headphones would normally be the technology of choice.

Mounting such headphones can simply be done by attaching them to the spectacle's ear handles with flexible wires. This is surely better than just squeezing them in.

Reproducing surround sound with these earphones (as with any) requires some signal processing. This function can be found in today's sound cards as well as in some soft or maybe even desk-top DVD players. It is state of the art. What is done is to emulate an artificial head recording, one that uses an original human anatomy to reproduce exactly the sound waves getting into the ear at the original site.

So far nothing special. What I would add is a dynamic sound field simulation that compensates for the user's head movements. So as with vision simulated scenes, it wouldn't be necessary anymore to stay in place or seat to enjoy the full 3D impression. Even this will be something that could easily be addressed with today's technology. CPU's hardly take notice doing that real time.

We would also need microphones for this design, be it for voice control or in order to use the vision simulator as a mobile phone or as a camcorder.

As stated already, a reasonable implementation would be to attach these microphones directly to the earphones, back to back, earphones pointing towards the ear channel and microphones outwards. Using this device as a 'natural head microphone', of course has the disadvantage that it needs the head to be fixed for a professional result. Some sound processing however could greatly compensate for head movements, and we could also convert such a sound recording to multi channel if we desire.

In case of speech recording, a microphone at the ear might not be what's currently considered the best way. A microphone closer to the mouth (although still beneath it, to avoid breathe noises), is more usual. Yet we have 2 microphones, and using their output for some intelligent signal discrimination could provide for a very good separation of the owner's speech from environmental noise. So we could probably well do without any separate speech microphone.

Last but not least, let's mention again that we could add active noise cancellation, by feeding an inverted signal from the microphone to the headphone, to just compensate incoming noise with an actively generated signal of exactly opposite amplitude. This technique is quite common in aviation, and could be useful anywhere, if anyone had a sufficiently equipped vision simulator. We could also do the opposite. If button headphones stick too close (normally I wouldn't like that all the time, but it's sometimes useful to produce good bass), then we could avoid the user being closed out from environmental sound by just sending some of the microphone signals to the headphones. Another application could be a hearing aid.

Very recently, a new technology has emerged that can pick up the user's voice from the ear's auditory canal [63]. The sound comes from the oral cavity through the Eustachian tube. Even whispering can be picked up this way, in presence of environmental noise. As the earpiece has to fit entirely tight in this case and any hearing can only occur indirectly through microphones, this is something I wouldn't like for everyday use. It's very interesting for professional applications of course.

As stated in the introduction already, a very important software feature of a vision simulator will have to be spatial sound impressions complying with the pictures of virtual objects.

In order to support a realistic impression for any simulation or media reproduction, sound has to come from the visible sources.

As the user can move his head relative to these sources, classical surround sound has to be converted to the true angle and timing, and the characteristic influence of the user's head also has to be simulated (synthetic artificial head stereophony). The operations necessary can be found in any current soundcard already, maybe not exactly fit to our requirements, but it's state of the art, so let's leave this to other literature (e.g.,[73]).

We will get back to sound in the media chapter once more.

Conclusion

I have tried to address the main technological aspects of vision simulators that should be able to generate really perfect virtual devices and objects.

Again, many of the ideas are still speculative, and what I have tried here is not only an overview of ideas, but also in some aspects a proof of concept (as far as possible in theory), i.e. to show that it should be achievable in a foreseeable time.

As to the status of technology, this can only be a snapshot, as new ideas and technologies keep arising every day.

I did not address sound too much, as this is all more or less state of the art and so much less difficult than the optical matters.

Although the difficulties of some approaches may seem to be overwhelming, and some are so complex that they also require large multi threaded research projects, we should not forget that this technology will not only replace many others, but also have a huge economical perspective. Substantial efforts are therefore well justified.

In the following chapter, I will address some aspects of a very large application area having its own requirements, i.e. (virtual) media technology.

Here we have to think about appropriate 3D recording technology as well as about the relation between vision simulators and conventional screen displays (that will still play a role in some areas). So I will include some more thoughts about 3D screen technology.

I will also use this theme to look into some basics of stereo pictures, hopefully useful for readers not too familiar with it, also better to understand some related topics in the preceding chapters.

Before imagination streaming, when media still needed hardware, possibilities were closely limited by available technology. This is a paper considering media technology at the edge of a vital intermediate stage called virtualization.

part 4: Virtual Media

Introduction

We have seen that a universal sensorial interface will allow for new media formats, greatly surpassing anything possible with classical screens.
Perfect 3D video is but one possibility, something very difficult to achieve with screens in near future.

Producing truly three dimensional, or even *screen independent* media formats is anything but trivial already. We will see that we need object oriented or synthetic holography recording, because if we want to get away from the usual pseudo plastic puppet theatre, any user perspective has to be individually generated for each person, during playback, in real time.

Large conventional screens, not fully able to match the 3D capabilities of the vision simulator, will nevertheless stay around for a long time. Not because the current monster varieties of 'flat' screens are so good, but because they will be replaced by much better ones.
Organic (OLED) screens will quite likely be cheaply produced in large sizes and huge resolutions, probably flexible as well and mountable on any surface. Projection screens may be greatly improved as well, by the introduction of holographic screens that are direction selective and offer the same contrast as any self luminating versions, or even better.
Both varieties mentioned essentially are thin plastic foils, promising a large potential for cost reduction with mass production, and they offer a much better energy efficiency than anything available today.
So we will have to discuss which applications will probably run on a vision simulator and which will remain on real screens.

We will further regard the possibilities and problems of media production methods that could unleash all of the new capabilities. A large impulse for the development of new recording technologies comes from the increasing popularity of synthetic animation.

Practically everybody could now use the 'levels editor' of a computer game to produce synthetic movies ('machinima'). Software for professional productions is many times more sophisticated of course.

What is inherent to all these productions, that anything is originally object oriented and fully three dimensional. Viewer perspectives have to be set by defining the 'camera positions', and only after this, a classical 2-dimensional movie emerges from the setup.

With these computer generated movies, producing for only one picture channel will, in almost any case, just be equivalent to throwing away information. Recording of multiple virtual camera channels would be the minimum requirement, to enable future reconstruction of 3D information.

Combining these virtual scenes with real ones is currently very difficult. At least it involves blue (or green) screen technique, where a single colored background is used to cut out the actors from it. First attempts to avoid all this and get the entire 3 dimensional scene just by stereo cameras are under way, but the difficulty is large.

Even the correct animation of virtual characters is still a problem. You may already have seen actors running around in black suits covered with white spots. These spots help the cameras to catch their movements in a way that can then be used to perfect the animations of a synthetic movie machine.

I'm nevertheless quite confident that an entirely three dimensional and object oriented production technology, perhaps with the help of additional 3D scanning equipment, laser scanners for example, will be accomplished in a way that could be routinely used even in less expensive projects.

What would basically be necessary is to record any scene with several cameras, in order to gather the raw material for any immediate or future 3D processing.

With audio, this has been a common practice for decades, not because surround or even simple stereo were already there, but because single instruments and voices were recorded separately and mixed down later on. Now the master tapes of these recordings allow to produce surround sound with them, completely unforeseen at the time they were recorded. The original sources can be re-mixed to any format desired, allowing to exploit the same assets again and again.

So even though we might not be able to make full use of it right now, recording with multiple camera arrays may be a good idea already.
For people still using a 70 mm movie camera this may sound lunatic, but HDTV cameras are getting very affordable already and even larger formats are only a matter of pretty short time. Cameras are steadily getting smaller and also less expensive. It may be possible to upscale resolution by correlating pictures from several cameras in an array, so each of them would become even cheaper (more on this later). Recording will also no longer be done on tape but directly and routinely on the computer harddisk, where the data streams even of many parallel cameras are not a problem to deal with anymore.
Together with some adapted editing software, this won't be more difficult to use than any of the current systems.

What is necessary here is a standard format to record information about camera positions, focus length (for correct perspective), and also additional data from dedicated 3D scanners. We would also need a standard format for video compression (encoding) and a standard media format for permanent master storage.
Regrettably, no format has yet been standardized for the recording of camera position information, even though some proposals for this have been made.

Encoding is something special here, as pictures from different perspective also have large common parts that can be exploited to reduce data, just by encoding a 2D base image, then enhancing it with additional data for hidden surfaces, depth and so on. With such an approach, the total data volume may be reduced to a little more than that of a single camera. The advantage would be that we could also transmit this entire information to any viewer, where it could optionally be used by high end display equipment to produce any perspective according to the viewer's individual position.

First experiments on encoding multiple camera channels in the context of advancing the MPEG4 standard yielded only small advantages [9]. Research however goes on, and recent results appear to be much better [112].

It should be possible anyway. Pictures from adjacent array cameras are identical to subsequent ones from one camera moved sideways, and MPEG is especially good at compressing motion by frame-to-frame similarities. I will return to this later on.

Already foreseen in the current standards, although not implemented except for research prototypes, is the description of three dimensional objects by a triangular mesh.

Approaches extending current encoding technology by depth or surface information may however fall short of expectations. It is just like doing collages with paper and scissors, while real objects can be transparent or foggy. I will later on also describe an holographic approach. Holograms are just an optimal encoding of anything that light can show, therefore they could possibly be much better suited for the task.

Standardization of certain frame formats or even certain camera array assemblies is not so important. At times of analog TV channels, even conversion of different image sizes has been a problem. Today we could almost do away with standards, at least these, because modern graphic chips do these conversions on the fly, all the time, without anybody even taking notice (even though many devices are doing this badly, and far too often). Likewise, object oriented formats would leave the actual display arrangement entirely to the disposition of the viewer, restricted by his technical equipment only.

Storing scenes with object descriptions or other appropriate structural information would later on not only enable us to freely select the reproduction technology, but also to seamlessly integrate artificial objects and scenes. It would also allow for a universal manipulation of content, i.e. we will get additional degrees of freedom so far only available in pure computer animations.

At last, the objects displayed could be made interactive and reacting. This way, we would get a floating transgression from film to computer game to virtual device.

Hence, concepts of augmented reality and of virtual media are essentially the same.

With hybrid projects, containing computer generated as well as natural scenes (hence, with any 'better' movie even nowadays), we see that such a technology would greatly simplify the integration of the different types of content. This should provide a strong motivation for further research in this field.

We may henceforward conclude, that the recording of three dimensional image information will become of fundamental significance in the foreseeable future and that it is absolutely urgent to develop standards for multi channel image recording as soon as possible.

In the following pages I will try a systematic description of the methods outlined, and give some overview of the technologies involved.

This may also be useful as background information for some things that I could only touch so far.

In addition to an assessment of possible technologies, we also have to try some predictions about new viewing habits that might also emerge with them.

The 3-step paradigm: hardware independent media

The entire process of recording, processing, storage, and intelligent reproduction can basically be parted into 3 steps:

1) Acquisition: Transferring reality (and artificial resources) into data storage.
2) Processing: Anything from signal processing to cutting and directing.
3) Playback: Transporting the finished product into the human brain (via eyes, ears etc.).

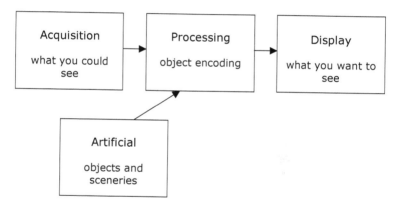

Step 1) would in conventional terms mean shooting raw scenes or recording live music. It could also mean production of cartoons, for example.

In this chapter, I will concentrate on the technical process of recording *reality*.

The central approach is to record exactly those signals that a human observer would acquire in the real scene. It is, in principle, based on conventional optimization of recording equipment

(avoiding any effort to record more than what meets the eye and ear but doing so perfectly and without redundancy), but I'll try to systematize this approach towards the extensive use of modern sensors and computing power to achieve a scene acquisition as complete as possible, including holography like pictures and sounds.
You say this may sound good but could never be achieved ? We'll see.

Step 2) would mean cutting etc. in conventional film or music production.

Here, the focus is on the technological process of conversion from crude recording signals into computer based reality models.

The idea is to use sensors as simple as possible, to extract the necessary data, to enhance the data where components may be flawed or missing due to limitations of the sensors, and to use reality and human sense models to achieve an optimal data storage and transport, including highest level and quality of compression.

At this step, artificial (entirely computer generated) scenes would also be inserted.

Step 3) in this approach comprises the optimal preparation of data for a diversity of available playback devices (displays, speakers etc.).

Computer power is used to generate individually tailored signals, for example driving stereo glasses as well as pseudo holographic displays, any number of speakers according to the specific design of any playback assembly, synthesizing artificial head stereophony for in-ear-phones, or simply optimizing the picture signal for a given projector.

In this part, our focus here is on the evaluation and suggestion of reproduction devices best suited to the computer based media processing concept.

In general, I suppose that computers will extensively be used to make recording, transport/storage and playback as equipment independent as possible, the only central standard being the encoding, which should be an object oriented approach based on knowledge about the requirements and limitations of human perception.

In part, such a development has already occurred, for example in the fact that modern equipment gets more and more flexible regarding image resolution. In earlier days, resolution was hard-wired in the equipment, and all devices had to conform to standards.
Nowadays, low and high resolution pictures can be displayed on any kind of screen, because the necessary conversions have become so easy. HDTV enters the living room with only minor requirement for standards, as many of the devices involved can be scaled to different resolutions, image rates, etc.

Signal formats have also become flexible. With analog equipment, minor changes would have made everything incompatible. Today, Video playback devices master several compression and media formats, and more could be implemented by software, if desired.
We could anticipate that a multitude of formats could be used, that come with a description of their properties in a common language to program any device for their proper playback.

The MPEG4 and MPEG7 standards [80] are steps towards this objective, introducing image and media objects, not just image compression. The aim is to resolve recorded scenes into objects, which are first described by shape, then texture (maybe involving conventional DCT* compression).

---

* Discrete cosine transform, used to encode 2-dimensional pixel arrays

For 3D, we would then add material properties, in order to be able to reproduce their appearances from different viewing angles, also such that are not identical to that of a real recording camera.

As stated already, it may be questioned if the current mainstream approaches are the ideal ones. Holographic or light field encoding may perhaps be alternatives.

The signal chain sketched at the beginning could for example look like this:

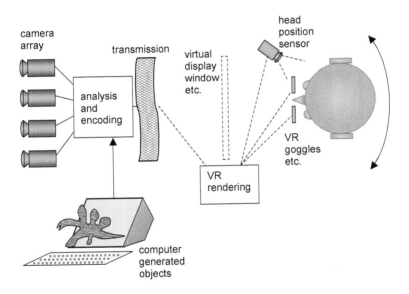

Here we have a camera array delivering - together with a signal processor - a 3D description of a scene, which is then encoded for recording and transmission.

At the receiver side, a virtual reality rendering processor together with a head position sensor delivers pictures to display glasses that emulate a virtual holographic display window.

An example for step 1
(perfect acquisition): color

The human eye has 3 separate types of color sensors: One each for 'red', 'green' and 'blue'. Blue is at about a wavelength of <450nm (0.45 µm), green at ≈530nm and red at >600nm. The sensitivity curves of these receptors are not well separated. For many spectral colors, 2 or all 3 sensor types are reacting, although with different sensitivity. The Picture below shows how far the sensitivity curves are overlapping. It is obvious that the human brain does a pretty good job on signal processing here, because we are able to differentiate millions of colors, from these three only vaguely discriminated signals.

A modern professional TV camera has filter characteristics exactly corresponding to those of the human eye (picture). The 3 color outputs are then sent over a matrix circuit that recalculates them into three standardized 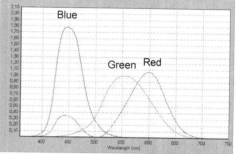 R, G, and B color values to match the dyes of standard displays. This may create an additional overlapping and reduce the color space a bit, but with smart signal processing it has already been shown that this process is reversible.

As the color curves exactly match the human eye characteristics, they contain all information that could be visible. Color *recording* is already optimal with today's equipment !

But how does this hold against the fact that no current display can reproduce all possible colors?

The answer is simple: Most Displays have only 3 standardized primary colors, so we get a problem with fidelity, because any primary color from a display is again intermixed with the others by the viewing process, so we just can't address either of the 3 sensor groups *separately*.

Perfect color reproduction

This diagram shows the color space of the human eye (the outer elliptical curve) and the area of reproducible colors for TV (black triangle).

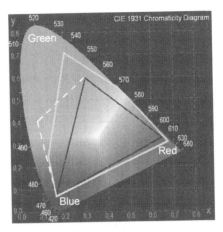

The corners of this triangle are the color locations of the three standard dyes for displays. All reproducible colors lie in the area between these three locations. We see that these dyes are not all monochromatic (spectral): Otherwise they would be located on the curved border of the diagram. We also see that especially green here is a mixed color, and that there is a large deficit especially in the range of blue-green (cyan).

If we add some more colors, we can produce a larger area from the theoretical range, because we can simulate the original color much better.

It is almost impossible to extend the range for extreme red or blue very far, because the eye's sensitivity there becomes very weak. In the green and cyan range, a greater improvement can be achieved, yielding a much more natural reproduction especially of landscapes (plants, sky, sea). Printing media already use 6 or more colors.

Genoa developed a 5 color system that shall be marketed in a high end projection TV together with Philips (gray line).

Eizo announced a computer display that uses an additional Cyan color (dotted white line) and is mainly targeted towards professional publishing and printing applications.

We have seen that any older video production could be reproduced with a color quality that only depends on the equipment. So color already conforms to the 3 step approach.

Evolution of 2D and 3D paradigms

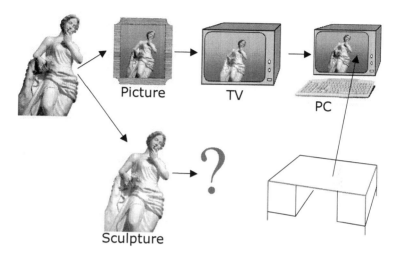

Let's add a little more systematics to see where the gaps are:

With visual media, traditional forms were painting and sculpture, representing 2D and 3D reproduction. In 2D, electronic technology led to the TV and then without any major change, to the usual PC screen. Natural environments like a desktop have been translated to a 2D screen representation, with all objects encased in that screen.

The classical 3D form (sculpture) has hardly any electronic counterpart until now, except for experimental augmented reality setups. Stereoscopic reproduction always lacks one or the other part of reality, be it dynamic perspective or focus. Also in all cases but VR , the object is always confined to a window.

Abandoning the window is useful for exhibitions (virtual sculptures), but also for certain kinds of entertainment media.
Characters in 3D real world games would also be of this variety.

Sound

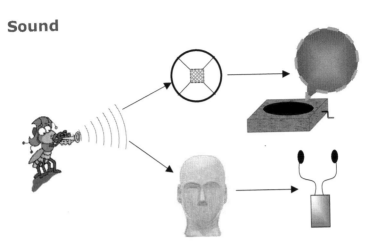

With sound, anything is much easier, not only because less processing power is required. The traditional monaural representation (microphone, gramophone or radio), could easily be expanded to a perfect 3D impression with an artificial head microphone and stereo headphones.

In the design part, some technologies suitable for the vision simulator were mentioned already. Talking about media, we'll just have to figure out what could become usual procedures with the assumed existence of the technology.

What could be a really new experience, with dynamic artificial head simulation, to go around the musicians in a virtual surround video recorded orchestra, being able to hear every instrument really separately.

Acoustic reflections in a room can be simulated quite easily. Current sound processors can even calculate multiple reflections in complicated environments in real time. This can actually be achieved with a PC soundcard and standard software.

Multi channel sound recording will remain standard in media production. Artificial head remained a niche technology for a reason, as it restricts proper playback to headphones in traditional technology and delivers much less directional separation even with current post processing methods. It is also ill fitted to usual soundtrack production methodology.

Encoding multi channel sound has just recently seen a big progress with the introduction of mp3 surround [32]. Before, it had been usual to encode each channel (almost) separately, although multiple channels carry a great deal of redundancy. Now they need only little more bandwidth than a single one.

Historic example: Phase encoded surround

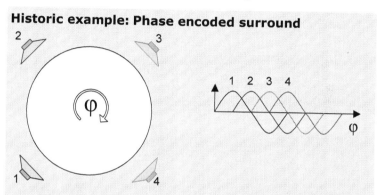

Imagine 4 speakers (1,2,3,4,) arranged in certain angles around one listener. We encode the 4 signals by adding all of them into channel A, and adding them with different phase shifts in channel B (this example is taken as simple as possible, so it is not identical to real surround systems):

If we want to decode a certain speaker channel, we add A and B with a certain phase shift that equals the direction:

The signal of the opposite speaker becomes zero, the signals of the neighboring speakers get through with about –3 dB (70%).

Hence, signal separation is not very good, but the system allows to decode signals for any speaker direction we could think of, so the number and arrangement of playback channels becomes independent of the recording situation.

All usual multi channel technology now relies on horizontal separation only. The more flexible usage habits that we may develop with vision simulators, could raise the interest in a really three dimensional sound recording.

Obviously, sound already carries more spatial information than picture. Simple screen formats come with surround and 3D sound

effects. In future, image technology will hopefully be able to catch up.
What should be developed, are flexible encoding technologies that allow to chose between several formats for different type of media. It may for example be useful to transmit virtual objects each with their own sound channel.

A virtual orchestra could in the extreme case come with one channel per instrument and could then be walked around and viewed and listened to from all directions even with the acoustics of any listening room desired.
In this case we could as well consider some kind of holographic sound description that would cover the entire sound field around the orchestra.
This sounds more difficult than it is, as we only need a real or virtual mesh of microphones arranged on a sphere, and to encode their signals with a redundancy reducing algorithm.

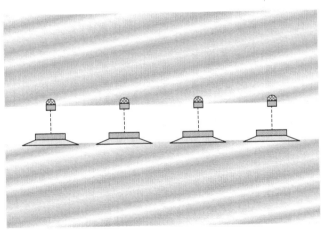

A nearly holographic effect can be achieved even with a modest number of sound channels. For example, if we record with microphones placed at one wall in one room and reproduce with a speaker array spread over an entire wall of a second room, these rooms virtually melt into one.

With speakers, the acoustics of the listening room will overlay with those of the recording environment, so usually we only get something realistic from the most unrealistic of all recording situations, the multi channel studio recording and mixing of separate instruments (which is the most common recording method not at last for just this reason).

If we virtually link two rooms with an holographic sound wall as in the picture, this is not a problem because we would just expect the resulting virtually merged room to have both acoustical influences.

Speakers can also do things that earphones can't: shaking the ground, or the stomachs of the audience. This could be a reason to install real speakers.

The reproduction equipment we would prefer in most cases is much simpler: button headphones, nothing else. Due to the almost direct coupling to the ear drum, they can reproduce any frequency free of artifacts and phase or pulse errors, and these devices have also reached a very high degree of perfection over a long space of time. Their only disadvantage: if they do not fit tightly to the ear they can't deliver full bass because of acoustic shortcut. If they fit tight, they are inconvenient and attenuate natural sound.

Conveniently wearing these things is normally impossible but not really the problem if we mount them flexibly with the glasses handles. Then they will sit loose however, and dealing with different levels of acoustic shortcut requires a little effort. Maybe an adaptive bass boosting could help here.

Otherwise if the phones fit too tight, natural sound could be passed through with help of the microphones that we would also install attached to them.

This is all quite simple. We could be glad if matters were so easy with *visual* media. There it's utterly difficult instead, but the sound example tells us what we should have: a display that is the optical equivalent of button headphones, i.e. that is as close to the eye as possible and just projects an image right into it, without any intermediate influences.

Perspective

For completeness, I will shortly recapitulate some basics of stereo viewing and display. The experienced reader may skip this.

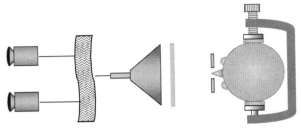

One problem with the conventional stereoscopic techniques described so far, is that for a correct perception of the picture, the viewer must literally have his head fixed in a screw mount.
The graphic shows a typical assembly with stereo cameras, a CRT display with a light shutter in front, and the viewer wearing shutter glasses. For a correct reproduction, display size and distance cannot be varied, zooming is almost impossible without very disturbing false perspectives, etc. Everything is defined by the recording equipment, once and for all. Any deviation from the right position and distance causes errors, and *sideways tilting of the head has catastrophic effects*, e.g. it's absolutely impossible to watch stereo TV lying on a couch (one would have to move one eye up and one down; try this). How could anybody ever have thought this could work anywhere anytime anyhow ? - And that's not all: an always present distraction  is false focus, e.g. the viewer for example looks to infinity according to eye parallax, but has to accommodate to a screen only 6 ft away. This hurts. In a cinema where everybody is sitting upright and focus is near infinity it may work (10 ft is the *absolute minimum* distance to be sufficiently free of focus issues), but for TV it's not an option. This task simply can't be accomplished without very advanced recording, image processing and display technologies.

I'll now shortly list the major corrections necessary for a good reproduction.

Perspective correction

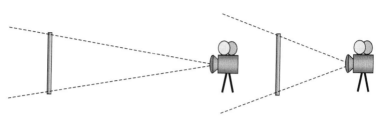

Tele and wide angle shots have very different viewing angles. Due to this, different viewing environments with different screen sizes would be necessary, and zooming has always been a major problem for 3D filming.

In order to reproduce the original perspective, the viewer would have to be precisely at the position of the recording cameras.

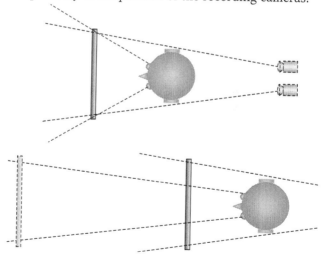

If viewer distance and original camera distance diverge too much, things get tricky. Images and objects appear very unreal, making the entire effort of 3D production quite useless.

In the example, in order to retain the original perspective, we would have to create a distant virtual screen window inside the real display. This would render most of the real display area useless and require a very good resolution for the still active part.
This would not be a very reasonable approach.
If we had the processing power to generate a different perspective, we could retain the full display usage as well as constructing a physiological perspective.
The only useful strategy to shoot 3D zoom and tele shots currently is to enlarge the stereo basis together with increasing focal length. This allows for the same distance separation in a tele shot as in a normal shot and makes a natural looking reproduction much easier.

Panning effects

Imagine being outdoors. There is a tree 50 yards away and some others a mile away. Now moving your head sideways by only 1 inch, you will already see the foreground tree move relative to the background. If it would not, you would know that something is wrong. That would not be a real scene.
Any 3D movie so far has this problem. In real world, we constantly use head movements to check perspective. So any 3D reproduction not dealing with this is significantly flawed.

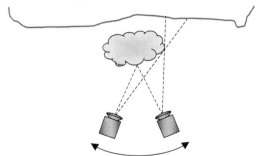

This powerful trick for cameramen (that only a few actually use), can make any still shot look 3 dimensional:

Simply shift the camera sideways or upwards a bit while fixing one point. Everything suddenly has depth !
(There has also been a 3D shooting technology that wiggles the camera all the time, but this makes people seasick).
A certain type of 3D displays exploits this fact, by showing only one picture, but changing the virtual camera position according to head movements of the observer. This allows for 'looking behind' and gives a very 3 dimensional impression even though there is no real stereoscopy. These displays work for one viewer only.
Combining panning with a stereo display (polarized or shuttered). gives a very realistic impression. It is of course necessary to have an image generator that delivers all viewing angles, corrects perspectives etc. Focus errors remain. I'll discuss this later on.

Viewer position correction

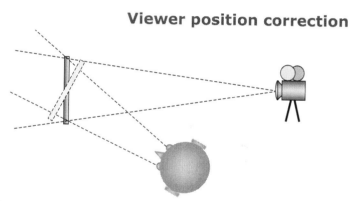

With enough processing power given, we could conceive a recalculation of perspective for the viewer's location. Though difficult, that's the only way to make things look real. What actually happens by itself with any conventional 3D screen, is that the virtual window seems to tilt towards the viewer and objects are distorted and start looking a bit unreal.
As large correction angles would be difficult to calculate even if we could, another way would be to allow for some tilting towards the user's average position and to perform dynamic perspective corrections for small head movements only.

Stereo perception ranges

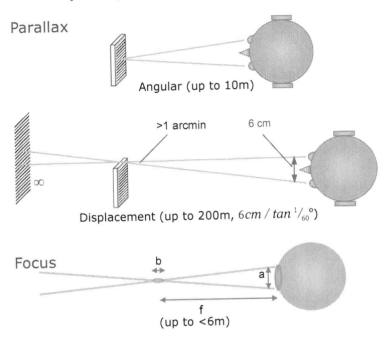

Parallax

Angular (up to 10m)

>1 arcmin   6 cm

∞

Displacement (up to 200m, $6cm / tan \, {}^1\!/_{60}{}^\circ$)

Focus

b

a

f
(up to <6m)

The most familiar hint we use for stereo seeing is parallax. This can be the angular displacement between the eyes, which usually cannot be sensed too good when it comes to very small and absolute angles. Therefore an absolute depth perception from this effect can only be expected for distances up to 10 m.

A more sensitive indicator is the different displacement of near and far objects between both eyes. Here the perception limit is given by eye resolution and eye-to-eye distance. It is the most sensitive stereo perception and works for up to 200m.

The third indicator is focus. Given the typical depth of field of our eyes, a real difference here can only be perceived for distances significantly below 6m, against infinity. Hence, focus simulation for example is no requirement for screens in distances of 3m or above.

3D displays: a review

We already know that a vision simulator can do many things not achievable with screens of any type. As screens will also be around for various reasons, I will now give a short overview of stereo display- and connected recording technologies.

The holography hype

Some decades ago, when holography was invented, many writers thought it would revolutionize film making. Pretty hasty indeed. True holograms need laser light to shoot, and film or displays with micrometer resolution to reproduce. They cannot be zoomed, adding color is difficult and may produce artifacts, and so on. Filming would actually require a studio with laser lighting and film formats several feet wide. Pretty weird. For shooting outdoors, no realistic ideas have arisen whatsoever. Effects like self interference are also severely limiting the quality of naturally recorded holograms. So the only still promising variety will be synthetic holograms generated by computers.

The VR disaster

In the beginning, many types of virtual reality glasses and goggles had been developed, most of them bulky, heavy, with primitive optics and low resolution displays that would make users seasick and send them to the chiropractic. Even now, no products have been sighted so far that were the opposite in *all* aspects. Technology strides forward, and without very high resolution, *eye trackers, mask displays* and semi transparent displays, nothing will really ever work perfect. So even the most developed VR glasses today are still not acceptable for our purpose. One reason may be that the bad reputation VR acquired from early experiments has slowed down development.

The anaglyphic headache

A simple and ancient method to reproduce 3D pictures is using red and green color to separate pictures. I only mention this for completeness as it tends to reappear every some years when some TV station tries to get some PR by a 'revolutionary' stereo transmission. Wearing red/green glasses may be something one can adapt to for a little while, but it is terribly inconvenient. Only black-and-white pictures are possible, and the method is at best viable to reproduce some 3D pictures in educational books.

Polarizers and shutters

A screen or projection display can show 2 pictures sequentially or in different polarizations. Shutter or polarizing glasses must be used to deliver the pictures to the appropriate eye. Both approaches have the disadvantage to require glasses (then we could better use our vision simulator), and to allow no 'looking behind'.

Given the fact that setting up a shuttered 3D display is very easy with any computer screen, and the shutter glasses aren't expensive, one may wonder why this technology is used so little.
It may just be that 3D is not considered necessary enough for most users, and it's certainly so that the problems with static 3D displays (false perspective, false size, false focus) are just annoying, especially with close-up computer screens.

Perfectly displaying 3D is absolutely necessary for the concept of a vision simulator, including operation systems and applications, and I think that 3D video will probably just come as a side effect when this equipment will be in everyday use and no further effort has to be taken rather than just playing the movie.
If the advanced recording and object oriented processing methods suggested here can be realized, this will also transgress into everyday use quite smoothly .

Auto stereoscopy

Auto stereoscopic displays typically use cylinder lens arrays to display different pictures for every viewing angle ('lenticular displays'). In Theory, this would work, but practically one can only display a very limited selection of angles and therefore has to cope with transition effects between them.

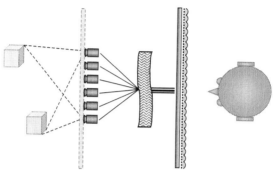

In an auto-stereoscopic assembly, two or more cameras pick up the scene. The cameras are arranged in an only horizontal row.
By arranging separate display stripes for each camera picture behind tiny lens stripes, each eye of a spectator should get only the image of a certain camera from a certain viewing angle. In practice, there are areas in between where the 2 images overlap.

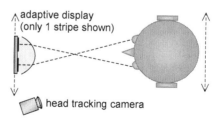

adaptive display
(only 1 stripe shown)

head tracking camera

If we move the display stripes sideways, we can adapt the optimal viewing points to different head positions, so that each eye always only gets its appropriate picture, and no overlapping or image switching occurs. This can only work for a single viewer.

We could further generate dynamic perspectives, allowing to view around objects.

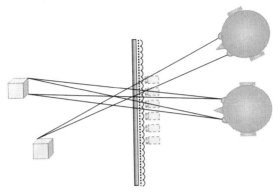

Here I have visualized how the screen with its display and lens stripes virtually reproduces the camera array.

It is obvious that this assembly can also provide a certain view 'around' objects (regard the upper viewer position).

It is also obvious that with freely moving observers, many perspectives will consist of an overlay of 2 images (regard the lower viewer and the lower edge of the upper cube).

We see that auto stereoscopy, in spite of the advantage not to require glasses, has the problem that it produces artifacts because intermediate angles are simply achieved by overlaying 2 images.

What also becomes difficult is the realization of large displays, with accordingly large viewing distances from the display. In order to give every eye its own picture, very small angular deviations have to be resolved, which in turn reduces the 'good' viewing area, requires more cameras and more display stripes, and a pretty high optical precision.

'Adaptive' auto stereoscopy, moving the stripes a little to avoid transitions, gives a 3D impression that works without glasses, but it is restricted to personal use.

So the main commercial application with this are notebook displays, that could as well be realized with shutter glasses (display and glasses switching between 2 perspectives) at very little disadvantage and little effort.

3D effects in the typical applications involved (construction, chemistry etc.) may also be achieved by just tilting and turning virtual objects by software, so the practical advantage of any stereo display in this case is limited anyway.

With all non holographic displays, there is also no correlation of focus and distance. The user has to focus on the computer screen, while the object depicted may be at a different virtual distance. Real holograms and vision simulators could do better.

Finally remember the already stated fact that the viewer would usually have to keep his head in an upright position all the time. Nothing realistically acceptable for a home TV.

Pseudo Holography

Experimental displays have been constructed using holographic optics, being able to deliver a much denser raster of viewing angles (0.8^0 for example) [30]. In essence, this is a non adaptive light field technology. The vast number of perspectives to be generated makes such approaches little realistic.

Really holographic displays?

Holographic interference patterns usually have a resolution better than 1μm. This means we will not need millions, but trillions of pixels, in case of big screens. It simply busts up any attempt to do it with current technology. From the fact that single pixels lead to ring structures in a hologram, one might speculate about injecting pixel data in a flat nanostructure that would then generate holographic patterns by propagating waves.

The non linearity of the pixel ring patterns, the necessity to limit patterns at edges of foreground objects, to also generate patterns that originate outside the display window, make this a tremendously difficult idea.

Auto holographic displays

Holographic effects cannot only be achieved with super resolution displays. In certain cases, considerably larger screen pixels phase modulating coherent light can produce 'larger' patches in space where entire stretches of waves are interfering, forming 'pixels' in the millimeter range. This can be used to direct light to individual eyes of a viewer, and even separate light values to separate parts of a single pupil, hence even enabling focus simulation [88].

The resolution required for the display panel, as well as the computing requirements are still tremendous (hundreds of high end graphic card processors currently), and several prerequisites and restrictions, especially regarding lighting. are making this approach a bit complicated as well.

Of course, individual pictures for multiple viewers have to be generated and multiplexed, requiring a tremendously high frame rate.

The focus simulation ability is interesting but also at least currently makes the approach almost unacceptably expensive compared to adaptive light field displays with micro lenses.

Adaptive light field displays

Using a lenticular array for directing light beams towards a viewer's individual eyes from all areas of the screen, offers the possibility to deliver this particular viewer his own individual images, separately for both eyes, hence a perfect perspective and stereo vision.

The screen pixels would simply have to be but inverted micro cameras with many sub pixels working as projectors.

We have already described this thoroughly at page 243, as it is crucial for understanding Fourier holograms. It is the only really promising screen technology so far.

In conclusion, except for the small versions for projectors or possible display glasses we have discussed, there is currently no concept in sight for a fully 'holographic' screen that could get to the market in less than several decades.

The only large screen alternative to glasses' displays seems to be the adaptive light field concept, that could probably be brought into existence within less than 10 years and deliver a cost effective solution for a few viewers concurrently, yet still in a very limited range of use compared to display glasses.

Vision simulators

The principal advantage of combining a vision simulator with computer based 3D recordings, lies in the possibility to calculate output pictures for different viewing positions and angles, according to the user's head movements, in real time. For example, a virtual holographic display window would be generated with appropriate coordinate transformations, making it appear at a fixed position in a real environment.

This technology requires fast computing and high resolution vision simulator displays for satisfactory results, but it would be more than rewarding.
Yet the tasks to perform for a perfect reproduction are less difficult compared to the *recording* of the pseudo holographic data we need as a basis, no matter if for screens or glasses.

We should also recall that personal vision simulators will already be of great advantage even if we could only simulate classical two dimensional screens, as these could be set up anywhere in any size at no cost, and also for surround cinema, where we wouldn't necessarily need dynamic 3D as well.

3D image recording

Holography had a big media attention when it was first discovered some decades ago, but it never worked out. With today's technology, we could at least try to record as much data as there is in a hologram and can be perceived by a real observer.
First we place several cameras in a plane similar to an intended display screen, recording many viewing angles simultaneously.

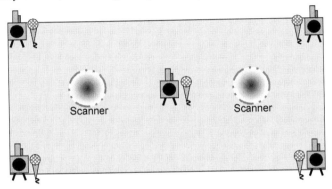

The recording plane erects a virtual window, that could be reproduced in a similar window at playback and through which the scene can be viewed from any distance and angle, giving a realistic three dimensional impression, even with the possibility of seeing behind objects, as in a true hologram. If we could generate intermediate perspectives, that is. Without this capability, the fixed window would be just as inflexible as conventional stereo video. As stated, it may anyway be wise to start with multi channel recordings at the present time, and hope that we could improve at a later date. We would need computers to differentiate the scene into objects of different distance and encode the entire picture in a descriptive, object oriented way for example. More about this thematic can also be found in [64]. In order to facilitate things, distance scanners (laser, ultrasound, radar, or other) could be used.
One of these solutions is time-of-flight measurement using laser pulses. An optical shutter with a very short slope (some nanosec-

onds) encodes arrival time into brightness [121]. Apparently this long known principle can now be implemented cheap enough for general use.

Another promising approach uses patterns (*'structured light'*), projected onto the scene. This way, features can be inserted into bald surfaces, allowing for a stereoscopic analysis even there. The patterns may also be encoded in a way allowing to distinguish individual locations for direct triangulation. Another method uses images sequences with varying binary patterns, delivering different binary words for the brightness sequence of any individual scene point. Patterns with soft modulated stripes can improve triangulation accuracy by exploiting their spatial 'phase' (gray gradient) [102]. Research on applying fringe projection to movie recording has been carried out in the 3DTV project [114].

A much simpler approach [117] works with a projector where a sweeping blind opens up from left to right, for example. The sharp border between dark and bright moves over all objects and seen from a camera at an angle, it looks distorted by the object surfaces. This works like a triangulation, for any point in the scene. If the camera shutter is left open for the entire sweep, the brightness of each scene location is modulated by the duration of lighting and this is also modulated by the triangulation angle. Divide this by the brightness from a picture with constant illumination, and we have a measure for depth.

With any of these methods, the projections should of course not be visible. Infrared light and separate recording cameras, or flashing projections inserted in between the picture sequences, could mend this. Reflections within the scene can affect all active projection methods. Outdoor light is a problem as well, but with narrow band filtering and flash operation, separation factors of up to 1:10000 are achievable. As 3D information gets less important with distance, the projection only has to cover about 20 ft.

With all techniques using multiple exposures, moving objects are another problem. This can partly be addressed by calculating motion vectors from simple image content, a discipline highly developed already from the MPEG or AVC compression used in almost any video recording today.

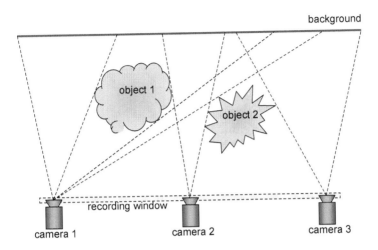

This picture shows the (idealized) viewing angles of 3 cameras, with the shadowing and 'see behind' areas with some simple example objects.

The recording is obviously not perfect, in that certain parts of a real scene will be missing as there is no real camera for all of the possible angles that a spectator could take when viewing the playback of this on a hypothetical, ideal 3D screen.

An array assembly would work better if more cameras and microphones were used. As cameras will rapidly get cheaper and smaller, we may expect to see arrays with many more cameras than depicted here, making the task much easier.

Such a recording technique that still confines the movie to a window view may be the usual type for a long time to come, but other possibilities, like surround, will also become more popular with vision simulators.

The following picture illustrates that there always are certain sections in the image of any of those cameras that resemble a section of the image a virtual camera behind the 'window' would have seen. By merging the appropriate image parts with some software help, the image of the virtual camera can therefore be constructed. This also applies to stereo viewing (two eye perspectives separately).

Upscaling

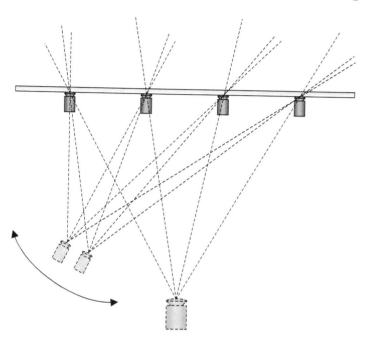

For a really perfect recording we will need many cameras. The more cameras, the fewer dead angles and the simpler the computing task. As it is practically impossible to align all cameras with single pixel precision (and also not reasonable, as they get slightly different pictures and perspectives anyway), we can assume their fine positioning to be random. So we would have to drop many pixels as they won't all fit into a common raster: a pixel in between just delivers no detail information

We could take advantage of this however. The cost of the array can be largely reduced if we use low resolution cameras and calculate a higher final picture resolution from overlaying and correlating their outputs. If the camera chips have pixels smaller than the raster size (some products have this anyway) as well as good optics, this is perfectly possible.

A resolution improvement of 2:1 or even 4:1 should be achievable, so an array of standard TV chips could as well record double HDTV as required for really large cinema applications.
Such an array may not be more expensive than just one dedicated double HDTV camera.
Let's explore this a bit further: smaller pixels are less sensitive or produce more noise, of course. Pixels with ¼ size have 2 times more image noise, for example. Adding up 4 signals just compensates for this (averaging n^2 signals reduces noise n times). For 4 times as many pixels, that is 4x resolution, the noise aspect would hence imply 16 cameras.
Under this aspect, an array of 16 times 9 cameras for example would be perfect to provide a resolution of 4x720 times 3x576, i.e. 2880x1728, which is really a cinema format (normal HDTV is 1280x720 in the US and 1920x1080 in Europe).
The computing equipment involved would first calculate raw correlations between different camera pictures to get the depth information, which is much easier here than with just 2 stereo cameras. Almost no dead angles will occur. With some additional depth sensors, this will be a cinch.

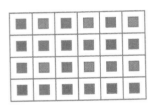 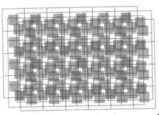

Section of a camera sensor with a sensitive pixel area of <100%, and random overlay of four pixel rasters (right)

In a second step, the computer would compare small image areas one by one, in order to find a correlation between pixel information from the single cameras and actual image detail. This way, camera pixels can be mapped to actual image pixels with high precision. This will only deliver actual fits if accidentally a camera pixel really fits into the higher resolution raster. Yet if we have 16x16 tries for just 4x4 raster points, the odds are good.

Again, nothing has to be precision aligned, not even the zoom factors, apertures and focus have to be 100% exactly fit, although they should be synchronized.

Every final alignment and adjustment can and should be taken care of by software, that would by the way also deliver a classical image stabilizing function, without the usual raster misalignment or blur. The entire camera array will in the end be really affordable compared to the usual prices for cinema equipment.

Calculating all influences precisely and concurrently would result in some average frequency response for the entire recording system. Deriving this would be beyond the scope of this book.

Let's just have a look at the average pixel coverage for different numbers of cameras (for calculations, see page 391):

pixel accuracy: $^1/_2$x$^1/_2$ number of cameras	resolution multiplication		
	2	**3**	**4**
4x4	0,356	0,637	0,777
5x5	0,199	0,494	0,675
6x6	**0,098**	0,363	0,567
7x7	0,042	0,251	0,462
8x8	**0,016**	0,165	0,365
9x9	0,005	**0,102**	0,279
10x10	0,002	0,060	0,207
11x11	0,000	0,033	0,149
12x12	0,000	**0,017**	**0,104**
13x13	0,000	0,009	0,070
14x14	0,000	0,004	0,046
15x15	0,000	0,002	0,029
16x16	0,000	0,001	**0,018**

Probability for a high resolution pixel not being aligned to at least one camera pixel by at least $\pm^1/_4$ pixel width in x and y direction

We see that 12x12 cameras, for example would already be very good for a 4 times resolution upscaling, and 6x6 if we want 2 times the resolution (only about 10% imperfect pixels).

The 'imperfect' pixels can be filled at a high probability or can also be smoothed out in the temporal axis, by averaging subsequent frames. Concurrently, this will result in a certain amount of

4x resolution information for any image pixel at any time, with a very high probability. Even with fewer cameras then, we would get some decent coverage already.

Real objects may of course be moving. The alignment will then be different for any frame. We will have to regard a certain displacement of image objects from frame to frame (motion vectors); hence, we won't average exactly the same pixels of subsequent frames, but those corresponding to the same (moving) scene pixels.

By the way, the method of upscaling from subsequent pictures from a single motion camera, called *super resolution*, is meanwhile available in several hard- and software products.

With the recording array, perspective processing and upscaling could be done in the cameras themselves, that could form a massively parallel processing unit if we equip them each with a little computing chip and wire these in an array, e.g. with high speed serial links. Still these camera units would be cheap, in a professional cinema context.

The entire video data picked up by the camera array will finally boil down to a partially descriptive format not bigger than that from two conventional high definition cameras.

With HD camera chips getting cheaper in the future, the upscaling effort will become less important, but the electronic precision alignment of pixels will still be necessary, and also ¾ of all pixels gathered will *always* have to be dropped, as they won't fit into the same common raster.

As mentioned already, it is simply not possible to ensure that all cameras get the same scene detail with the same alignment of their own pixel raster versus that detail. Natural scenes are not just flat test patterns but have a three dimensional structure that results in a different perspective for each camera. It's also not realistic to believe that we could precision align several optics. So we can really expect any raster alignments to be random anyway.

Hence, upscaling isn't just a weird and complicated idea, but a logical and consequential approach to turn some principal and unavoidable problems of camera arrays into a virtue.

Array camera requirements

Would we need expensive cameras for light field recording ?

The answer is no. Light field cameras should deliver as much depth of field as possible, as the ideal light field has to be crisp for any distance, same as a hologram. Lowering pixel noise by using larger lens apertures will therefore not work (the only way is by averaging, parallel to the upscaling process).

The small apertures necessary will limit the camera resolution possible, so upscaling may get even more interesting, but then the camera pixel crispness itself has certain restrictions.

It would now be interesting to determine the *optimum camera design and number of cameras* to use with a possible integrated light field/upscaling approach. This is a fairly complex problem, but let's try a simple approach for a first guess.

At page 380 you will find an unusually simple derivation for the depth of field to infinity, which is about all we need in addition to the formulas about lens resolution.

One solution would be:

- a lens size of $a=1mm$,
- hence a field depth of $b_i \approx 1m$ to infinity,
- probably good enough for a typical hologram recording,
- and an angular resolution of 2 arcmin,
- yielding ≈ 2000 pixels
- at 60 degrees image width.
- equaling an HDTV screen at a viewing distance equal to screen width.

This could for example be implemented with somewhere between 4x4 and 16x16 standard resolution pinhole cameras, for a target resolution of 1..2x HDTV.

Amateur video

The average video amateur would hardly be walking around with a huge camera array, of course.

This is something suited for big cinema or home movie theater, targeted at many spectators at different positions or even walking about.

Simply taking the vacation or family video in a „what you've seen is what you've got" style is better done with the device we've already been talking about, all the time: the vision simulator has stereo (HD) cameras, picks up anything anyway.

The recording conditions are good, as we're usually holding our head quite steady.

Focusing could not only be supported by looking at a target, the eye trackers could also deliver distance information right away by analyzing our squint, and we could even just show a frame border overlay instead of a complete viewfinder image.

Other than with the large cinema equipment described, the viewer position here is tied to the recording position.

One major disadvantage of conventional stereo pictures however, the intolerance against sideways tilting of the head, could be compensated by some not too complicated software. It would nevertheless necessary to take care about one's own head movements, for recordings that one would like to view later on.

Much less inconvenient than with any current equipment anyway: no fumbling around with straps and cases and switches, no waiting, no peering into a viewfinder, no dragging and towing.

The cigarette box sized pocket unit that we expect to persist for the first generations of vision simulators might still be there, but then it wouldn't be larger than the smallest current camcorder, serve a thousand more purposes anyway, can stay in the pocket all the time, and will easily be able to store days after days of video.

So equipped with a vision simulator, a video camera with many bells and whistles will be available anytime, at no weight or cost, and it will work almost unattended and unnoticed. Could we imagine any better ?

Smart cameras

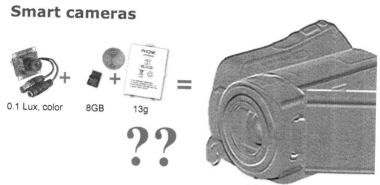

0.1 Lux, color   8GB   13g

2009 !!
The technology runaway: Solutions calling for products

Cameras today aren't only thick as a brick, they're stupid, too. Our eyes, in contrast, are very smart designs. Their optics aren't totally corrected, as it is quite simple to deal with geometrical corrections and even with chromatic aberration, by software. A smart camera should follow these *bionic* principles.

Superb plastic lenses can today be manufactured by simple molding. Full correction may be difficult, because large refraction indices are not available, but aspherical surfaces for example are easy to make. Geometry correcting the image by signal processing is just as easy.

Not only this: low resolution pictures can be converted to high resolution, exploiting raster shifts between subsequent images, as analyzed in the upscaling chapter already. Acceleration and perpendicularity sensors could deliver data for image stabilizing and easier MPEG encoding. These corrections wouldn't have to be made in the camera. Motion data can be integrated into an MPEG stream without compatibility issues, and a home computer can later on perform stabilizing and upscaling in one pass.

What we are talking about here is a HD camera as small as a sugar cube, weighing but a few grams, recording several hours of video into its own solid state memory, powered by its own internal accumulator. Such a camera you could just clip to your glasses' handle and almost forget, as the only notice you'd take of it, would be when pressing the record button.

As a viewfinder, a simple light frame mirrored into display glasses would do, as the viewing perspective of camera and eye are almost identical. Even without display glasses, there is still another way: include laser pointers into the camera, marking the corners of the image area right onto the scene. Placed a little outsides the recording window, these markers would not appear in the picture.

After recording, you'd simply plug the camera into your computer screen, use it as a webcam, let it load it's battery and let the computer render the previously recorded video, in the background.

Combining two cameras for stereo would be just as easy, if we simply equip them with some wireless connection, that could also ensure a microsecond accurate synchronicity for pictures and for a seamless, extended stereo sound.

And where would we leave this pretty large 10x zoom of our classical camcorder? Forget it. If these old fashioned cameras have one problem, it's their insufficient wide angle range. A powerful wide angle, without even the necessity of being optically perfect because of our smarter approach, with a moderate zoom range if desired, would be a much better solution for most practical purposes, especially with HD, where wide angle is the natural choice because of the larger screen size.

Wouldn't such a little camera come in handy? An approach using the same smart principles as our eye and brain, simple sensors and smart processing, far more capable than optical perfectionism. Simply the fittest.

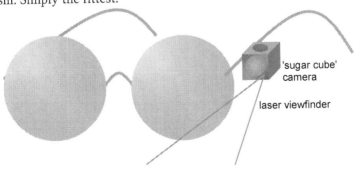

'sugar cube' camera

laser viewfinder

Encoding

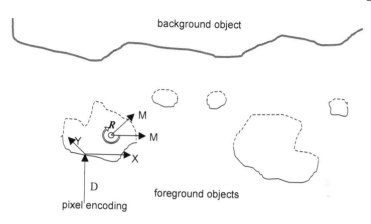

background object

M

M

Y

X

D

pixel encoding

foreground objects

A computerized encoder should be able to separate all background and foreground objects, and to encode all the information gathered. Of course there are more difficulties than illustrated here; for example, transparent objects, fog, etc.

With glassy objects, the software must try to derive their properties from the pictures from different camera angles. A certain 'intelligence' is necessary to derive a geometrical representation as well as a correct description of material properties, at least enough of it also allowing for a correct calculation of intermediate viewing angles between the original camera positions.

Even though the software does not have to 'understand' what it sees, obviously at least with glassy, foggy and reflective objects, deriving a good object description becomes very difficult.

In theory, current MPEG standards allow extensions for objects and surface textures as well as motion vectors, which would also allows for a high level of compression. It's however for a reason that so little thereof has actually been implemented.

While PC graphics cards will soon be able to synthesize arbitrary complex scenes so well that they look perfectly real, the opposite, i.e. deriving a description for such a synthesis from a real scene, is a lot more difficult.

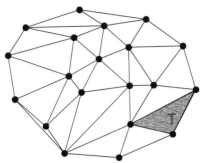

In principle, 3D objects in graphics or game engines are usually modeled as triangular surface meshes describing the spatial shape of the object (the more triangles, the better the fit), while textures (T) are used to fill the areas in the mesh. These textures can well be encoded and compressed like conventional images. With a sufficient number of texture elements and some smoothing applied, we can get a perfect reproduction of any real object. Game engines are based on predefined object descriptions as above, together with physical data describing the possible interactions of objects. A rendering engine then simulates a virtual camera to derive a perspective view of the scene as well as lighting and shadows according to virtual light sources that also have to be defined beforehand. The big advantage of the approach is that it profits from the huge advances of high end graphics cards driven by the game market.

Generating an object based representation of a real scene, requires to derive the object descriptions (mesh, textures) from real camera pictures. This has already been subject to intense research for a couple of years. It is not necessary to resolve the light sources in this case and to restore lighting later on (although this would facilitate the merging with virtual scenes). Lighting can be recorded as a property of the texture. Glassy, reflective and foggy objects, as said, cause difficulties with this approach, and time will tell how this will be resolved. Nevertheless, we may expect to see sophisticated encoding schemes of this type, and they'll seamlessly integrate with synthetic scene generation, enabling some very advanced hybrid production methods.

Light field encoding

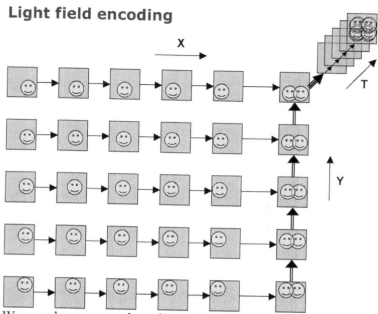

We may however neglect object recognition at recording time, if we just manage to encode several camera channels in an efficient way. Let us consider this a bit further.

Pictures from neighboring cameras show similarities identical to those in a time sequence from a single camera move. Classical motion encoding (MPEG) can therefore encode such a sequence at ease (the illustration may resemble [112] by the way, but the method is very different).

Encoded line picture sequences could be treated the same way again, compressing the columns, with the sole complication that some meta data has to be treated as well. Finally, the entire compound including all meta data, could be encoded exploiting similarities over the time axis (T).

The method would require no „intelligent" image processing, nor would it deliver any hint about depth. It could however be a feasible approach to encode all camera pictures for later retrieval. Intermediate perspectives would be derived at playback time only, then requiring sort of „intelligence" of course.

Holographic encoding

Object oriented and multi camera recordings are not the only possible formats. Holograms (or complete light fields, which is just another way achieving similar results) would of course be better, if we only could find a way to do this.

- Holograms can contain any of the nasty objects and reproduce them perfectly (they encode just anything light can show).

- The patterns of a hologram have a great deal of redundancy.

- Holograms can be computed (synthesized) from three dimensional picture data.

- The mathematics of the transformations are well understood.

- We could conceive a recording method where a hologram is recorded, then scanned and the vast amount of data it contains is reduced by computer algorithms, removing any unnecessary redundancy. Theoretically, this should be possible up to a point where the amount of data remaining is not much bigger than with the conventional methods regarded.

- Such a redundancy reduced hologram could be transmitted and a receiver could use it to reproduce not a hologram, but single custom tailored perspectives for single viewers instead.

One question is certainly left wide open, how to get at a hologram at recording, that could then be processed. Probably we would still have to derive this from camera arrays.
As this is still utterly difficult, experiments have been carried out with synthetic image data. After a huge amount of simplifications and optimizations, finally the only holographic motion picture displays realized were indeed viewer adaptive Fourier holograms (see p.248). Although these were also optimized for compression, the effectiveness of this technology left a lot to desire.

The downside of a holographic encoding would also be that we wouldn't get at an object based description and therefore the merging of real and computer generated data in movie production wouldn't get much easier this way. Objects however may just be one possible abstraction. Procedures based on the mathematics of holography could perhaps enable us to merge 3D scenes as easy as a collage of paper clips, without any need for abstract description of surfaces, textures, materials and so on.

But what is it that makes holographic data for large screens so vast? Is it the large number of perspectives? Not necessarily, as the hologram can't record much more than superficial information.

There is another fact that greatly contributes to the amount of data: a hologram is, theoretically, utterly crisp. Light wavelength is the limit (those little holograms that you can buy are not as crisp, but that is because they are viewed in white light and the lamps are not point like). A large screen image with 1/1000 mm resolution doesn't make any sense. And we can't reduce this data sufficiently by just blurring the picture, as many attempts have shown. We could use a smaller window, what is actually one ingredient of the adaptive Fourier hologram approach.

But there is yet another way to do it: use a larger wavelength. We can't simply use microwaves for photography, of course. A millimeter wave hologram could theoretically be taken by a large area of micro antennas and wouldn't even need a reference beam because these elements could directly work with an electrical reference frequency, and an image could be read out from the array like with a giant camera chip. These waves however penetrate clothing and other non conducting material, as we know from the recently introduced 'naked scanners' for security control. This is useless for normal photography applications.

Ultrasound could also be an option, I've already considered this for medical applications in [1]. There a sensor array could be made from a single silicon wafer, but ultrasound of this wavelength doesn't work in plain air, beneath other problems.

The better way to do this kind of reduction would be to use a light hologram and then recalculate the patterns, synthetically that is, to look as if they were recorded with longer waves, ½ millimeter perhaps instead of ½ micrometer waves. Such a hologram would essentially carry all superficial and spatial information, yet with less detail resolution, in the order of ½ mm, only as much as we need for a large, apparently sharp natural image. The reduction factor possible is about one million. From the information theoretical view as well, we should indeed not need a much larger number of pixels than with a classical image. It's nothing less than fully implementing step 1 of the aforementioned 3 step paradigm. Actually, anything 'you could see' is contained in the hologram, with the little constraint that we confine this to seeing through a certain window frame.

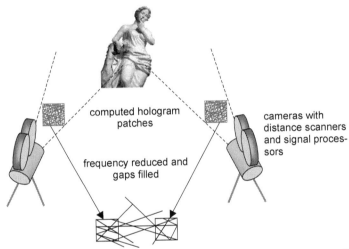

One might speculate about alternative recording methods as well, for example recording many little keyhole holograms by a camera array (each just the size of the camera aperture) and somehow merging them into a big one. Yet there is no hint so far if this would lead to anything useful.

Since the idea of millimeter wave holograms has been brought up in the 1st edition of this book, such an encoding has actually been tried out with synthetic image data, using the immensely powerful processing engine of a current graphics card [83]. Not only this, conversions from hologram to light field representation and back have also been carried out. The principle has been proven, and the images can e.g. be rendered for different perspectives and depth of field ranges from the same scene data.

Although the practical usability of the principle is still more of a futuristic theme, the interest in it justified and looking into this yields other insights about 3D imaging technology. So I'll now explain it more thoroughly.

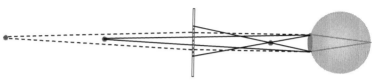

Let's compare the millimeter wave approach to a light hologram. There, a certain image pixel (d) can only be represented by an area of fringes ('fringelet', actually a tiny zone plate).
In case of a pixel at infinity, this zone plate cannot be bigger than the pupil. For nearer pixels, it becomes smaller, and for virtual image pixels before the hologram plane it can also be bigger than the pupil.

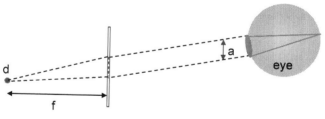

For general considerations we can simply assume this zone plate to be as big as the pupil. Instead of analyzing various configurations with different reference beams, we can simplify the situation by assuming the zone plate to focus light to a pixel with diameter d at distance f. This is even accurate, when the distance between the eye and the hologram becomes very small.
This also implies that the theoretical resolution in the micrometer range is not achieved in practical viewing situations.

From the lens resolution formula, we know that $d \approx \lambda f / a$. With a viewing distance $f = 1$ m, $\lambda = 500$ nm, $a = 3$ mm, we get a pixel diameter $d = 0.2$ mm. Due to our small eye aperture, viewing a real hologram we therefore don't see all of it's theoretical crispness (which can be about 300 times better).

Nevertheless, this very pixel has to be encoded over the entire screen area, because viewers could come from any direction.

It becomes quite obvious here, why it is possible to make holograms that show entirely different pictures from different directions or unreel a film sequence as one moves by.

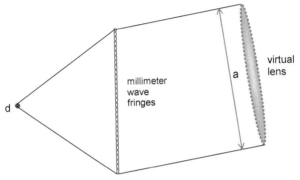

In case of the millimeter wave encoding scheme, the decoding algorithm would use the entire area in any case, somehow equaling a virtual lens as large as the screen. So we get about the same practical resolution as with the viewing situation for a real light hologram shown before (if $f = a$, then $d \approx \lambda$).

A difficulty would be remote objects that can only be seen through gaps between more proximate objects, as these could only be represented on a smaller screen area. It would be necessary to care for this, for example by partially inserting layers with smaller wavelengths (virtual holograms allow for such tricks). Strange perspectives would also arise, e.g. seeing objects from 5 sides at once because of the huge lens size. This has all to be dealt with.

One problem remains with these synthetic holograms: even in spite of the larger wavelength we use, the amount of computation we need will likely be tremendous. From some basic considerations concerning diffraction, we may guess that a millimeter wave hologram would at least need about twice the resolution of a classical picture, i.e. 4 times as many pixels.

Let us first consider what a 'brute force approach' to hologram synthesis would involve.

With only basic algorithmic tricks applied, we would have to add up the interference patterns for all image pixels as they appear in the area of the holographic window. For 1 million pixels (very roughly 4x the count of a TV image), we'd have to add about 1mio. x 1mio. individual gray values. It is necessary to find algorithms that reduce theses calculations by several orders. We may partly apply Fourier holograms. We may also greatly parallelize the process. Let's develop this a little further:

Assume we have a scene description consisting of surface pixels (a simple case). The number of pixel we have, will just be a little larger here than the number of screen pixels, as anything else is hidden.

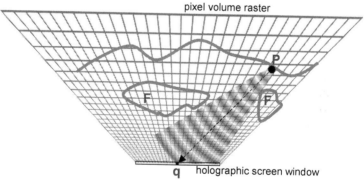

pixel volume raster

holographic screen window

The further away scene objects are, the less resolution we need. Here we try to use a raster expanding with an angle corresponding to the viewing angle of the recording cameras (more can't be recorded).

The raster could expand up to a few hundred ft. of distance, anything more distant actually appears as infinite and can be allocated to the last pixel plane.

Actually this results in a pattern of single pixels, but from the distance they should appear as a solid surface.

Now we have to map all scene pixels (P) to every single screen pixel (q). The illustration shows the virtual wavefront coming from one scene pixel and getting to one screen pixel (wavelength shown larger than real).

Getting the wave amplitude that the scene pixel will cause at a given screen pixel, involves calculating the proper distance, then calculating the amplitude. The amplitude calculation at q can in principle be reduced to cutting off decimals before the point (if we just normalize wavelength to 1), then looking up a sine wave function in a simple table. Calculating the distance may be a bit more difficult but we shall find something easy as well. Then we compare the phase of the pixel wave with the local phase of a virtual reference beam. So this are still about 1mio. x 1mio. operations.

Yet if we use a large chip and dedicate *one complete calculation circuit* to any screen pixel, it's 'only' 1 million calculations/image in each of them. This is 60 millions per second, not a big deal at all with current chips easily reaching billions of clock cycles per second. Current high end CPUs or graphics processor chips have up to 1 billion switching elements, this would result in 1000 per pixel if we want 1 mio. parallel circuits. Actually, we may hardly need more than this. So this is not SciFi, it's quite possible.

High definition pictures would of course need about an order of magnitude more processing power, but even this is not too far fetched, and the approach considered here is far from being optimal.

But there is still one more difficulty: Not all P/q combinations would contribute to the result, as certain pixels are covered by foreground objects F in certain areas of the hologram window (above picture).

This masking of distant pixels is not simple, as we have to tell any pixel element in our chip if to process this input or not. Doing this all the time would entirely spoil the gain expected from parallel computing. We could try to load this information only once and re-use it for neighboring pixels by just shifting it within the computing array and only reloading some pixels where necessary. We see that while there are some obvious tricks for true hologram synthesis, this requires a lot more.

At least, our synthetic approach will not suffer from the self interference (light scattered back from object surfaces) that haunts natural holograms [65] and spoils them with noise. Digitally produced hologram patterns can also be optimized to deliver less diffraction effects than natural ones.

A Fourier approach

As we have seen, approaches to real-time hologram synthesis so far are just light field displays (p.243), making up the 'hologram' display from little patches of Fourier holograms (p.248).

If we use this however, any of these patches will have to be 1...2 mm wide for a sufficient angular resolution. In this case, a keyhole hologram broken out from the area would have no focus information (Fourier holograms just don't), while a real hologram would.

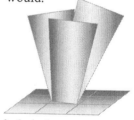

The Fourier patch would just define a large number of light beams by angle and intensity (like a small lens), but the angle would not change over the patch. If we try making the patch smaller, the number of different angles than can be resolved, hence the picture resolution of the keyhole hologram and the entire encoding will decline, as we know.

Now if for example we would not use smaller patches, but shift the entire raster of patches by e.g. ½ a patch width, we would again get no focus effects (different angles for the same scene point) for single patches, but the light beams defined by the patterns would again just have the right angles for a look through the center of each patch.

If we shift the patch matrix around in small steps just often enough, we could most likely combine the hologram patterns from all patches and get a complete, real hologram including focus information as well. It will still be a lot of computing, but maybe less than with the brute force approach considered before. We may also consider using different patch raster sizes for different pattern wavelengths (hence, angular ranges, as hologram pattern wavelengths depend on beam angles) and combining them afterwards. A lot of ideas that I will not continue speculating about here.

This is not comparable with the speculation about deriving a hologram from keyhole camera patches of a camera array mentioned before. There we have no means of simply calculating these patches at any position, as we have here.

Color

Dealing with *color* will in principle increase the complexity of holographic encoding by less than ¼, because we can just add 2 color difference channels of half or even quarter resolution, as with classical video (here, half the wavelength).

Decoding

Another demanding task is the decoding of a hologram into actual viewer perspectives for display glasses. It can be nearly as complex as generating the hologram.

Last but not least, we also have to consider if we want a holographic display in the glasses themselves as a last stage in the transmission chain, and it may be rewarding but will get pretty complex to sort out possible simplifications with this, if the original picture source is already a hologram.

Just viewing a synthetic wavelength enlarged hologram, could easily be accomplished with a micro display exactly small enough to translate the mm wavelength back to light wavelength, and viewing this micro screen with a magnifier (that could as well be the mirror glass of a vision simulator).

For a realistic appearance, we would of course need to simulate head movements that would be possible in front of a real hologram screen. Otherwise seeing around objects - for example - would be impossible, and the entire reproduction would be no better than with a simple stereo movie. We could maybe accomplish this by shifting and tilting the micro display opposite to actual head movements, measured with position sensors. This would include a lot of mechanics, but it could be quite simple.

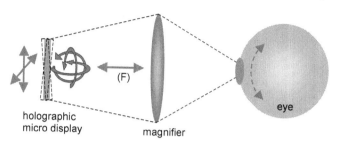

holographic
micro display   magnifier

Simulating movements to and from the screen (F) would be difficult however, as it would require to change the focus length of the magnifier or at least its distance to the eye, something almost impossible with the vision simulator optics we have discussed so far.

The ideal solution would of course try to do all these compensation movements electronically by changing the display image itself. Just shifting would be easy, but some other changes would require quite sophisticated mathematical operations on the hologram itself.

Another task with holographic displays in this context is a seamless integration of virtual objects with scene holograms, which will be necessary in several applications.

We see that this thematic is very complex, and a lot of research will be required to explore it.

Nevertheless, it's an interesting topic worth keeping an eye on it, even though the method of choice for 3D media will most probably be multi channel encoding for recording and light field displays or 'classical' vision simulator displays for viewing.

Giant screens

OLED displays are in a process of rapid development. These self luminating devices can be produced on flexible substrates. A simple production process is to print them, with inkjet printers. It's only natural to make them im stripes, roll them up and sell them as wallpaper. If this works, then the customer could just cover a wall with this at any desired size, screw some contact clamps on to interconnect everything, and a flat, cheap and efficient display would be ready.
Even 3D light field displays will be possible, as micro lens stripe arrays can be imprinted into plastics at high precision.
Another possibility are holographic projection screens, that can work with little projectors and deliver the same contrast as a self luminating screen.
A display panel with a very short reaction time could also deliver individual pictures to several viewers wearing simple shutter glasses.
All these things will become very cheap, We see this with large LCD screens already and OLED will be *a lot* cheaper in the end.
As some people might still prefer real screens to glasses in certain applications, we will look at the following from both points of view. This all applies to general TV and home cinema as well.

Virtual households and conference rooms
The impact of bandwidth

Glass fiber cables have a far higher potential than is widely recognized:
A single glass fiber could theoretically transport over 10^{15} bit/second (visible light has about 10^{15} Hz, and perfect modulation could yield more than 1 Bit/second per Hz of bandwidth). HDTV signals can be compressed to about 10 Mbits/second,
hence, 100 million HDTV channels would be the possible. With realistically achievable modulation technology (multispectral modulation), it would still be about 10 million. Given the fact that

even a single overseas cable has a bundle of many fibers, up to about a billion simultaneous HDTV connections of any kind wouldn't be a problem.

The result of more and more bandwidth available is already becoming obvious. A recent study showed that only 2% of the already available bandwidth of transatlantic fiber cables is currently in use. No wonder that distance phone calls almost never go by satellite anymore, and they are already cheaper than local calls. These millions of channels available will make a permanent private HDTV connection affordable for anybody.

Who would need this, anyway ?

One possible application could be virtual households. Guess mom and dad live in Europe, grandma in the US and junior has a job in Japan. Or a company would like to have one or more permanent virtual connections between distant offices.

They could just cover a wall with display wallpaper, add some micro cameras with small lenses that hide in this large display area, and create a virtual wall breakthrough that would extend the room into another one at the other side of the globe, 24 hours a day if necessary. If everyone used vision simulators, the display wallpaper could be omitted, of course.

In case of such virtual wall breakthroughs, or windows, most of the time the scene would be very static, and the display would have to generate pictures for existing viewers only (it would be possible to track them or use data from their vision simulators to determine what they can see), so the originating source would have to send only that, and in high resolution it would be necessary only at the center of their field of vision.

Tracking is also absolutely necessary to generate the right perspective from the available camera perspective, otherwise the impression would not be entirely realistic.

With only necessary pictures transmitted, the average bandwidth requirement could in this case go well below 1 Mbit/second. Indeed, *billions* of high definition virtual wall breakthroughs could be held open permanently, at very moderate costs.

Properties of large scale 'holograms'

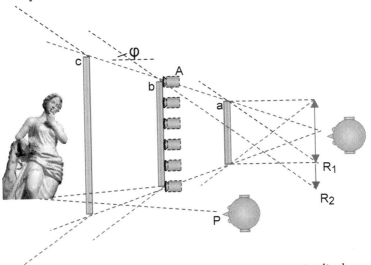

No matter if hologram, light field or auto stereoscopic display or virtual screen rendered b a vision simulator, we have to consider certain properties and restrictions if we stick to a certain 'screen window' (as will certainly be the case for many years ahead).

We regard a hologram taken by a camera array A, with a lens opening angle φ.

Holographic screens act like *windows*, hence screens of appropriate size in different distances (a, b, c) can give the spectator an *entirely identical viewing experience*, if the display holograms for them are individually adapted.

The horizontal viewing range usable will depend on the screen size: R_1 in this example for screen a, but at least R_2 for screen b. Note that the useful edge angle is not the same for all object distances, and that a for a viewer (P) using a screen larger than the recording array, R is still limited, as not all side edges could be resolved.

The array cameras have to deliver pictures that are *crisp from zero to infinity*, if we want to record the light field correctly. Depth-of-field blur with holograms occurs at reproduction only. A properly recorded hologram is entirely crisp anywhere!

Perfecting the virtual wall break-through

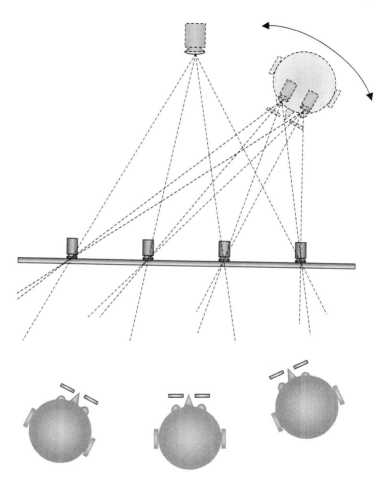

A wall display in a tele-conferencing assembly. A camera that would take up the viewpoint of a participator at the other side is impossible to make. Yet with a display this large, several pinhole cameras can be mounted in the panel without being noticed. There are always certain sections in the image of any of those cameras that resemble a section of the image a virtual camera behind the wall would have seen. By merging the appropriate image parts with some software help, the image of the virtual camera can therefore be constructed. This also applies to stereo viewing (two eye perspectives separately).

This way, we could also dynamically construct the right perspective for a viewer at any place at the other side of the wall.

If two rooms are equipped with this hardware, and we use a lightfield display as described before, every participant gets a perfect stereo perspective all the time, e.g. the scene should look 100% real.

We could complete the assembly by a microphone array and a corresponding speaker array in the wall (flat speakers that fit behind wallpapers and even reproduce a lot of bass, are already on the market). Such a sound assembly would have pseudo holographic properties and perfect the illusion.

Single person applications like this have been tried several times, one of the most recent being the Immersive Meeting Point by HHI [10], that implements a few of the techniques discussed.

Screen based 3D: conclusion

We have taken a short but quite comprehensive look at 3D screen varieties, and all of them exhibit some problems

Many require to occupy a certain viewing position, or even to hold one's head straight. Even worse, many will cause headaches due to false perspective or focus.
A huge obstacle for general application is the inflexibility with display size and perspective. Modern media should work on a mobile phone display as well as on a wall sized screen.

The solution to the mentioned problems will definitely be computerized image processing. Computers have already overcome any format restrictions in conventional productions. Getting rid of formats, a generic description of recorded objects is called for, that later on allows to produce a device independent performance, and synthesize in real time whatever the desired display arrangement requires.

Large screens will only be widely acceptable for 3D usage, if any viewer gets his own custom generated perspective. Which in turn limits applications a lot.

I therefore anticipate, that the technology of choice will finally use VR glasses and integrate seamlessly into the wider and more general paradigm of a virtual environment including all sorts of virtual devices.

As soon as this technology is in widespread use, a virtual wall breakthrough, for example, will only need a camera array to be installed, all else will be just one more piece of software for already existing hardware.
One more bodily contribution to the implementation of virtual screens and windows may perhaps be a blackened wall in order to make the virtual objects insertion more easy.

Beyond the screen
Optical surround

For special applications, it will be desirable to record objects, actors, scenes from everywhere, or from at least 180^0 up front.

A chamber orchestra, a theater stage etc. would be good applications. This is only logical, if we use vision simulators, to get away from the screen paradigm and create a virtual stage that can be viewed from all around, for example.

It is necessary to do a lot of perspective calculations and object separation for this to work, and it will lead to an object oriented encoding of scenes, that would be similar to that of a scene synthesis like in 3D games. This is difficult but the logical course of further development anyway.

With such capabilities, the virtual orchestra could just sit in the middle of the living room, the virtual stage or the news speaker as well. Specific application patterns will evolve that we could hardly imagine today. It may seem as if this type of recording would not work with the holographic or light field encoding scheme we have discussed. Where is the 'hologram' screen with surround technology?

We could conceive a virtual hologram screen as a *sphere* around the recorded objects. This would likely get very big, but then we could use a coarser resolution. Otherwise, as holograms can also show objects before them, we could also choose any smaller diameter desired, even *inside* the recorded objects.

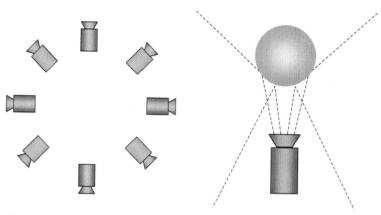

The other kind of surround video is available right now, and will become an everyday experience in the future. Either camera arrays or special optics (other than the simple mirror ball assembly shown above, there are a lot of sophisticated professional surround lenses available) can be used to record the required data. This type of recording should have many practical applications if vision simulators would become common equipment, as any place could then instantly be turned into a perfect surround theater and many program types as there are nature films, sports events etc. could use it to produce an immersive experience.

We might even see both types of surround video in the same event, enabling us to walk in a virtual room and see the objects in it as well as the walls and ceilings on all sides in full 3D.

In this case we may chose the same large virtual hologram sphere to encode the outside and inside scenery. Outdoors scenes are also possible, of course.

The holographic circle

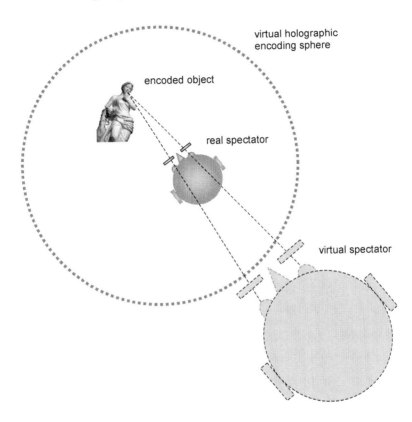

virtual holographic
encoding sphere

encoded object

real spectator

virtual spectator

A virtual encoding sphere for the holographic method can be positioned far outside the depicted scene. The visual impression can later on be generated for a virtual spectator outside the sphere in a way that it entirely resembles the impression a real spectator inside the sphere would get, except for a different scale. The hologram patterns encoded could in this case be much coarser than with a small encoding sphere, according to the scaling factor involved, so the use of a large sphere does not increase the amount of data to be generated and recorded.

In and out of the sphere

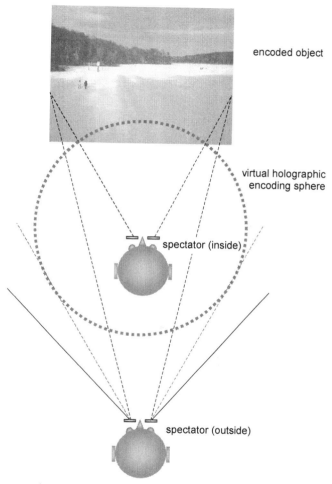

encoded object

virtual holographic encoding sphere

spectator (inside)

spectator (outside)

The same virtual sphere could encode a scenery outsides of it. In fact, for a totally immersive cinema experience, it should be best to use a sphere as large as possible, because if a spectator gets outsides, we will still be able to generate images for him as long as the sphere is in the viewing angle, but not otherwise.

Virtual cinema

Today it is very dangerous to enter a US movie theater with a camcorder. Even only a suspected attempt of filming the movie could send you to jail. What if everybody had a personal vision simulator with all the cameras belonging to it? Would they collect all these items at the wardrobe ?

Or would movie theaters go out of business anyway, because everybody could perfectly simulate a big screen at home ?

Maybe not, indeed:

If anybody had a vision simulator, movie theaters could just stop projecting films but instead transmit the picture by wireless networks. Viewers would get the picture by their own vision device. So everybody would always sit at the best place and the overwhelming expense for current Imax or surround projectors could be saved.

As the micro headphones of a vision simulator could produce quite good sound but not as well surround, and certainly not let the ground shake, movie theaters could invest in a good sound system (frankly, today's sound systems often are a torture, nothing but loud). Sound could even be diverted between the theater system and the user's headphones, to provide the same impression at every place.

The video transmission could be copy protected (recording inhibited) and encrypted. Admissions would not be sold in paper but as an electronic key sent to the user's device at payment.

Would anybody really visit such a cinema ?

Maybe. At least if the movie was new and couldn't be viewed anywhere else.

The technology would also offer new possibilities: Perfect 3D, just like holography, would be possible, and special effects like smells, moving seats, water splashing on the audience, like in some monster cinemas today, would be the real attractions.

So indeed cinema could survive the vision simulator.

Virtual media - a conclusion

Cinema productions are frequently using synthetic scenes already, and merge them with reality. These scenes are inherently 3D and object oriented, and enable us to render perspectives according to the viewer's own position rather than to a fixed camera position. These viewer perspectives could best be rendered and displayed in the viewer's own vision simulator glasses. This would, for the first time, deliver perfectly realistic 3D.
The bottleneck to this approach is the capability to record real scenes in a similar manner, i.e. to separate objects and gather their 3D surfaces, just like with the computer generated ones.
Therefore I did emphasize the necessity of multi channel, multi position camera recording and 3D processing and encoding.

Virtual media is a very wide field, and so far we did only scratch the surface a little, as far as it concerns the most important aspects in conjunction with our thematic.
Vision simulators could change our entire attitude and habits with media objects. For example, movie characters could appear without image frame and background, our living room could become a theater stage or that of a concert hall. We could as well imagine total surround cinema, ideal for documentaries and outdoors themes, to be possible everywhere. If that isn't an attractive technology, then I don't know.

For the scope of this book, I think this may suffice. A little more is in the fiction chapter, and much more is left to your imagination.

The end of hardware – an outlook

In the course of this text it should have become obvious that the further development of computer communications and computer interfaces will inevitably include to move these as close to the brain as possible (i.e. towards the eyes and ears for the time being), which in turn will result in an ubiquitous and - hopefully - seamlessly integrated augmented reality.

I also hope to have proven that simplistic approaches may have been good for first experiments or specialized applications, but that the course now has to go towards more perfect implementations that - first and foremost - have to solve the problem of merging the virtual with the real.

This also implies lots of new applications, situations, usage habits, security problems, and so on, that couldn't realistically be addressed in a comprehensive way, even less in the course of a single book and surely not without a lot of experimentation and experience with the fully implemented technology. Nonetheless I hope my limited fantasy could shed some light on it and inspire the spirit of others.

Even if there certainly are some contradictions remaining in the scenarios envisioned, especially as far as it concerns implications on society, laws etc., I think this may serve even the better to initiate, and contribute to, discussions on the thematic.

As with any technology, perfection will not be achieved in one step, so we have to expect many intermediate solutions and applications to come. An entire field that I did not really address here is about thinking out and implementing such intermediate products. It's of course about impossible to foresee such a certainly very complex development.

What I tried here instead, was to define the aim and the technologies necessary to approach the target, so we could easily determine the strategic relevance of this or that development for our final objective.

We have seen some applications that could do without one or the other feature, hence allowing to get to a product easier and faster.

The applications for vision impaired people discussed above, need about anything but the displays. So they are perfect test beds for camera based orientation systems, spatial sound synthesis, finger and maybe even eye pointing. The entire difficulty of high end main displays or mask displays is however avoided in this case.
Other varieties could need just these, but not sound: office applications, for example. So we could think about special office models.
For home entertainment, very simple models could be developed that would need the highest quality displays possible but could do without part or all of the spatial orientation functions. Other varieties of such devices could work with spatial orientation but without mask displays, instead requiring real black areas on the walls to insert virtual display screens.

For outdoor activities as well as driving, glasses without mask displays could be sufficient in many cases, with the advantage of lower light attenuation and some weight savings. These couldn't provide the intelligent sunglasses function of course.

A mobile phone integrated in glasses, as already described in the introduction, could be a great product and an ideal test bed for displays eye trackers, acoustic components and more.

The most difficult application area in the end would be night driving, if we want an anti blinding function, that of course wouldn't be possible without a mask display of very low light attenuation. It's also a tough application under security aspects, as we have to guarantee that nothing important is covered up accidentally, or disturbed otherwise by the displays.

I think we have seen that there are many special applications that could be used to develop parts of the full featured vision simulator and address fairly big markets already. People may own

several different ones for different occasions, until it finally becomes easy to include all features into one device.
It will anyway remain hard to say what the further course of development will be, and how fast it will go.

Having thrived through so many aspects of the field, we could at least try to compile a short list of things to do:

1. A display design based on the presence of eye trackers, that allows for high resolution, viewing angle and brightness at minimum weight.
2. Technologies for a good mask display. This is even more basic research than (1). Very important.
3. Develop the best eye tracker possible, fully integrated with the display design.
4. Micro and nano technologies for laser, holographic and other displays as well as optical and mechanical elements.
5. Very low power image compression and decompression as well as serial communication chips.

There are also tasks that have already been performed somewhere but may have to be adapted, reinvented, revived or improved:

1. Anticipative motion sensing and rock stable rendering of objects.
2. Camera based position sensing and scene identification (not recognition).
3. Virtual keys. Add eye pointing !
4. Dynamic sound rendering.
5. High performance, low power, very light pocket computers.
6. All sorts of application software.

That's enough.

In order not to disrupt the flow of arguments, some calculations still infesting have been banished to the end of this book. Nevertheless, only simple things are elegant. Here we have some approaches to high tech optics, using most simple mathematics.

Appendix: optics and more

Laser beam deviation

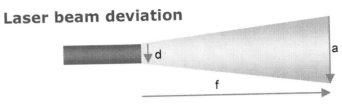

Deviation of a laser beam with source diameter d

Laser beam deviation can be assessed from the resolution of a lens. The resolution a zone plate or a lens can deliver, follows very simply from the actual pixel sizes light wave fronts from different parts of the lens are able to form. With a slight simplification for larger focus lengths, the following picture allows us to see this easily:

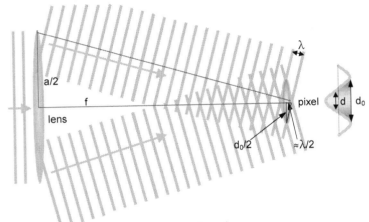

We straightforwardly get $^a/_2/f \approx {^\lambda/_2}/{^{d_0}/_2}$, hence $d_0 \approx 2\lambda f/a$. Given the way d_0 refers to the amplitude pattern, the actual pixel diameter d is less than half of it, depending on the contrast value desired. Wavefronts from inner parts of the lens (smaller a, larger d_0) will however spoil the result towards larger d values. Hence we could simply define:

$$d = \lambda f / a$$

An exact but more complicated calculation may result in the usual Gauss solution but this is only about 20% different.

The formula also resembles the schoolbook Gaussian Beam solution* for laser beam focusing. If we imagine a laser beam with diameter a, originating from the eye and being focused by a lens positioned in the screen area, we see the analogy. Again, a wider beam can be focused to a smaller point than a narrow one. These standard formulas carry additional factors of 1.27 resp. 1.22, but this largely depends on the edge amplitude definition, anyway.

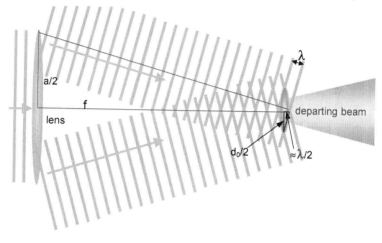

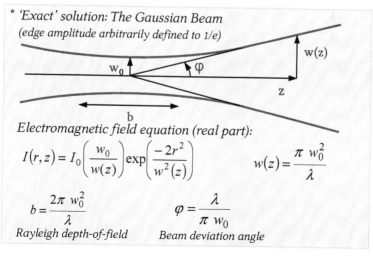

* *'Exact' solution: The Gaussian Beam*
(edge amplitude arbitrarily defined to 1/e)

$w(z)$

w_0 φ

z

b

Electromagnetic field equation (real part):

$$I(r,z) = I_0\left(\frac{w_0}{w(z)}\right)\exp\left(\frac{-2r^2}{w^2(z)}\right) \qquad w(z) = \frac{\pi\, w_0^2}{\lambda}$$

$$b = \frac{2\pi\, w_0^2}{\lambda} \qquad\qquad \varphi = \frac{\lambda}{\pi\, w_0}$$

Rayleigh depth-of-field   *Beam deviation angle*

Hence:

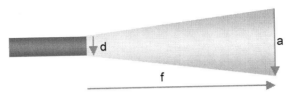

Beam deviation $\qquad a \approx \lambda\, f\,/\,d$

The Gaussian beam solution would be $\quad a \approx \dfrac{4}{\pi}\lambda\, f\,/\,d$
(just a matter of contrast definition !)

Beam deviation angle* $a\,/\,f \approx 2\,\varphi \approx \lambda\,/\,d$

The Gaussian beam solution would have been $\quad 2\varphi \approx \dfrac{4}{\pi}\lambda\,/\,d$

The formula also applies to both sides of a lens likewise, so it can tell us about the resolution of telescopes.

A spy satellite with a large telescope (aperture a=1m) for example at λ = 500nm and an altitude of f = 100km could resolve d = 5cm (2") on the ground. We can also derive that it would take a lens or mirror almost a mile wide to see the remainders of lunar missions on the moon, or prove that an HDTV camera including lens could fit into an 1/8"(3mm) cube. Applied to the eye (a $\approx$ 2...5mm, f $\approx$ 20mm), we get the strange result that theoretical crispness is lower at bright light, when the iris contracts and our lens aperture gets smaller. Actual d values for different lens apertures are between 3 and 6 µm, or $\approx$ 0.4 and 1 arcmin of angular resolution.

Actually, 1 arcmin, corresponding to a lens size of a=2mm, is what physiologists have found to be the human average and what TV standards are considering as 'crisp'. No wonder, as much bigger lens sizes are seen at low light conditions only, where making the receptor cells smaller would only increase noise, technically spoken. So evolutionary optimization is indeed responsible for our eyesight.

---

*With small angles, $\tan\varphi \approx \varphi$

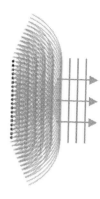

The picture to the left illustrates many coherent light origins. forming a planar wave front. In this case, we have drawn sources constant distance from each other. With a continuous large surface and arbitrarily narrow light origins, the edge waves will wipe out each other almost entirely.

Macroscopically, what we get is nothing but a typical laser beam.

Depth of field

The same simple assessment shown for resolution can likewise be used to calculate the *depth of field* of a lens:

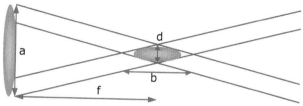

Depth of field (max.): $b \approx 2d\, f/a \approx 2\, \lambda\, f^2/a^2$

Gauss/Rayleigh result in comparison: $b \approx \dfrac{8}{\pi} \lambda\, f^2/a^2$

In case of limited camera resolution (< lens resolution) we get:

$$b \approx 2\, \lambda\, f^2/(a_o a) \quad \text{for} \quad a_o < a$$

where a_o is the aperture corresponding to this resolution. Interesting remark: the depth of field **b** for optimum aperture ($a_0 = a$) depends on the object pixel size **d** only

$$b \approx 2\, d^2/\lambda$$

Hence, depth of field becomes quadratically lower with shrinking dimensions (microscope effect).

Depth of field to infinity

A closest distance b_i, for a depth of field from b_i to infinity we could simply derive as follows (usual calculations take pages):

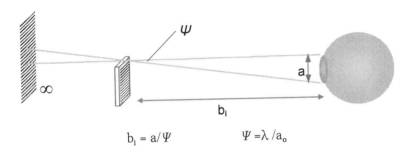

$$b_i = a/\Psi \qquad\qquad \Psi = \lambda/a_o$$

Assume eye focusing to distance b_i. Towards infinity, the rays should not deviate by more than an angle Ψ, that should equal b_i/a at small angles, and also the eye resolution given by λ/a_o (min.1 arcmin, at a_o=2mm). As the same deviation can be allowed before b_i, a factor of 2 has to be introduced for the full depth of field:

$$b_i \approx (a_o a)/2\,\lambda \quad \text{if } a_o < a$$

$$b_i \approx a^2/2\,\lambda \quad \text{otherwise}$$

One solution would be a lens size of a=1mm, hence a field depth of $b_i \approx$1m to infinity, probably good enough for a basic light field recording, and an angular resolution of 2 arcmin, yielding $\approx$ 2000 pixels at 60 degrees image width.

This could for example be implemented with somewhere between 4x4 and 16x16 standard resolution pinhole cameras, for a target resolution of 1..2x HDTV.

Illumination and coherence

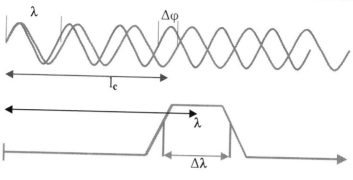

$$l_c / \lambda \Delta \varphi \approx \lambda / \Delta \lambda$$

$$l_c \approx \lambda^2 / \pi \Delta \lambda \quad \text{(for } \Delta \varphi = 1/\pi\text{)}$$

$$\Delta \lambda \approx \lambda^2 / \pi l_c$$

$\Delta \lambda$ is the *bandwidth*, for convenience
(some optics texts use this for *half bandwidth*)

Explanation: consider a small light source with a bandwidth $\Delta \lambda$ (we use wavelength instead of frequency, as usual with light). After a certain distance, two signals at the band edges will erase each other. Going further, the entire signal get irregular and lose its phase information.

We can define a coherence length l_c (as above) up to where the signal is sufficiently in phase. A usual, haphazard assumption is a phase difference of $360^0/\pi$ (*2rad* or 114.59^0). Anything using constructive interference will only work within approx. the coherence length.

For hologram *photography*, the coherence length limits the useful distance range. Therefore huge coherence lengths are desirable (laser light).

For hologram *reconstruction*, we only need a coherence length just allowing constructive interference from the contributing fringes.

What would be the coherence length for light to produce sufficient constructive interference with a display hologram?

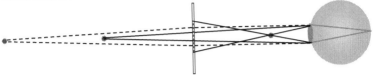

A certain image pixel (d) can only be represented by an area,
actually a tiny zone plate. In case of a pixel at infinity, this zone
plate cannot be bigger than the pupil. For nearer pixels, it becomes smaller, and for virtual image pixels before the hologram
plane it can also be bigger.

For general considerations we can simply assume the contributing
fringe pattern or 'zone plate' to be just as big as the pupil
Calculating the influence of timely coherence, hence we need the
size of the fringe pattern forming a pixel, and the distance of the
pixel from the fringe.

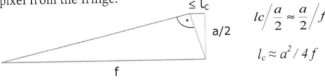

$$lc \left/ \frac{a}{2} \approx \frac{a}{2} \right/ f$$

$$l_c \approx a^2 / 4f$$

The viewer's eye has a lens that delays the inner part of the
beam, but this is negligible. The differences occur at the source
pixel. Hence, we take f= f$_p$.

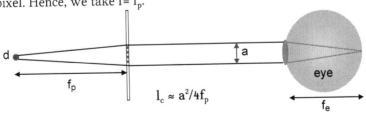

$$l_c \approx a^2/4f_p$$

Example: with f$_p$=200mm and a=2mm, we get l$_c$≈5 μm. With
λ=0.5μm, we then get for the source bandwidth:

$$\Delta\lambda = 16 \text{ nm.}$$

Hence, as any display hologram must define any pixel only within a pattern size as big as the viewer's eye aperture, a light source with e.g. 16 nm bandwidth should be sufficiently coherent in many cases !

An interesting effect of it: As 16 nm are about 1/20 of the human visible spectrum, it's obvious that the selective characteristics of a volume hologram may enable the selection of the necessary wavelengths from a white light source just by the hologram itself. Hence the ability to show holograms in halogen light, as practically any photographic hologram is thick enough for it.

Spatial coherence

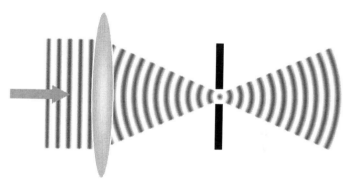

The focusing of a laser beam, and a pinhole
as often applied for beam collimation (cleaning)

A laser source delivers waves in phase for all of its surface. If we want to use a different source, such as an LED, any part of its surface emits its own light phase.

A laser beam can be focused down to about wavelength. This defines a fully coherent wavefront as we require for good holography.

A light source that cannot be focused this tight, is spatially less coherent. We could use a pinhole to enforce coherence, but we may lose a lot of light this way.

What remains, defining a measure for spatial coherence and calculating how   spatially coherent a light source has to be for certain applications.

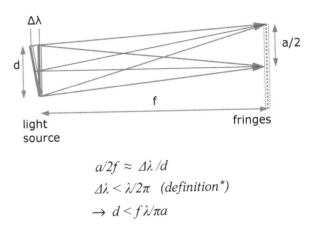

$$a/2f \approx \Delta\lambda /d$$

$$\Delta\lambda < \lambda/2\pi \quad (definition^*)$$

$$\rightarrow d < f\lambda/\pi a$$

Consider a light source of diameter d illuminating a fringe pattern of diameter a from distance f. Beams from the edges of the light sources travel the same distance to the center of the fringes but different distances to their edges.

This difference $\Delta\lambda$ should be smaller than one wavelength, otherwise we get   destructive interference. We define $\Delta\lambda<\lambda/2\pi$[*] or $\approx60^0$, which over the full pattern width a results in $\approx120^0$ or a max. amplitude loss of ≈0.5.

We get: $d < f\lambda / \pi a$

---

[*] People seem to like using cool-looking factors like π (3.14...). Some sources allow only half as much, but we try to stay consistent with timely coherence.

Reflection laws

Just for completeness, some schoolbook formulas about partial light reflection (at sharp media boundaries) without explanation. The reflection angle trivially equals the incident angle. The refraction angle follows from the index ratio (Snell's law):

$$\sin \gamma = \frac{n_1}{n_2} \sin \alpha$$

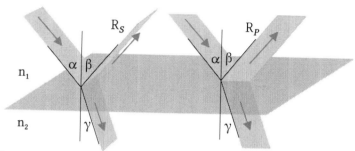

The ratio of reflected light intensity vs. incident light intensity also depends on polarization.
Reflection intensities for polarizations transversal (s) and parallel (p) to the plane spanned by the rays (Fresnel equations):

$$R_s = \left(\frac{n_1 \cos \alpha - n_2 \cos \gamma}{n_1 \cos \alpha + n_2 \cos \gamma} \right)^2 \qquad R_p = \left(\frac{n_2 \cos \alpha - n_1 \cos \gamma}{n_2 \cos \alpha + n_1 \cos \gamma} \right)^2$$

Non Polarized light accordingly results in different polarized partitions for the reflected beam. The total reflection intensity for non polarized light is:

$$R = \frac{R_s + R_p}{2}$$

The remainder gives the intensity of the refracted light, of course.
Total reflection intensity for perpendicular light ($\alpha = 0^0$):

$$R_0 = \left(\frac{n_1 - n_2}{n_1 + n_2} \right)^2$$

At $\alpha + \gamma = 90^0$ (Brewster's angle), all reflected light is s-polarized.

The Grating Equation

We'll shortly explain how constructive interference can be calculated (just skip this page if you're not interested).

A planar mirror pattern with only straight and equidistant lines would resemble a small section of the zone plate we discussed already. Just imagine an even wavefront approaching a surface with very narrow reflecting lines. Any of these lines will become a source of a cylinder wave, and all these cylinder waves have different phases according to the angle of incoming light and pattern line distance. They will add up to another planar wave of a certain angle, very different from the reflection angle of a simple mirror surface. As this actually describes the behavior of any pattern detail of any hologram, it should be interesting enough to examine it in more detail (this is similar to the behavior of a 'diffraction grating'):

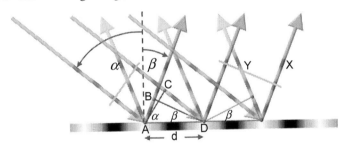

With a reflective hologram as depicted above, it can easily be seen that 'constructive interference' of waves from the different wave origins (the bright parts of the pattern) occurs when

$$CD - AB = n \lambda$$

(a multiple n of the wavelength λ), but also when

$$CD + AB = n \lambda$$

(the underlinings denote distances).

Hence, 'conjugated' departing wavefronts X and Y are generated.

$$n \lambda = CD \pm AB = d \sin \alpha \pm d \sin \beta$$
$$\text{(the 'grating equation')}$$

$$\beta = \pm \arcsin (n \lambda /d - \sin \alpha), \quad n=1,2,3,... \text{ (only n=1 is of interest)}$$

Bragg diffraction

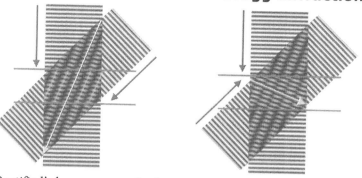

'Rectified' laser waves (both maxima and minima turned to black), showing the real exposure effect. Especially on the left side of the picture, we can easily see straight dark lines arising from the (steadily moving) interference patterns, marking exposure. Note that the left and right cases are essentially identical, if we just change the angle between the two wavefronts and turn them both around. The only remarkable difference resulting is, that the beams are coming from the same or from opposite sides of the substrate. We will neglect refraction a the substrate border. Deriving the standard formulas for the patterns can be quite simple:

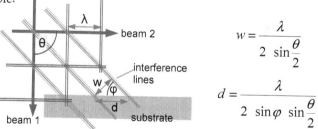

$$w = \frac{\lambda}{2 \, \sin\frac{\theta}{2}}$$

$$d = \frac{\lambda}{2 \, \sin\varphi \, \sin\frac{\theta}{2}}$$

The resolution formulas also yield the pattern size, and inverting them gives beam angles (beams generate pattern, pattern generates beams, the principle of holography). Simply setting $n\lambda$ instead of λ, we get all reflected and diffracted modes:

Bragg's Law : $\qquad d = \dfrac{n \, \lambda}{2 \, \sin\theta} \qquad\qquad n \, \lambda = 2 \, d \sin\theta$

HOE characteristics: Angle

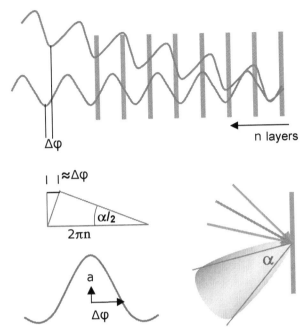

Note that these very rough approximations are just intended as an example. Exact calculations of HOE's would be very complex. HOE's don't just have a single response angle but a certain range, depending on their thickness, hence the number of reflection layers contributing. Smaller angle variations result in minor phase variations:

$$\Delta\varphi \approx 2\pi\, n\, (\, 1\text{-}\cos(\alpha/2)\,) \quad \textit{or for small } \alpha: \Delta\varphi \approx \pi\, n\, \alpha^2/4.$$

Hence we get a relatively wide α range. With $\Delta\varphi{=}2$ and $n{=}10$ layers for example, we get $\alpha \approx 30°$.

Higher orders are less likely to occur in near eye displays as to the limited angular range for possible beams from the display to the eye (but some effects with environmental light may still be possible).

HOE characteristics: Frequency

The spectral bandwidth of HOE's is quite narrow. Not quite as good as with dichroic mirrors however.

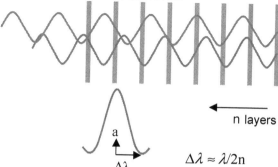

n layers

$$\Delta\lambda \approx \lambda/2n$$

Example: Approx. 10 effective layers, λ=500nm
⇨ Δλ ≈ 25nm

1 : 1.4

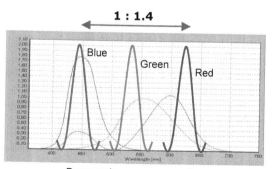

Base color range << 2
⇨ higher orders unlikely to occur

complex layer sequence

refined filter curve

More sophisticated characteristics: Subtle layer variations would allow for improved, custom tailored characteristics. Could this be accomplished e.g. using several wavelengths in construction?

A practical HOE construction setup

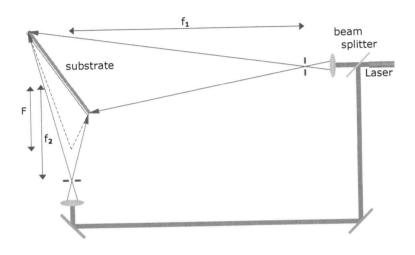

A huge lens to imitate infinity as we have used in the simplified headup display manufacturing scheme, may give an easy explanation but is impractical and expensive to produce. With a little trick, we can avoid this. We use the lens equation

$$1 / F = 1 / f_1 + 1 / f_2$$

to form an equivalent holographic mirror with beams coming from finite focus points. This works because of the angular range that any HOE of finite thickness still maintains.

The picture also shows the pinholes used for beam cleaning.

Upscaling evaluated

The following example shows the mapping of a group of 4 camera sensor pixels to 16 high definition (4x resolution) image pixels in one dimension. We see that some image pixels get more properly aligned camera inputs while some may get almost none.

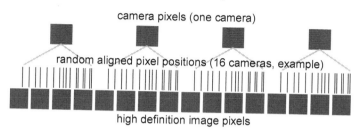

Calculating how well this would work is quite simple: that a certain high definition image pixel is aligned with one camera pixel by ±25% of the pixel width, has the probability $1/8$ in one direction (as we regard an 4:1 pixel relation and an alignment to 50% of a pixel width) or $1/8^2$, i.e. $1/64$ in two dimensions.

Inverse probabilities are easier, because they multiply*: that it's *not* the case, has a probability of $63/64$. We have 256 tries with 16x16 cameras and (assuming random alignment) this results in an overall probability of $63/64^{256}$, actually 0.018, or < 2%. So only about one in 55 pixels will get no good input to derive the high definition information.

---

* Mathematically inclined readers may stumble over this as generally we would need the more complicated formula for the binomial distribution: with n trials at a probability p, the probability for k hits is

$$P(k) = \begin{cases} \binom{n}{k} p^k (1-p)^{n-k} & \textit{for } 0 \leq k \leq n \\ 0 & \textit{otherwise} \end{cases} \qquad \textit{where } \binom{n}{k} = \frac{n!}{k!(n-k)!}$$

As we only want to know the probability for 0 hits ($k = 0$), n above k and p both are 1 and we get $P(0) = (1 - p)^n$, as stated.

The light field camera

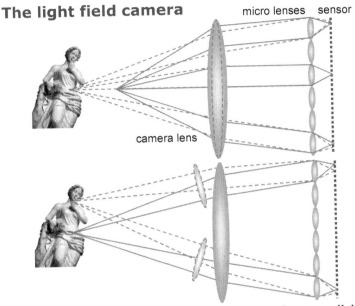

Replacing any pixel of a conventional camera by a small lens, addressing many tiny sub pixels behind it - a tiny camera of its own - allows to select certain rays out of the image from the large lens by selecting the appropriate sub pixels [99].

Any sub pixel together with its lens selects rays as if seen through a pinhole camera located at a certain position on the main lens. Sub pixels may be selected to collect light rays as if we had focused the main lens nearer or farther.

Sub pixels may as well be selected to form sub images seen from different points on the main lens, hence different perspectives. The selection rules may be combined to render and entirely crisp 2D or 3D image, or a 2D or 3D image with almost any focus distance and depth of field desired.

Most important advantage: with a conventional camera, the depth of field **b** for optimum aperture ($a_0 = a$) depends on the object pixel size **d** only (ref.p.379): $b \approx 2d^2/\lambda$.

The light field camera overcomes this restriction. It can be used for focus or perspective synthesis, but also the following purpose:

Depth pointing: monocular if you like

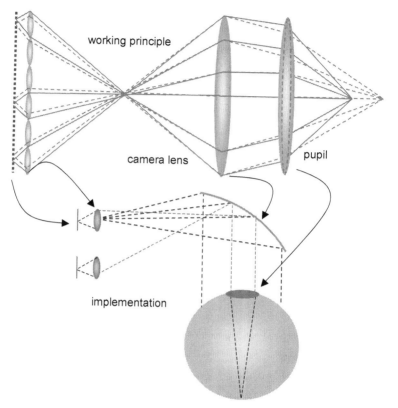

Eye focus could for example be measured using the light field camera principle.

The first obvious method of measuring the actual eye lens focus would be, observing the retina through the pupil with an autofocus camera. Taking pixel displacements between several sub camera images, like with the light field camera, might work as well.

Just a few small sub cameras at sample positions should be enough. Any sub camera however can only deliver useful pixels where it sees (through) the pupil.

References

This is an individual selection from the many materials existing on the issue. It can't be comprehensive and isn't intended to be. It should be a collection of the most remarkable things I found, especially in the recent time. I also generally preferred to list materials that can be quickly accessed by the web. Some items are mainly included for completeness, because their title suggests that they would contribute to the theme but actually they might not, or use the same words for different things. You'll easily find out when checking abstracts or looking up book descriptions in online stores.

If there are keywords in the text that you'd like to know more about, you'll surely find something very quickly by a web search. If computer scientists were more up to date, you would also surely find lots of papers on the arxiv servers. Maybe next year.

Remark: I can't guarantee that the web links listed here will stay current. I'll try to list updates on http://www.theendofhardware.com.

[1] Rolf R. Hainich: Echtzeitdiagnostik und Sichtsimulation für die minimal invasive Chirurgie, 1993. Proposing Augmented Reality in medicine, as well as in mass market applications.
http://www.theendofhardware.com/materials/Echtzeitdiagnostik.pdf

[2] Rolf R. Hainich: Integrative 3D Visualization. Conference opening paper, Workshop on Integrative 3D Visualization, Wiesbaden, 1994.
A paper already defining and outlining all of augmented reality and technology solutions. http://www.theendofhardware.com/materials/i3p.pdf

[3] Steve Mann: Smart Clothing': Wearable Multimedia Computing and `Personal Imaging', 1996. http://wearcam.org/acm-mm96/

[4] Tim Suthau, Marcus Vetter, Peter Hassenpflug, Hans-Peter Meinzer, Olaf Hellwich: A concept work for Augmented Reality visualisation based on a medical application in liver surgery IAPRS, Corfu, 2002
http://www.cv.tu-berlin.de/forschung/AR/medizin_AR.phtml

[5] Henning Schaefer, Kalibrierungen für Augmented Reality. Diplomarbeit at Technical University of Berlin, 2003.

[6] IBM Continous Data Protection:
ftp://ftp.software.ibm.com/software/tivoli/flyers/fl-tsm.pdf;
http://www.redbooks.ibm.com/abstracts/SG246844.html?Open

[7] Gursel Sonmez et al., A RGB Polymeric Electrochromic Device, University of California, Los Angeles, 2003
http://www.wiley-vch.de/contents/jc_2001/2004/z52910_s.pdf

[8] Ulrich Hofmann, Beamer für die Westentasche, FhG-ISIT, 2004
http://www.fraunhofer.de/fhg/press/pi/2004/11/Mediendienst112004Thema6.jsp

[9] MPEG.org Report on 3DAV Exploration
http://www.chiariglione.org/mpeg/working_documents/explorations/3dav/report_on_3dav_explor.zip

[10] HHI Immersive Meeting Point: http://ip.hhi.de/imedia_G3/impoint2.htm

[11] George Orwell, 1984. Signet Book; Reissue edition (May, 1990), 336 pages, ISBN: 0451524934 (many other sources)

[12] Jeff Hawkins: On Intelligence, Owl Books, 2005, ISBN: 0805078533
http://www.onintelligence.org/

[13] US pat. 5,572,343, concerning LCD displays as light valves,
http://patents.uspto.gov/

[14] MicroOptical Corporation
http://www.microopticalcorp.com/Products/HomePage.html

[15] Microvision, Inc. http://www.microvision.com

[16] James Fung: http://www.eyetap.org/~fungja/

[17] Wearable Computing Library: http://about.eyetap.org/fundamentals/

[18] Universal Display Corporation :http://www.universaldisplay.com/

[19] Oliver Bimber, Ramesh Raskar: Spatial Augmented Reality: Merging Real and Virtual Worlds, A K Peters, Ltd.,2005, ISBN: 1568812302
A very different approach, see also http://www.spatialar.com/

[20] Woodrow Barfield (Ed.), Thomas Caudell (Ed.): Fundamentals of Wearable Computers and Augmented Reality, Lawrence Erlbaum Associates, 2000, ISBN: 0805829016

[21] Tobias Hans Hollerer, User interfaces for mobile augmented reality systems, PhD thesis, 2004, Advisor: Steven K Feiner, Columbia University, Published Jun 2004, ISBN: 0-496-62842-6

[22] Bolan Jiang, Robust hybrid tracking for outdoor augmented reality, PhD thesis, 2004, Advisor: Ulrich Neumann, University of Southern California, Published Jan 2005 ISBN: 0-496-87626-2 (available as e-book)

[23] Grigore C. Burdea, Philippe Coiffet: Virtual Reality Technology, 2nd ed. with CD-ROM, Wiley-IEEE Press 2003, ISBN: 0471360899

[24] MIT wearable computing link collection:
http://www.media.mit.edu/wearables/lizzy/wearlinks.html

[25] Wearable Computing Library, eyetap:
http://www.eyetap.org/research/eyetap.html

[26] Virtual keys, US pt. 5,767,842 (1992/1998): http://patents.uspto.gov/

[27] Turner, Stuart L., Coupling Retinal Scanning Displays to the Human Vision System: Visual Response and Engineering Considerations. PhD thesis, University of Washington, 2000

[28] GP Markham: The ORIGINAL Illustrated Catalog Of ACME Products. *have fun !* http://home.nc.rr.com/tuco/looney/acme/acme.html

[29] EST-Engineering System Technologies. http://www.est-kl.com

[30] Tibor Balogh et al.: A Scalable Holographic Display for Interactive Graphics Applications. In Proc. IEEE VR 2005
http://www.crs4.it/vic/data/papers/ieeevr2005ws-holo.pdf
http://www.crs4.it/vic/cgi-bin/bib-page.cgi?id='Balogh:2005:SHD'

[31] Light Blue Optics / Cambridge University, Holographic projection display: http://www.lightblueoptics.com/
http://www.eng.cam.ac.uk/news/stories/pocket_projectors/

[32] Jürgen Herre et al.: An Introduction To MP3 Surround
http://www.iis.fraunhofer.de/amm/download/flyer/dl.html?f=introduction_to_mp3surround.pdf
http://www.iis.fraunhofer.de/amm/download/mp3surround/index.html

[33] CRLO Displays Ltd., microdisplays, http://www.crlopto.com/

[34] Claude Shannon, Communication in the Presence of Noise, 1948 Reprint: Proceedings of the IEEE, VOL. 86, NO. 2, Feb. 1998, also:
http://cm.bell-labs.com/cm/ms/what/shannonday/paper.html
http://cm.bell-labs.com/cm/ms/what/shannonday/shannon1948.pdf

[35] Oliver Bimber, L. Miguel Encarnação, and André Stork: Seamless integration of virtual reality in habitual workplaces - a website about some fundamental research projects in augmented reality.
http://www.uni-weimar.de/~bimber/research.php

[36] Michael L. Huebschman, Bala Munjuluri, and Harold R. Garner: Dynamic holographic 3-D image projection; see also:
http://innovation.swmed.edu/research/instrumentation/res_inst_dev3d.html

[37] C.E.Rash (ed.): Helmet mounted Displays in Aviation SPIE Press Monograph,Vol. PM93,ISBN0819439169, also: http://www.usaarl.army.mil/
http://www.usaarl.army.mil/hmdbook/cp_0002_contents.htm

[38] AR-NAV, FhG-FIT, http://www.fit.fraunhofer.de/projekte/arnav/index.xml

[39] Metcalfe, R.M., Boggs, D.R.: Ethernet: Distributed Packet Switching for Local Computer Networks. Coomm. ACM, 7/1976 (see also US Patent # 4.063.220, http://patents.uspto.gov/)

[40] Project ARVIKA: http://www.arvika.de/

[41] Tim Suthau: Augmented Reality – Positionsgenaue Einblendung räumlicher Information in ein See-Through Head Mounted Display für die Medizin am Beispiel der Leberchirurgie. Dissertation at TU Berlin, 2006

[42] Thorsteinn Halldorsson: Farbdisplays und holographische Bildschirme, EADS- Corporate Research Center, Ottobrunn. Darmstädter Kolloquium für Messtechnik, DAKOM 2005. http://www.eads.com

[43] Abramson, N.: The ALOHA System – Another Alternative for Computer Communications. AFIPS Conf. Proc. vol.37 (1970), p.281-285

[44] Lars Bönnen: FOHMD: The Fiber-Optic Helmet mounted Display and its Applications. CAE, Stolberg, Germany. In: Proceedings of the Workshop on integrative 3D visualization, Wiesbaden, 1994

[45] Jim Vallino's Augmented Reality Page (link collection): http://www.se.rit.edu/~jrv/research/ar/index.html

[46] Ronald Azuma: A Survey of Augmented Reality. In Presence: Teleoperators and Virtual Environments 6, 4 (August 1997), 355-385. http://www.cs.unc.edu/~azuma/ARpresence.pdf

[47] Wikipedia article on Augmented Reality, contains many links: http://en.wikipedia.org/wiki/Augmented_reality

[48] George Ou (http://blogs.zdnet.com/Ou) Is encryption really crackable? A short and thorough sweep-out of myths about 'cracked' encryption http://blogs.zdnet.com/Ou/?p=204&tag=nl.e550 [01.05.2006 22:29:28]

[49] Cyclon Systems, UK, manufacturer of wearable cameras for police, military and other services, http://www.cylonsystems.com/

[50] Stereo3d.com HMD comparison: http://www.stereo3d.com/hmd.htm

[51] Holoeye Photonics AG, spatial light modulators http://www.holoeye.com/spatial_light_modulators-technology.html

[52] LC Technologies, inc.: The Eygaze communication system, http://www.lctinc.com/PRODUCTS.htm

[53] Mirage Innovations, Manufacturer of the LughtVu glasses,http://www.mirageinnovations.com/

[54] Liteye Systems, producer of miniature displays, http://www.liteye.com/

[55] NVIS, manufacturer of head mounted displays, http://www.nvisinc.com

[56] Arrington Research, manufacturer of head mounted eye trackers. http://www.arringtonresearch.com

[57] Thomas Schnell, Applying Eye Tracking as an Alternative Approach for Activation of Controls and Functions in Aircraft http://cosmos.ssol.iastate.edu/isgc/RES_INF/VRR2000/Schnell_SEED.pdf

[58] Peter B.L.Meijer, vOICe, http://www.seeingwithsound.com/

[59] Larry Leifer and David Grossman: Blind Navigator: using object recognition to enhance blind mobility. http://mediax.stanford.edu/news/conference_nov03/dave_grossman.pdf

[60] eMagin head mounted displays, http://www.emagin.com

[61] Qualcomm, iMoD display technology, http://www.qualcomm.com/qmt/

[62] Jan Fischer, Interaktive Spezifikation von Domänen und Detektion partieller dynamischer Verdeckungen in Augmented-Reality Umgebungen; http://www.gris.uni-tuebingen.de/~fischer/janfischer.com/publications/fischer2002-thesis.pdf J.Fischer and H. Regenbrecht and G. Baratoff, Detecting Dynamic Occlusion in front of Static Backgrounds for AR Scenes, EGVE, Zürich, 2003 http://www.gris.uni-tuebingen.de/~fischer/janfischer.com/publications/DynamicOcclusion.pdf

[63] Think-A-Move, Ltd., InnerVoice Pro http://www.think-a-move.com/products.html

[64] Michael W. Halle, "Multiple Viewpoint Rendering for 3-Dimensional Displays", Ph.D. Thesis, Program in Media Arts and Sciences, MIT 1997, http://www.media.mit.edu/spi/spiPubs.htm http://www.media.mit.edu/spi/SPIPapers/halazar/thesis-orig.pdf

[65] Mark Lucente, Diffraction-Specific Fringe Computation for Electro-Holography, PhD thesis, MIT1994 http://www.media.mit.edu/spi/spiPubs.htm http://www.lucente.biz/pubs/PhDthesis/contents.html

[66] Cyberkinetics Neurotechnology Systems inc. http://www.cyberkineticsinc.com/

[67] Donoghue Labs, http://donoghue.neuro.brown.edu/

[68] Privacy and Human Rights http://www.gilc.org/privacy/survey/intro.html

[69] UN Universal Declaration of Human Rights http://www.hrweb.org/legal/udhr.html

[70] Cryptool, free cryptography learning software by Deutsche Bank. Siegen University, TU Darmstadt, Secude, FZI: http://www.cryptool.com/

[71] Bernhard Esslinger (Ed), 2006 The Cryptool Script (cryptography): http://www.cryptool.com/downloads/CrypToolScript_1_4_00_en.pdf

[72] Steven Feiner, links on user interfaces f. mobile & wearable computing, http://www1.cs.columbia.edu/graphics/courses/mobwear/reading.html

[73] Durand R. Begault, 3-D Sound for Virtual Reality and Multimedia http://human-factors.arc.nasa.gov/publications/Begault_2000_3d_Sound_Multimedia.pdf

[74] Wayne Piekarski, Interactive 3D Modelling in Outdoor Augmented Reality Worlds, PhD thesis, http://www.tinmith.net/wayne/thesis/

[75] Electronic Frontier Foundation, working to protect your digital rights. http://www.eff.org

[76] Thilo Womelsdorf et al.: Dynamic shifts of visual receptive fields in cortical area MT by spatial attention. Nature, 2006 http://www.nature.com/neuro/journal/vaop/ncurrent/abs/nn1748.html

[77] Kiyoshi Kiyokawa et al. 2003, An Occlusion-Capable Optical See-through Head Mount Display forCollaboration of Co-located Multiple Users http://www.hitlabnz.org/fileman_store/2003-ISMAR-occlusion_hmd3_kiyo_final.pdf

[78] Rolf R. Hainich, An Improved Ethernet for Real Time Applications, Real Time Data, Versailles 1982
http://www.theendofhardware.com/materials/ImprovedEthernet.pdf

[79] Rolf R. Hainich, Backoff Strategies for CSMA/CD with Real Time Applications, internat. conf. Kommunikation in Verteilten Systemen, GI/NTG 1983
http://www.theendofhardware.com/materials/CSMA-RT.pdf

[80] Home page of the Moving Picture Experts Group (MPEG)
http://www.chiariglione.org/mpeg/index.htm

[81] Peter K. Kaiser, The joy of Visual Perception : a web book
http://www.yorku.ca/eye/

[82] Eyes Tea, Berlin/Boston, http://www.eyes-tea.net/, with an interesting linklist at http://www.roetting.de/eyes-tea/who.html

[83] R. Ziegler, P. Kaufmann, M. Gross : A Framework for Holographic Scene Representation and Image Synthesis. To appear in ACM SIGGRAPH 2006 Sketch, Boston, USA, 30.July - 3.August, 2006
http://graphics.ethz.ch/Downloads/Publications/Papers/2006/Zie06a/Zie06a.pdf

[84] Aurora Systems Co.,Ltd., Manufacturer of high resolution LCOS micro displays, http://www.aurora-sys.com/home.htm

[85] Augmented Reality: Hyperlinking to the Real World, TechNewsWorld Nov.2006, http://www.technewsworld.com/story/54364.html

[86] Fraunhofer IDMT - Ultrafast 1-Chip-Eyetracker
http://www.idmt.fraunhofer.de/de/projekte_themen/ultrafast_eyetracker.htm

[87] Zeiss - Head Mounted Displays project:
http://www.zeiss.de/C12567A100537AB9/Contents-Frame/83F3D3C1FDFB5168C1256EA9002A8166

[88] SeeReal Holographic Display Technology
http://www.seereal.com/en/holography/index.php

[89] Hinckley, K., Sinclair, M., Hanson, E., Szeliski, R., Conway, M., The VideoMouse: A Camera-Based Multi-Degree-of-Freedom Input Device, ACM UIST'99 Symposium on User Interface Software & Technology, pp. 103-112. http://research.microsoft.com/users/kenh/papers/VideoMouse.pdf

[90] R. Ziegler, S. Bucheli, L.Ahrenberg, M.Magnor, M.Gross: A Bidirectional Light Field - Hologram Transform. To appear in Computer Graphics Forum 26(3), Proceedings of Eurographics 2007.
http://graphics.ethz.ch/Downloads/Publications/Papers/2007/Zie07c/Zie07c.pdf

[91] New Scale Technologies, Inc. - Manufacturaer of piezo electric micro motors. http://www.newscaletech.com/

[92] FhG-IPMS, Fraunhofer Institute for integrated photonic microsystems: micro scanners and micro mechanical light modulators.
http://www.ipms.fraunhofer.de/en/products/microscanner.shtml

[93] S.C. Barden, J.A. Arns and W.S. Colburn "Volume-phase holographic gratings and their potential for astronomical applications", Proc. SPIE 3355, 1998. http://www.noao.edu/ets/vpgratings/papers/spiepaper.pdf

[94] D. H. Close and A. Graube, "Holographic Lens for Pilot's Head-up Display", NTIS Rep. AD/787605, 1974.

[95] A. Lu , R. Maciejewski and D.S. Ebert: Volume Composition Using Eye Tracking Data. Eurographics/ IEEE-VGTC Symposium on Visualization (2006). http://web.ics.purdue.edu/~rmacieje/research/comp.pdf

[96] US patent 5682210: "Eye contact lens video display system". http://patft.uspto.gov

[97] Erik Sofge: Souped-Up Contact Lenses Promise On-Demand Bionic Eyesight. In: Popular Mechanics, April 2008. http://www.popularmechanics.com/science/health_medicine/4252012.html

[98] Noah Shachtman: Pentagon: 'Augment' Reality with 'Videogame' Contact Lenses. WIRED Blog Network, March 2008. http://blog.wired.com/defense/2008/03/darpa-wants-con.html

[99] Ng, Duval et al.: Light Field Photography with a Hand-Held Plenoptic Camera. Stanford Tech Report CTSR 2005-02. http://graphics.stanford.edu/papers/lfcamera/

[100] Photosynth picture merging technology. http://photosynth.net/

[101] K. S. Beev, K.N. Beeva, S. H. Sainov: Materials for Holographic 3DTV Display Applications. In: H.M. Ozaktas, L. Onural (Ed.) Three-Dimensional Television, Springer 2008, ISBN 978-3-540-72531-2

[102] Frankowski, G., Hainich, R.: DLP-Based 3D Metrology by Structured Light or Projected Fringe Technology. Proc. SPIE Photonics West 2009.

[103] O. Cakmakci, S. Vo, S. Vogl, R. Spindelbalker, A. Ferscha, J. P. Rolland: Optical Free-Form Surfaces in Off-Axis Head-Worn Display Design. Proceedings of The 7th IEEE and ACM International Symposium on Mixed and Augmented reality, ISMAR 2008, Cambridge, Sept.15-18, 2008.

[104] Hyung Min Park, Seok Han Lee, Jong Soo Choi: Wearable Augmented Reality System using Gaze Interaction. Proceedings of The 7th IEEE and ACM International Symposium on Mixed and Augmented reality, ISMAR 2008, Cambridge, Sept.15-18, 2008.

[105] Rolf R. Hainich: New approaches to 3D displays. Guest lecture, University of Weimar, 2007

[106] Rolf R. Hainich: The End of Hardware, 1st Ed., April 2006.

[107] Rolf R. Hainich: The End of Hardware, 2nd Ed., October 2005.

[108] Superwise Technologies AG, Apollo Engine: http://www.superwise-technologies.com

[109] P. Surman, K. Hopf, I. Sexton, W. K. Lee, R. Bates: Solving the 3D problem - The History and Development of Viable Domestic 3D Displays. In: H.M. Ozaktas, L. Onural (Ed.) Three-Dimensional Television, Springer 2008, ISBN 978-3-540-72531-2

[110] Fourth Dimension Displays, manufacturer of LCOS displays for near-eye-systems http://www.forthdd.com/

[111] A. Koz, G. A. Triantafyllidis, A. A: Alatan: 3D Watermarking: Techniques and directions. In: H.M. Ozaktas, L. Onural (Ed.) Three-Dimensional Television, Springer 2008, ISBN 978-3-540-72531-2

[112] A. Smolic, P. Merkle, K. Müller, C: Fehn, P. Knauff, T. Wiegand: Compression of Multi-View Video and Associated Data. In: H.M. Ozaktas, L. Onural (Ed.) Three-Dimensional Television, Springer 2008, ISBN 978-3-540-72531-2

[113] Brombach, B., Bruns, E. and Bimber, O.: Subobject Detection through Spatial Relationships on Mobile Phones. Submitted to International Conference of Intelligent User Interfaces (IUI2009), 2008

[114] E.Stoykova, J. Harizanova, V. Sainov: Pattern Projection Profilometry for 3D Coordinates Measurement of Dynamic Scenes. In: H.M. Ozaktas, L. Onural (Ed.) Three-Dimensional Television, Springer 2008, ISBN 978-3-540-72531-2

[115] Physik Instrumente (manufacturer of piezo motors). http://www.physikinstrumente.com/

[116] Saxby, G.: Practical Holography, Prentice Hall, 1988

[117] Pat. appl. DE102007023920 (Siemens)

[118] ISTAR-project: Interactive See-Through Augmented Reality Displays. http://www.istar-project.org

[119] Wolter, A.: Untersuchungen zu einem hochauflösenden Flächenlichtmodulator mit einstellbarem Profil einer Flüssigkeitsoberfläche zur optischen Musterwiedergabe. Dissertation, Fachbereich 9 , Universität Duisburg, 2001. http://deposit.ddb.de/cgi-bin/dokserv?idn=981604471

[120] Rolf R. Hainich: Universal Caching with Hash or Random UUIDs (2004). http:/www.theendofhardware.com/materials/Internet-draft.pdf

[121] R. Gvili, A. Kaplan, E. Ofek and G. Yahav: Depth keying. 3DV Systems Ltd.,2002. http://www.3dvsystems.com/technology/DepthKey.pdf

[122] Rohstoffe für Zukunftstechnologien, 2009. ISBN 978-3-8167-7957-5 http://www.irb.fraunhofer.de/bookshop/artikel.jsp?v=229184

[123] Rolf R. Hainich: Near Eye Displays - a look into the Christmas Ball. Keynote Lecture, 7th IEEE and ACM International Symposium on Mixed and Augmented reality, ISMAR 2008, Cambridge, Sept.15-18, 2008. http://ismar08.org/wiki/doku.php?id=program

Index

W

X

Z

Acknowledgements

There are many people who helped me with this effort. I can't honestly list them all, so I just wish to express my gratefulness to all of you, and for the reader I list a few of you here:

First of all, Sigrid, my beloved wife, who patiently endured me 'staring into the computer' for many months.

Walter Kroy, former head of research at MBB Aerospace, has supported this work since the very beginning, chaired the first conference, and provided useful hints and links for this book. Thorsteinn Halldorsson of EADS gave helpful comments on holography. Lucilla Croce-Ferri of FhG-IGD/IPSI provided advice about watermarks.

Dietrich Grönemeyer, who created interventional radiology, supported my ideas in their early stages already. Georg Vallender and his colleagues at CAE contributed a lot of motivation. Günter Hommel of TU Berlin, gave me that outstanding programming course very long ago and also provided some interesting links for the book project.

Olaf Hellwich of TU Berlin enabled valuable research in AR; Tim Suthau, who worked at his institute, provided me with rare materials about virtual retina displays. Corell Nowak of EST helped with product pictures.

David P. Keith, world's best flight instructor, did that gorgeous painting (p.121) on the cut out back of my T-shirt (after drying it). Klaus Rebensburg of Hasso Plattner Institute and Uli Weinberg of Film Academy Babelsberg provided many inspirations with their 'n-space' invited lecture series.

Oliver Bimber, outstanding researcher, professor of Augmented Reality at Bauhaus-University Weimar, played a great part in motivating the work on this 3rd edition.

The people at Booksurge made this publication possible in the fastest and most innovative way. For a book about innovation, that's the way to do it, isn't it.

Finally, the honorable Balduin Egghead, who posed so patiently for many of my illustrations.